On Celtic Tides

On Celtic Tides

ONE MAN'S JOURNEY AROUND
IRELAND BY SEA KAYAK

Chris Duff

St. Martin's Press ⚏ New York

Design by Maureen Troy

Library of Congress Cataloging-in-Publication Data

Duff, Chris.
    On Celtic tides : one man's journey around Ireland by sea kayak / Chris Duff.—1st ed.
       p.   cm.
    ISBN 0-312-20508-2
    1. Sea kayaking—Ireland.   2. Duff, Chris—Journeys—Ireland.
3. Ireland—Description and travel.   I. Title.
Gv776.467.174D84   1999
914.1504'824—dc21

                                                                        99-21989
                                                                        CIP

First Edition: August 1999

10 9 8 7 6 5 4 3 2 1

this book is dedicated with love

to my mother and father

We shall not cease from exploration

And the end of all our exploring

Will be to arrive where we started

And know the place for the first time.

—T.S. Eliot

Contents

Foreword

Sea kayaking is about taking journeys: trips around the bay on a sparkling summer's day; exposed passages along lines of cliffs with dark sea caves to explore; around promontories that spawn tide races where ten-knot currents can kick up huge waves on the calmest of days; grueling crossings when settled weather and trained muscles are essential; crossings accompanied by dolphins and broaching whales; journeys in foul weather when the hiss of spray sets the adrenaline racing and the final landfall to safety through the surf is exhilarating and chilling to both mind and body. The physical list is endless. And there is also the inner journey.

Back in 1986, a man I'd never seen before walked into our showroom and asked for his boat. Chris Duff, the invoice said, all the way from the U.S.A. Strange, we sent many kayaks over to the States, but this was the first time a customer had traveled four thousand miles just to pick up his boat. One of the shop workers walked across the yard with us, as I would need a hand to pull the boat out of the storage unit. "Are you paddling the boat over here while on holiday, or are you taking it back to the States right away?" I asked, by way of making conversation. "Oh, I'll be taking it back to the States," replied the stranger, "but first I'm going to paddle it round Great Britain." There was a quickly suppressed guffaw from my helper within the container; we rolled our eyes at one another, but nothing was said. Over the years, many canoeists have walked into our workshops with grandiose plans for expeditions, world records, kayak designs, and aspirations almost always beyond their reach. The kayak was located, lifted down, and the plastic tube acting as a dust cover was pulled off. There was

Chris's kayak, spanking new and looking great. I remembered now: the letter detailing very carefully the exact specifications for the kayak and asking for it to be stored until his arrival in the spring.

As Chris examined his boat, I realized that he was an experienced paddler. He looked in all the right places as he checked the quality of construction. His choice of deck fittings and other accessories left me in no doubt that he knew precisely what he was undertaking. He slid his legs out of the cockpit, obviously pleased with what he'd purchased, looked round the parking lot, and asked, "Is there any place I can camp?"

Industrial areas are not the most salubrious of places, and we were on the wrong side of the tracks anyway. I phoned my wife and told her an American had turned up who wanted to paddle around Great Britain and that he had a tent but no campsite. I suggested that we could put him up for a day or two. It was clear he was well prepared to accomplish this feat. He just needed a few days to complete last-minute preparations. We would give him those few days.

"Where's a good place to start?" he asked.

"Well, anywhere really," I replied "It depends where you want to finish. Why not start from Nottingham? It's eighty odd miles from here to the North Sea, just paddle down the River Trent, turn right at the end, and keep going."

And that's exactly what he did.

So, ten years later, when I heard through the grapevine that Chris had completed a solo circumnavigation of Ireland, I was delighted. Here was a man who first thought carefully about a project, decided what were the basic criteria, and then, after carefully laying his plans, made it all seem very simple—he just did it.

Journeys on the ocean are essentially in wilderness. It starts at the beach, often crowded and unthreatening. Beyond the lines of sunbathers are the shallows, where children shriek as the waves curl around their shins; there may be other lines: body surfers, board surfers, and the white sails of windsurfers pushing a little further out into the bay. But go by kayak to the headlands, where the savage rocks below shudder under the brunt of the swell and the smallest bush above is combed to the cliff face by the prevailing wind. Here you will find true wilderness—a world unique and wild in unspoiled beauty, but where if things go wrong, rescue, if it is possible, can be hours away. Sea paddlers know this, and take precautions. They still go, of course, because this wilderness offers excitement and exhilaration, apprehension and introspection; the element of risk being taken as part of the price paid in visiting these pristine places.

If you tackle this unpredictable world alone, then you increase the risk factor—by ten, twenty, a hundred? The trade-off is of course heightened awareness. You alone must decide whether conditions will remain stable for a long crossing; you must tune in to the slightest change in wind or tide when your route demands calm seas. Only you can fully appreciate your own emotions when a careless reading of a tide table has meant hours of bucking the tide at best, or, at worst, a disaster of epic proportions.

Ireland is remarkable for its artifacts. The west coast particularly is a treasurehouse of ruined monasteries, stone crosses, burial sites, and beehive huts. It was here, close to the howling Atlantic, that early Christians lived their lives in spiritual contemplation. Maybe times have changed. Few people nowadays spend time in beehive huts contemplating their place within the universe; however, these age-old questions still tug at our hearts.

Maybe the approach is more dynamic now. Perhaps a kayak journey allows the ocean to speak in ways that have been known to all ages of man, if they cared to listen. Chris has been listening. This remarkable book allows us a glimpse into this world. *On Celtic Tides* is a fine experience.

Over the years I have spent many weeks paddling the shores of Ireland, not alone, but I know something of this wild coastline with its Celtic and early Christian remains scattered over headlands and islands. *On Celtic Tides*, with its stunning descriptions of many places I have visited, also paints brilliant pictures of the places I have missed. Chris helped me to see and feel this magnificent coast as only a solo paddler can.

—Frank Goodman,
Founder of Valley Canoe Products,
Nottingham, England

Acknowledgments

There are many correlations between my solo circumnavigation of Ireland and the writing of this book. Both appear to be endeavors of solitude and for the most part are just that. However, without the help of dozens of people, neither the journey nor this book would have been possible. It is an honor for me to recognize the contributions of family and friends.

To my parents, I offer a great thank you for the gift of spirit which I have inherited and the wonderful lesson of childhood—"You can do whatever you set your mind to." The continual support that my mother and father have offered over the years is a lesson in true love.

In writing this book I became aware of how much more difficult the writing was than the actual paddling. To David, I say a special thank you for wading through structural, grammatical, and spelling errors, and greatly assisting me in producing a solid first draft. Your insight and enthusiasm pulled the book through a difficult time. To my paddling friend and computer doctor, Erran, thank you. Your patience and skill at unscrambling my computer errors is greatly appreciated, as are your editing skills and advice. Thanks to Gay for all your support during the circumnavigation, the hours of reading and rereading the manuscript, and the friendship that has always been there. To Dave and Ann, and now, little Waverly, who was listening from the womb while her mom and dad shared their stories of world travels with me and kept the fires of our writing aglow—thank you. Thanks to my brothers and sisters, who offered encouragement and belief in me when the project seemed endless and too daunting. To Anna, who gave me my first computer, a hearty thanks for the opportunity to enter the twentieth century and attempt to become computer-literate. To all my friends with whom I did not ski, hike, paddle, or socialize enough during the "working-on-my-book" phase of my life, I offer this book as payment-in-lieu.

To Werner Paddles of Sultan, Washington, I owe a great debt. You were there with your support on the British circumnavigation in 1986. Your enthusiastic support and Molokai graphite paddle went the distance again on the Irish circumnavigation. Many thanks for your faith in me and for a great paddle.

To everyone I met along the wave-battered coast of Ireland, I offer my thanks for your hospitality, generosity, and the memories of the trip, which I can now share with you.

Finally, thank you to Marc Resnick, my editor at St. Martin's Press. Your enthusiasm and commitment to this book has been invaluable!

This book is an offering of thanks to all the people who helped make not only the journey possible but also the actual recording of it. Each of you played a part in these endeavors and it is to you that I offer the entire story of my journey.

On Celtic Tides

Shannon River Reflections

... Yet I cannot tarry longer.
The sea that calls all things unto her calls me,
and I must embark.
For to stay, though the hours burn in the night,
is to freeze and crystallize and be bound in a mold.

—Kahlil Gibran, *The Prophet*

In the gray of dawn I rolled over in the sleeping bag and slowly came out of my dream world. I looked up at the peak of the tent and remembered where I was: camped on a patch of grass above a cobbled beach at Kilbaha, near the mouth of the Shannon River. Memories floated through my mind as the waves broke gently on the cobbles. I recalled waking up on Scattery Island this same time yesterday morning. I had paddled ten miles upriver to explore the tenth-century monastic ruins on the island. The evening ebb tide had carried me back to the north side of the mouth of the river, my present camp. I wanted to be in a good position to get around Loop Head, which was now just a few miles around the cliff shoreline.

I slid out of the bag and unzipped the tent flap. Droplets of condensation from the sagging nylon fell on my back and I shivered, looking out on another overcast morning. The sea had a cold look to it, a greasy smooth blackness that made me want to curl back into the warmth of the bag. There was a breeze on the left side of my face—a northeast breeze. The mornings had been dead calm lately and this breeze made me edgy. My

1

mind kicked into gear. I would be sheltered under the cliffs until I reached Loop Head, then the approaching weather would be on the bow. I would have to hurry if I was to get around the headland before the winds picked up. Thoughts of retreating into the bag were forgotten as I pushed handfuls of its warmth into the stuff sack and started breaking down camp.

Within an hour I had eaten breakfast, reluctantly pulled on my damp paddling clothes from the day before, and carried all the gear and the boat to the water's edge. The tide was dropping, leaving wet rocks where there had been the lapping of wind-driven wavelets. I finished packing the gear in the three compartments of the boat: the heavier items, the stove, tent, and food bag, as close to the cockpit as possible; the lighter bundle of cloths and tent poles jammed in the far ends. There wasn't room for an extra pair of socks by the time everything was carefully packed. I ran back to the tent site as much to get warm as to make sure I hadn't forgotten anything. Only the bent grass where I had slept remained.

I returned to the boat, sat on the rear deck, and slid into the warm confines of the cockpit. As I snapped the spray deck in place I went through my pre-paddle checklist: hatches secure, map folded for the day's route and sealed in the chart case on the foredeck, camera tied off to its tether, and the spare paddles held on the rear deck with the bungie cords. The last thing I did was to fasten a two-inch-wide safety belt around my waist. It was attached to a length of one-inch webbing that ran to the rear toggle. A short length of webbing tied the paddle to my wrist.

I threw my weight forward and the boat slid off the algae-covered rocks. The northeast breeze of an hour earlier was now more of a wind. It was building faster than I thought it would. It caught the boat and drifted it toward a rock ledge extending out from the cobbles. I leaned the boat over on its starboard side and with a sweep stroke pulled it away from the ledge and onto a course leading to the mouth of the river.

Beneath the cliffs, gusts of wind curled from their heights and hit the water in a broad fan. To my left across the ten-mile-wide river, I could see where the ebbing tide collided with the winds in standing waves and white-caps. In front of me, Loop Head was hidden by the curve of the cliffs to the north. At the furthest point where the cliffs met the open ocean, heavy bands of rollers and an occasional breaker advanced from beyond the cliffs. The wind was holding at Force 3—fifteen mph—not strong but steady enough to build the seas running against the tide. Yesterday, when I pulled into Kilbaha, a fisherman had warned me about the headland. "She can be the devil to get around in a wind." I had also been warned about it three days earlier by a fisherman on the south side of the river. The mouth of the Shannon, and Loop Head in particular, had a reputation for being rough.

As I paddled within a mile of the final cliff approach to Loop Head, four-footers wrapped their way into the rivermouth and smashed against the base of the cliff, sending spray flying up the wall of rock. The rebounding waves turned the seas into a steep chop and the boat began a familiar twisting and pitching.

Against the cliff, washed in breaking waves, was a white lobster boat pitching wildly in the seas. I recognized the shear of the boat and the stout build of the yellow-clad fisherman. It was Gerry O'Shea, the fisherman from Kilbaha. He had said he would be out this morning checking his pots and that he would keep an eye out for me. I paddled toward him as he waved, then swung a pot on board and rested it on the gunwale as I approached. I paddled within a dozen feet of his hull, which was rising and falling like a pile driver, then stopped and struggled to hold my position.

" 'Morning, Gerry, it's a bit bumpy out here," I yelled above the sound of the waves and wind.

With a shake of his head and a cheery smile he called back in a strong Irish accent, "Aye, 'tis a northeast wind. She might slack by tomorrow but then there's fog due in. Are ye goin' round the point?"

Before I could answer, a wave surged me almost under his bow. I struggled to back away as another wave washed over the stern, hit me in the back, then swept over the cockpit. Finally I yelled back, "I think I'll have a look, but if it's too rough I'll find a place to sit it out and wait. Have you been out this morning?"

"Around the point? Oh aye. Earlier I was and I tell you she's dirty, very dirty on the outside. Ye might get outta the wind if ye stay in close, but I tell ye she's right dirty today. I won't be goin' out again meself 'til the mornin'."

We were drifting close to the rocks. Gerry eased the engine into gear and slowly moved to more open water. We both needed to get further offshore and put a buffer between the rocks and our boats. I paddled ten yards off his bow and called out a final farewell. His bow split a wave, throwing water to both sides as he lifted a gloved hand and yelled, "I'll be watchin' out for ye and tellin' the other boats to do the same."

With a quick wave I dug the paddle into the next swell and pulled away from a lobster buoy Gerry was headed toward.

The closer I paddled to the mouth of the river, the bigger and steeper the waves became. I felt myself tighten up: elbows in close to save the shoulders, and feet pressing against the forward bulkhead, jamming my hips tighter in the seat. I concentrated on an imaginary circle twenty yards around the boat as I paddled toward the final rock that blocked my view of the headland.

The bow buried into the face of a swell, then climbed the gray-green wall and hung suspended for a second before dropping into the following trough, leaving my stomach somewhere midway in the fall. The boat hit with a jarring crash and immediately started to rise on the next wave. A hundred yards to my right the seas exploded against the cliff in concussions that reverberated in my chest. I was too close, being pushed by the tide and wind toward the rocks. I pulled harder, deeper on the right paddle, and moved further out. Again the boat climbed, fell into the trough, and twisted with the rebounding waves hitting the stern and throwing it sideways into the northerly seas. The wind carried the spray off the bow, flinging it in cold buckets into my face and chest.

Progress was measured slowly, the cliff falling away and revealing for the first time an intimidating view of the coast to the north. A half mile in front of me a wall of rock like that of a towered cathedral rose into the strengthening winds and gloomy weight of sky. It stood craggy, shadowless in the dull light but powerful in its bulk that separated river from ocean, sky from land. This was Loop Head.

Beneath the headland and the lighthouse that seemed to scrape the layered gray of the sky was a thirty-five-foot fishing boat rolling broadside in the heavy swells. As she rolled over each crest I could see ten feet of her planking, the sea streaming off in sheets before she rolled the other way and came within a couple of feet of taking water over the far gunwale. Thirty-five feet and ten tons of boat looked as fragile as a child's toy.

Beyond the boat and the headland the ocean appeared possessed, angry and blackened, throwing itself in fury against the cliffs that extended as far as I could see. Rebounding waves, spray, the noise of the wind, and the ocean crashing against the land were more than I wanted to deal with. A wave washed over the bow and hit me in the chest, sending cold seawater into my nose and eyes. I shook my head clear, refocused, and waited for the right moment to turn around. I had paddled over four hundred miles to reach this point. With another eight hundred to go, the risks of rounding the headland weren't worth jeopardizing the rest of the journey. It would have to wait for another day.

Turning the boat around in the confused seas was like balancing a bicycle in a slow, tight turn. All forward momentum was lost and for a few agonizingly slow moments the boat wallowed broadside to the waves. A wave hit solidly from the port side and buried the boat in rumbling broken water. I reached into it with a left brace, leaning on the paddle for stability until the wave flooded over the cockpit, then quickly finished the turn as the wave swept past the bow.

With my back to the oncoming waves, I was now blind to whatever was breaking and rolling in from behind. Around me the sea was a heaving, chaotic world of noise and spine-twisting breakers. The boat pitched, dove, and climbed in a different direction every few seconds. I needed something to focus on, something solid to give my eye and inner ear a reference point. I locked onto the tip of the bow and blocked out the sights and sounds that overloaded my senses. I was working on instinct, my mind focused and calm while my body somehow responded to the boat being thrown around by the sea.

From the corner of my eye, I saw a wave over my right shoulder. It was huge, steep, and beginning to peak. A second later, I felt the stern rise sharply and my eye was immediately back on the bow, searching for that point that told me the boat was being pitch-poled, the bow corkscrewing into a rebounding wave while the stern lifted and started to throw the craft end over end.

I sucked in a lungful of air, waited for the shock of seawater to flood my sinuses and ears and to bury the noise of the sea and winds in a capsize. My mind shifted from paddling to setting up for an Eskimo roll. I knew what I would do, how my body would feel as I went over, then rapidly tucked into a curl and began to unwind in a smooth arc of the paddle back to the surface. I didn't question my ability to roll. I knew if I went over I was going to come back around.

The boat was almost on its nose and twisted sharply to the right, a second away from finishing the swing of the pendulum. A wave suddenly peaked to the right of the cockpit, even with the paddle blade. I jammed the blade into the wave and snapped my hips, instinctively bringing the boat back under me and breaking the momentum of the stern wave. The boat came down with a crash, teetered on its edge, then miraculously stayed upright. A surge of adrenaline rushed through me, quickening my heart rate and filling my arms, chest, and legs with enough power to pull the boat through the wave pouring over the foredeck. The mechanics of the roll were forgotten. My mind was back on the surface, dealing with the waves again and matching the energy of the seas crashing around me.

I slowed my paddling pace, giving my body and mind time to come off the adrenaline high that was using too much precious energy. The adrenaline was what saved me from going over, but it couldn't sustain me for the two-mile paddle back to calm water. I breathed deeper and slower, trying to calm myself. The boat continued to get shoved around, to surf off the face of a wave one minute and the next second to bury its nose deep into a rebounding wave. Twice more, waves peaked at just the wrong time and sent me to within a couple of inches of going over. Each time it was a combination of timing and reflexes that kept the boat upright. Slowly the seas relinquished their hold and let me retreat into the protection of the river.

I passed Gerry on the way in and waved. There was comfort in someone knowing where I was. The size and power of the sea, plus the overwhelming scale of everything around me, was a reminder of how fragile my grasp on the trip was at times. The danger and exposure of the last hour made that very clear.

In another half hour the calm of the river soothed my nerves and welcomed me into a sheltered cove. The keel of my boat slid onto a patch of sand between two rocks. It felt strangely solid. I jackknifed out of the cockpit, straddling the rear deck as the sea gently washed over my calves. I looked back toward the headland. Once again the curve of the cliffs blocked my view and it was hard to believe that beyond those rocks was a world of breaking seas, wind, and miles of wave-battered cliffs. From a distance it looked so benign.

I pulled the boat above the reach of the tide. It was time to set up camp again and wait for the ocean to allow me to pass. I was cold and needed to get out of the wind and the drizzle that was just starting.

This waiting game wasn't anything new. It was part of the routine of ocean paddling. The tides, wind, fog, and sea conditions dictated whether I paddled or sat. As I unpacked the boat, reversing the steps of a few hours earlier, I thought how many hundreds of times I had packed and unpacked my boat in over twelve thousand miles of sea kayaking. I knew this transition of ocean to land as well as I did the actual paddling. There were three or four trips up and down the rocky beach before the boat was light enough to shoulder and carefully thread my way with its weight through the slippery rocks. I set it gently down beside the pile of nylon bags and stood looking out at the sea, partially veiled in the soft drizzle. When the seas calmed, I would continue. Until then there was nothing to do but wait.

MAP 1.

DUBLIN to MIZEN HEAD

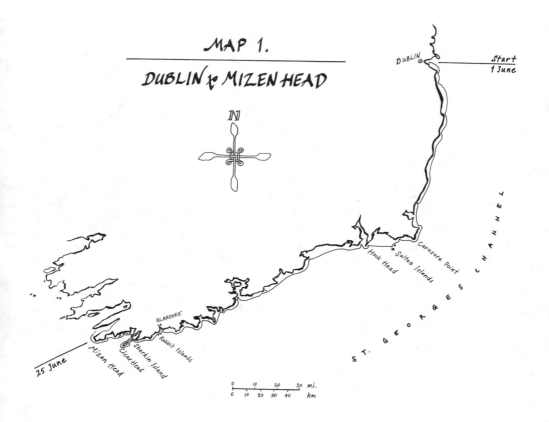

DUBLIN

Start
1 June

N

Carnsore Point

Saltee Islands

Hook Head

GLANDORE

Rabbit Islands

Sherkin Island

Clear Head

Mizen Head

25 June

ST. GEORGES CHANNEL

| 0 | 10 | 20 | 30 mi. |
| 0 | 10 | 20 | 30 | 40 | km |

Blisters and Dreams

A man who is not afraid of the sea
will soon be drowned
for he will be going out on a day he shouldn't.
But we do be afraid of the sea
and we do only be drowned now and again.

I found that quote while planning my solo kayak circumnavigation of Ireland. It was spoken by a fisherman, someone who knew the sea as only an islander could. And though the words were from another generation, the advice is as sound today as it was for those who took to the sea in their tarred, canvas-covered currachs. The unashamed fear, and the admission that the sea is the ultimate master, shows the humble wisdom of the author. I pinned the quote beside a wall map of Ireland, and during the planning phase of the trip, read those words often.

Ireland was not the first big trip I had planned. It was the third and shortest; but because of the exposure of the west coast, the seas to which the Aran Island fisherman referred, it was going to be the toughest. It seemed that the first two trips, and, in fact, my life before I started paddling on the sea, had been focused toward this journey. My adventure was to be the culmination of twenty-one years of working and paddling on the sea.

In the fall of 1982, I was part of a U.S. Navy dive team working on ballistic missile submarines in Holy Loch, Scotland. My job was to supervise the underwater repair and maintenance of the nuclear-powered submarines that patrolled the Atlantic and countered the nuclear threat of the Soviet Navy. Military life was filled with protocol, security clearances, and the exposure to the realities of the Cold War. We worked in bitter cold water, bolting on steel flanges, inspecting the subs for damage sustained during their seventy-day silent patrols, and doing security swims, our eyes sweeping the rounded black hulls for magnetic mines that an enemy swimmer could easily place against the floating missile platforms. The subs were moored sometimes three abreast on each side of the mother ship: as one sub prepared for deployment, another would appear on the horizon, and the work routine would continue. Missiles and torpedoes were loaded into launch tubes; pallets of food were lowered by crane from the mother ship; last-minute jobs, including those of the divers, were hastily completed, and another sub would slip out of the loch for its patrol.

For the last seven years I had worked as a navy diver beneath everything from tugboats to aircraft carriers, and now submarines. The work was exciting and challenging, but I was beginning to feel the constraints of higher rank. My second enlistment was almost up and another would put me over the halfway mark to retirement. If I reenlisted, I was headed for a desk job, pushing papers instead of doing the actual diving. Most of the guys were happy to take the ease of that job rather than jumping into the frigid waters, but I wasn't. The physical work, the freedom of weightlessness, the sound of my exhaled breath bubbling to the surface in silver globes of air was the world I loved. If I was going to be pulled out of the water and set behind a desk, then perhaps it was time for a change in careers. I didn't want to leave the navy, but it looked like I wasn't going to have a choice.

In the final weeks of my enlistment, I was torn by indecision. Each morning I put on the same uniform I had for the past seven years: the polished boots, the ironed shirt with the markings of my rank on the shoulder, and the coveted dive pin—a silver hardhat with dolphins, worn over the left chest pocket. As my reenlistment date approached, I had the feeling of squeezing into a uniform that no longer fit. It was as if my heart knew it was time to move on. In truth, I wouldn't miss the egos and the heavyhanded military way of getting the jobs done. It was a life that I had signed on for and didn't waste time complaining about, but it was never the way I wanted to work. I wouldn't miss the uniform, the exchange of salutes, or the privilege of rank that I was just beginning to "enjoy." The dive pin was another matter, however. Working in the water was the only job I had known and it was the reason for staying in the navy for as long as I had. I was more at home in the water than I was on land and I couldn't imagine life away from the sea.

One month later, I walked off the ship for the last time. A fellow diver, a friend who had made the decision to stay on in the navy, gave me a ride to the airport. He was on his way up through the ranks and would one day be the senior diving officer in the service. I wasn't sure where I was going. I was following my heart, an urging that tugged at my idealistic mind, but one that didn't lead down a secure path like my friend's.

We wear many kinds of clothes in life. Layers and colors that we outgrow and leave on a hanger, or give away to someone we think might want what we have worn. Sometimes it's out of boredom that we make a change. We get tired of the same old clothes. Sometimes it seems it's the other way around; the clothes are tired of us, they're worn through like a pair of jeans tired of the same hands shoved in the top of the pockets. They finally rip where the fabric is so thin that they can't be sewn. They force us to go out and try on something new. Something that doesn't fit anywhere near as well as what we had; but in time we either forget how the old garment fit, or maybe we just adapt until the new one softens and takes on some of the old one's character.

It isn't only the outer clothes that we hang up or trade for new ones. Sometimes we change the outer garments because the inner fabric of our soul, or spirit, is tired. Maybe by switching colors on the outside we can tighten the bagginess or patch the worn places inside. That helps for awhile, but soon the new clothes take on the same worn spots of the spirit and we need to look deeper at what the cause of the weakened threads really is.

As I boarded the plane, I had plenty of time to think of old and new, of changing clothes, or in my case, a uniform, and of what it really was that made me leave the navy. It wasn't the uniform, or what the uniform stood for. It was what I stood for, or maybe what I didn't know I stood for, that made me take the starched uniform off and feel the loss of the coveted pin. Maybe the stuff of my soul had had enough of the routine, the security, and was finally talking loud enough that I had to listen. I think it was tired of summer whites, winter blues, ribbons of achievements, letters of commendation, dress shoes for inspections, and work boots polished black. For seven years it had let me grow into an adult, disciplined and secure in who I was and what I needed to do at that stage in my life. Now when I was ready—or maybe even if I wasn't—it was shaking me up, turning things around, and making me look at where my life was headed.

The jet roared down the runway, forcing me deep into the cushioned seat and making it easy to lay back and think of what I was doing. I had shed the protective skin of the past and now knew what a crab must feel when it has done the same thing—it grows too big for its old shell, and crawls out the back of it, discarding the old for the new that will slowly harden around it. For a week, the crab's body is soft and vulnerable to the life that just days ago had been secure and unthreatening. Somewhere behind me, along the shore of a Scottish loch was my discarded shell, seven years of protection that I no longer had.

As the jet cleared the runway, I caught a few parting views of Scottish countryside. The first wisps of clouds flashed over the wingtips and seconds later all sight of the land was lost. The jet continued to climb, pulling me swiftly from the past and racing me on to what lay ahead. Part of me was excited about breaking out of the mold of the military. Another part was frightened by uncertainty, by the fear of maybe making a mistake, and of failure.

A memory from my late teens came back to me. It was a mural, a collage of life experiences; people's faces, travels, and earthy colors; greens, blues, and browns. Trees and water. While other kids were thinking about jobs and college, I had come up with this image of what I wanted my life to be. Where it came from I didn't know. Was it rebellion, or something deeper? Perhaps intuition? I had made the decision to "Join the navy and see the world," as the saying goes. Now, years later, I was changing direction. While others stuck to a known career and something that promised security, I was questioning the norm and setting off to explore other options. Maybe my decision to leave the protective shell of the navy was part of that mural, another stroke of the brush dipped in a new color. I knew the change would be difficult, but I wanted to believe we are artists of our own lives. We create what we live, and though there is uncertainty in change, I had to trust that I had made the right choice.

The jet broke through the clouds, and sunlight streamed into the small windows. I looked out beyond the wingtip. Blinding white clouds, thick with piles of loft, billowed into a sky bluer than any I had seen in months. I was glad to be in the sun. It seemed to soak into me, drying out the corners of fear and doubt, and assuring me that I had made the right decision. I settled into the flight and tried to imagine how the next months of my life would unfold.

I returned to upstate New York, a place of family, to sort out my new life. I tried my hand at carpentry—a different set of tools and clothing; work boots, nail bags, measuring tape, hammer and nails. The work was creative and relaxed. Instead of steel decks and welded seams painted with multiple layers of the same gray paint, there was wood: sawed, fitted, and spiked with sixteen penny nails. Nails that at first came awkwardly out of a pouch on the left hip, fingers fumbling for the heads while the right hand reached for the hammer. There was the satisfying *thunk* of a nail set deep in sweet-smelling wood and the occasional searing red pain of a carelessly placed thumb or finger. The learning curve was fast. It was a world of hard physical work, the whine of circular saws and the slam thunk of hammers echoing across hillsides covered with oak, maple, and ash. At the end of the day there was sawdust between boottop and socks, and blisters where the hammer handle heated the flesh of my hand.

In the winter, when the carpentry jobs slowed down, I worked with a semiretired Irish couple in their meat shop. Mr. and Mrs. Kelly taught me how to cut meat, and shared stories of growing up in depression-era Brooklyn. While sides of beef and pork were broken down and packaged, I heard about horses being trained, and pigs running in fields where today there is only blacktop and high-rise apartments. Another set of stories was of a visit to Ireland. Stories of horses being lowered from a dockside boom; harnesses around their bellies, eyes white with fear as they were swung over the water and lowered into an open boat. Men in black jackets, white shirts and ties, all wearing the same kind of cap. Farmers watching their livestock being loaded for the mainland. No money but for the price the animals would get at the market, plus the salted fish that was already in the hold.

"What part of Ireland was it?" I asked.

Mr. Kelly's knife found a joint. He worked the stainless blade around, slipped it through sinew and cartilage, and separated bone from bone.

"The Aran Islands, on the west coast," he answered.

An Irish tune from the fifties was playing on the eight-track player high on a corner shelf. Mr. Kelly wiped his hands on a bloodied apron and reached beside the player for a book edged between others. Books on horses, livestock, and gardening crowded the one he was looking for. He pulled it down and set it on a side counter: *Ireland: Its Land and Its People*. He flipped through the pages and found a photo of one of the Aran Islands. It was an aerial shot of blue seas breaking white around an island that looked more rock than green. There were photos of the people as well; ruddy, square faces with blue eyes and a weathered toughness from winds and sea salt. In the background were black-tarred boats overturned on a crescent of sunny beach. Another photo was of raging seas, storm clouds, and waves surrounding the island and not a soul in sight.

The book was closed, a few more memories were shared, and it was slid back into place on the shelf. Knives were slashed across sharpening steels and we went back to work. While meat was cut, wrapped, and frozen, another slab of beef was brought in from the walk-in cooler and a seed was sown for a future adventure. That seed would lay dormant for fourteen years while the pictures of the Aran Islands stayed fresh in my memory.

The carpentry and the work in the meat shop satisfied two things for me. They kept me fit and they gave me an opportunity to learn new skills. The problem was, I longed for the sea. I missed working in the water, or maybe just being around it; the smell of the salt air, the tides, and knowing there was another world of life just beneath its surface. The sea had become part of me, and though family and friends were supportive and loving, I felt like I was drying out from being away from it.

All the résumés I had sent out to commercial diving companies had come back with the same reply: "Due to current economic conditions we are no longer hiring at this time. Your résumé will be kept on file for future consideration." Most of the diving jobs in the civilian sector were for oil exploration and the recession of the early eighties had halted much of that work. I could have waited for the wheels of industry to begin turning again, but I was too impatient. Six months or a year was too long. I wanted to get back to the water sooner than that.

It was a magazine article about sea kayaks that grabbed my attention and eventually led me back to the sea. The article explored the design of these boats, the watertight hatches, the seaworthiness of the sealed cockpit, and the ability of the paddler to roll the boat upright if it was knocked over by a wave. The hatches could be loaded with gear and the boat used for coastal camping trips. After the third time through the article, I started imagining my own travels. If the boat could be used for short day trips, why couldn't it be used for longer adventures? I wrote for more information, and between work began dreaming. By the time the catalogue of boats had arrived, I had come up with an idea for an extended trip.

Before being transferred to Scotland, I had been assigned to a navy base in Washington State. The Northwest was a land of fir and cedar forests, and glacier-tipped mountain peaks that towered over the inland sea of Puget Sound. It was an environment where I thought I might want to settle down. I had purchased a piece of land a few miles from the shores of Hood Canal, then soon after had been transferred to Scotland. It was that land and the memories of the snow-capped peaks that gave me the idea for a trip.

If I could learn the basics of paddling, how to deal with the waves and tides, and how to roll the boat as I had seen whitewater paddlers do on TV, why couldn't I paddle to the West Coast? From New York I could head south to Florida, along the Gulf Coast to Texas, then somehow get the boat and myself overland to Southern California. From there it would be a straight shot up the coast to Washington. I was fit and confident from the years spent diving, and in my enthusiasm I saw this trip as a transition toward a new place of living as well as a new time in my life. In my naive enthusiasm I saw only possibility and no obstacles. The plan was born and a boat was ordered.

I knew nothing about kayaking when I began the twelve-month journey in March 1983. I also didn't know that halfway through the trip the route would change, and I would end up paddling a thousand miles up the Mississippi River, into the Illinois River, through the Great Lakes, out the St. Lawrence Seaway, around the Canadian Maritimes, and eventually back to New York. By the time I had changed my route, the original destination was no longer important. When I returned to New York, to the same beach that I had left a year earlier, there was a sense of completing a huge circle; not only the paddling circle but an inner one that was related to the simple life I had lived as a child. After eight thousand miles of paddling, I had come back to a place in myself that I had known years before. A place of discovery; of wonder and satisfaction with the simple things of life.

Two of the greatest gifts that I became aware of during that first trip were time and the pace of my daily life. A week into the trip, I realized the glances at my watch no longer had any relevance. Time was measured differently when there wasn't a schedule. There was no need to track it hour by hour, assign a dollar value to it, or be anywhere other than where the tide allowed me to go. Without the constraints of hourly time, a different measure became apparent. High and low tides measured dawn to dusk, and the amount of daylight waxing or waning indicated the change of seasons. It was this broader view of time that I became aware of, segmented not by minutes but by the forces of the planets; the moon pulling the oceans, and the earth tilting on its axis.

I remembered seeing the first faint signs of spring and feeling the wonder, the magic of seasonal change. I was several weeks into the trip and still dealing with mornings of ice in the water bottle, fingers that hurt with a cold that ran into the bones and stiffened the joints. I would lay the paddle across the spray deck and swing my arms in a circle, driving the blood into the tips and making them sting with pink warmth. It was the first week in April, the days were slowly growing longer, but where was spring? For three hundred miles I had nursed frozen fingers and toes, and paddled along shorelines of gray-black eastern hardwoods. They reached into the gray skies, bent crooked with alternating limbs brittle in the cold air, yet hopeful in the fidelity of the seasons. It was that sky, a winter sky in spring, and a stand of oaks that awakened me to a change that was slowly occurring. A change so subtle I would never have noticed it but for the slow progress southward and the hours of observation, of time spent looking more intently both inward and outward, that are part of paddling.

At first I didn't see anything different in the silhouetted trees. The oaks raked the sky with the same naked limbs of winter that I had seen all along my route. Yet something was different. I looked again, not at the individual limbs but at the outer reach of all the branches. There against the raw winds was a touch of delicate green. A breath of life so subtle it almost didn't exist. It was as though I had caught the moment the tiny buds were just breaking open. After months of winter, the sight of that first tinge brought hope for the warmer weather that couldn't be far off. Soon my fingers would no longer ache from the cold, and the waters that I paddled through would slowly warm as the sun climbed higher and burned brighter. In that first spring paddle, the season's changes had never felt so pivotal.

By the end of the trip I had seen eagles and alligators, manatees and finback whales, fiddler crabs and even a wolf as it trotted through the crisp autumn colors along the shores of Lake Huron. The paddling life was full of these moments of discovery; moments that stopped all thought and left me awed. My navy days of ships, and high technology that could destroy all life with the turn of matched keys, felt absurdly foreign. Had I really lived that life? Nuclear weapons, secret clearances that allowed me to work on board billion-dollar submarines, and shipboard life where a thousand men lived in a world of gray steel. Instead of the polished boots and the coveted dive pin that I had worn with pride, I now wore the sun-bleached and rumpled clothes of a traveler. They were clothes that fit physically, soft and comfortable. Clothes that fit spiritually as well; a bit untidy from the demands of living with the winds and weather, but clothes that were honest and didn't hide who I was. The collage of life that I had imagined in my teens now had another image: a kayak painted in the forefront of the mural. A kayak whose bow rose out of a broken wave and was heading into my future. A future of adventure and travel.

When I left Scotland at the end of my navy days, I knew in my heart that I would go back. I remembered telling an older Scottish lady that it was difficult to leave a country where I felt so at home. She listened, smiled, and with motherly advice said, "Ye canna come back unless first ye go away." I didn't understand her words at first but they proved prophetic. Four years later, with one kayaking journey behind me, I was heading back to the British Isles with a plan for my second one.

The idea of paddling around England, Wales, and Scotland had started as a daydream somewhere along the last portion of the American/Canadian trip. Sea kayaking had become a passion for me and I didn't want the paddling to end when that first trip did. I loved the fitness of pulling the boat through thirty miles of water each day, the focus of having a defined goal. The camping, the simple food, and the adventure of seeing new places and meeting interesting people were all reasons to dream away the last miles of the first trip while starting to plan the second.

By the time that first trip came to a close in 1984, the daydream had become a fixed plan. I would need money and time to figure out the logistics of buying a boat and mapping out a route, but I was already convinced the trip was possible. The first circumnavigation of mainland Britain had been completed by a team of two in 1980. If a team could do it, why couldn't one person? What I didn't know was that there had been several attempts to solo Britain over the years. Whether it was the distance, the unstable weather, or the seas, each attempt had failed. It wasn't until I was well into the trip that I realized just how big an undertaking Britain was and why it hadn't been successfully solved before.

The trip was approximately three thousand miles long and took five and a half months to complete. Although the distance and time were less than half that of my first trip, the sea conditions were far more difficult. Extreme low tides like those in the Thames Estuary, and again in the tidal flats of Liverpool, left me stranded on sandbars with the retreating ocean miles away. At other places the tidal currents were so fast, they piled the waters in standing waves eight to ten feet high and raced me along at speeds of a whitewater river. I capsized a half dozen times in big surf, and wrecked the boat on the rocks near Lands End on the southwest tip of England. In the first thousand miles I understood why the previous attempts had failed. British paddling was nothing like anything I had done before.

The trip was not all hardship and difficulty, though. There were many days of startling beauty on relatively calm seas, the same freeing wonder that I had known on my first trip, and moments of memorable experiences with the people I met along the way. One such meeting stands out vividly, and is the reason why these solo journeys are not only possible but also inspiring.

I had been stranded on a beach near Liverpool, waiting for the winds, the fog, and the tides to allow me to continue. I was less than halfway into the trip and frustrated by the unusually strong winds that seemed always to be against me. A middle-aged couple who ran a pony-trekking business on the beach had befriended me, and we had spent a day passing the time, chatting about our different lives. On the evening of the third day, the forecast called for fair winds and no fog. I told them I would be leaving at three-thirty the next morning to catch a north-flowing tide. We said good-bye and I thought that was the last I would see them.

The next morning at three o'clock I was loading the boat by moonlight and headlamp, when Robin and Barbara drove up. In the light of the moon they walked across the beach, laughing and balancing a silver tray with three crystal glasses and a bottle of champagne. While the town slept and the tide began to run north, we drank a toast to life and to journeys. Robin and Barbara shared their enthusiasm and their cares for me as if I was a brother. We laughed, cried, and hugged, then parted company in the silver ripple of moonlight on water, voices in the dark calling out farewells.

By the end of September 1986 I had succeeded in closing another circle of paddling. This one had taught me more about the sea, about the technical aspects of strong tides and heavy surf, about unstable weather and persevering when all the odds were against me. Unlike the first trip, where the destination was not important, this trip had a definite goal. I had set out to circumnavigate mainland Britain, and perhaps because it had been far more difficult than I had imagined, I finished the trip with a great sense of accomplishment. The skills learned, and the memories I had of the three thousand—mile journey, were enough reward for the five and a half months of work. I headed back to the States content, and happy to put the paddle away for a few years.

Over the next ten years I worked as a carpenter and learned the trade well enough to support a life of travel and adventure. I lived in upstate New York for awhile, then Nova Scotia, and finally moved to Washington State, where sea kayaking, whitewater kayaking, and telemark skiing shared equal time with work. I had made a choice to live my life as simply as possible, and to be conscious that every day was a blessing, a day I would live only once.

Sea kayaking was still a big part of my life, and on several week-long, or longer, trips with friends, the rhythm of my previous travels would surface and the urge for another adventure began to stir. Long after I had returned from these trips, memories from past journeys would slip into my mind like treasured photographs found in a cluttered drawer. I would sift through the images, turning them over in my mind and bringing them back to life. The pictures of peaceful camps, high rugged coastlines, and simple living began to build a momentum of their own. I played with the thoughts of another journey, letting my mind skip from the memories of a past adventure to the dreams of a future one. I reread journals, laying one upon the other on the top shelf of my bookcase. Ten-year-old entries stirred emotions of the past and spoke passionately of those adventures. The more I explored the memories, the greater the urge to travel became.

Since completing the British trip I had dreamed about returning to that part of the world and paddling around what I called the last piece of the Celtic puzzle: Ireland. During my navy days I had toured this land on a motorcycle, visiting quaint villages, meeting the people, and camping beside tea-colored bog streams. I remembered it as a country of stone cottages, warm friendly folk, and roads too narrow for modern cars; roads that eventually led me to rocky headlands above the sea. I had stood on the Cliffs of Moher and looked down at the mist of broken waves throwing themselves against the base six hundred feet below. If someone had told me I would one day attempt to paddle a kayak through those waters, I would have thought they were crazy. Now, fifteen years after my first visit, the circles of my adventurous life were about to overlap. It was 1996, and I had made the decision to visit Ireland again, not with the motorcycle of my youth but with a paddle, a sea kayak, and a much slower perspective of life. I would see the country as if for the first time—from the sea looking up, rather than from the land looking outward.

In the years since I started kayaking I had amassed twelve thousand miles of paddling, yet the Aran Island fisherman's warning seemed to brush away those miles and leave me feeling like a novice. The last two lines of that warning were a reminder of how careful I would have to be on this trip: ". . . But we do be afraid of the sea and we do only be drowned now and again." There was both wisdom and wit in those words, and I wanted to visit the seas that inspired a fisherman to speak of them with such poetic respect.

Ireland lies between 52 and 55 degrees North latitudes. It sits in the path both of the westerly swells of the North Atlantic Ocean and the cold air masses and high winds that pour off Iceland to the northwest. Were it not for the Gulf Stream sweeping up from the south and touching Ireland's west coast, the Emerald Isle would have a climate more like that of Newfoundland. For generations the fishermen of Ireland have pulled from these clear ocean waters their livelihood and sustenance. Their tarred canvas boat, the currach, is an adaptation of skin-covered craft thousands of years old. They are still used today where the rockbound coast allows only a boat light enough to be easily pulled from the water when it gets rough. In the time of the poet-fisherman of the Aran Islands, the currach was also known as a canoe—a term for any boat small and nimble enough to be rowed or paddled. It was in a kayak, or as they say in both England and Ireland, a canoe, that I planned to paddle around the waters of the Emerald Isle.

It is hard to say where a solo kayak journey begins because there are months of preparations that lead to that first pull of the paddle. If a journey of a thousand miles begins with a single step, then perhaps a kayak adventure, no matter the length, also begins with that first act of motion. Once the boat is afloat, its weight held by the waters lapping inches from the cockpit opening, the adventure begins. Ties to the point of departure are cast off. The handshake of a friend or stranger is loosened as reluctantly as the line tied to the dock. The boat drifts from the land and the wind or tide hastens the months of planning. Solo suddenly means exactly what it says.

On June 1, 1996 I sat just outside the shipping channel near the middle of the Liffey River and let the falling tide pull me down to the sea. Two miles upriver the clamor of Dublin and the bustle of the docks was carried away by a breeze that brought the smell of low tide. Pungent odors of brown seaweed clinging to rocks, mixed with the freshness of salt air, a smell of the intertidal zone where land meets sea and every six hours the tides bring a change.

The Liffey River was the starting point, and if I was lucky, the point of closure for my circumnavigation of Ireland. I dipped my hand into the river, then ran my fingers and palm rapidly over the paddle shaft. First my right, then my left. I did it unconsciously, a ritual that I perform before setting out for a paddle. I want to wash my hands and the paddle with the water that I'll be passing through. It is also a baptism, a place of beginning.

I could see the end of the seawall a half mile in front of me and the squat red brick tower at the end. A freighter was coming in from the open water, its blunt red bow heading straight upriver. Rusty anchors snubbed tightly in their housings looked like a pair of eyes staring down from the heights of the bow. The oncoming ship looked too big for the narrow river and I paddled a dozen yards closer to the seawall. Beyond the wall and the approaching bulk of the ship was the Irish Sea, a straight horizon where overcast sky met the washed-out color of gray waters. I drifted to the end of the seawall as the freighter passed the last sea buoy and entered the river. The massive weight of the ship, tall as a six-story building and as long as a city block, glided soundlessly upriver twenty yards away. I looked to my right, then sharply up, almost overhead, to the flash of light on the tower. I felt pinched between the red steel of the ship and the seawall a paddle length away. The backwash of the ship swirled around the rocks as I pulled the boat beyond the seawall and out to open water. To my left the stern of the ship swept by, and suddenly I was out of the shadow of steel and stone.

With a few strokes of the paddle, I pulled away from the mouth of the river and into the sea. The change was dramatic, a mix of excited freedom and nervousness at the exposure. I looked around for something to focus on, something definite on an empty horizon. A hundred yards back, there had been steel, stone, and brown churning water. Now all that was gone.

I swung the bow to the right and watched the compass rotate from east to southeast, then settle on a southerly heading. Ten feet in front of the bow, the riverwater met the sea in a line of dull brown, washed suddenly clear with blue-green. The bow buried into an oncoming wave, lifted as the swell rolled beneath the hull, then lowered us again. Droplets of sea-water clung to the bright yellow foredeck, until the next wave washed over the bow and set them free. I was on my way.

A gannet circled against a backdrop of broken gray clouds, then dove headfirst into the waves. A plume of white against the sea marked its disappearance. Seconds later it bobbed to the surface and took to the air with glistening droplets falling back to the water.

The sun had reached through the overlapping layers of clouds and for a few brief moments the dark, cold-looking waters didn't feel so threat-ening. Whitecaps curled off the tops of steep-sided waves, and with a hiss, slid down the face and into the troughs. The oncoming waves lifted and set the boat down in a steady rhythm that felt comforting and familiar from my past ocean travels. My senses were adjusting to the new world that I would be immersed in for the next twelve hundred miles.

I let my eyes play over the fine lines of the bow and foredeck, then back to the fullness of the paddling compartment and the spray deck stretched tight across the cockpit. Behind me were two more watertight compartments, the life jacket tied across the first hatch and the spare breakdown paddles lashed across the second. The lines of the hull swept back to a graceful point where the trailing seas met again.

I loved the feel of the boat snugly wrapped around me; the firmness of the bulkhead against my feet, the touch of the deck on my slightly bent knees, and the padded cockpit lightly holding my hips within the seat. While my eyes wandered across the waves, out to the distant shoreline and always back to the bow gracefully slicing into the next swell, my body felt each rise and fall of the sea. I reached forward, slipped the paddle into the bow wave, pulled back, and felt shoulder, arm, and stomach muscles tense. Fingers tightened around the shaft of the paddle, pulled smoothly, then relaxed as the blade exited at the rear of the cockpit. Rotate, reach, plant, pull. Again and again. Through the skin of the boat I could almost feel the caress of the waves, two worlds meeting in the rhythm of muscle, and the rise and fall of swell. I closed my eyes, smiled, and paddled for several minutes, wanting to live these first moments as deeply as I could.

As I opened my eyes, I tried to grasp the size and scope of what lay in front of me. All the months of training and planning had brought me to this moment, the first paddle strokes of the trip. The newspaper interviews, the warmth of friends at a going-away party, and the last-minute phone calls to family, all seemed so distant. I thought of familiar faces, solid hugs, and eyes that looked deep into my own with caring and love. Part of me wanted to find a place where I could hold on to all of that warmth and not think of the challenges ahead. Within the forward compartment of the boat was a light blue prayer flag the color of a summer sky. On one side of the flag were the snow-covered peaks and ravines of the Olympic Mountains, framed by green fir trees. On the other side were blessings of safe travels, smooth seas, and dozens of friends' names printed in brightly colored inks. It was a reminder of my physical home, the mountains that I could see from my living-room window, and the close friends I would symbolically take along on this journey. That blue flag would hang from the peak of the tent wherever I camped during the next three months.

As I settled into paddling, I was drawn deeper into the excitement of the first day of the trip and at the same time I feared the very thing that

I was excited about. What was I doing turning my back on everything that was secure and safe for a life that was full of the possibility of failure? All of the "what ifs" that people had been asking me since I came up with the plan of paddling around Ireland came drifting into my mind. The big surf of the west coast, the headlands and the expanses of rocky shoreline, where there would be ten or fifteen miles between landings; wasn't that reason enough to stay at home and be satisfied with adventures that I had already lived?

After the British trip I remembered telling a friend that I had had enough of long-distance paddling. At the time, the risks and sacrifices necessary for that kind of expedition were something I didn't want to do again. She reminded me of those words when I told her of the upcoming trip. I nodded and smiled. Time has a way of erasing hardship and coloring memories with sunny days and the promise of adventure. Now, here I was sitting a mile offshore, driving the boat into oncoming waves and feeling a mixture of elation and doubt. Three miles in front of me was Dalkey Island. I had plenty of time to sort out my feelings in the next hour and let my mind settle into the rhythm that my body had already found.

I remembered walking into the downstairs bedroom of my house, which I had turned into a planning room. In the far corner was a jumble of colored nylon bags, paddling clothes, camping and camera equipment, and two breakdown paddles leaning against the wall. There was an AM/FM radio for weather reports, a leatherbound journal, and a list of items yet to be purchased.

There was also a large map of Ireland stuck to the wall with colored pushpins. All of the counties of the Republic of Ireland and Northern Ireland were pieced together like a color-coded child's puzzle. Light greens, yellows, pinks, and blues interlocked and floated on a background of blue ocean. The Atlantic and the Irish Sea seemed to flood into every crevice and crack along the coastline. A few months earlier I wouldn't have known where County Galway was or if Counties Mayo and Sligo were in Southern or Northern Ireland. I hadn't known what counties were on the coast or where exactly the Shannon River flowed into the sea. But in the preceding weeks the map of Ireland had become my life. Every time I walked into that room, it pulled me from whatever task I had meant to accomplish and

I would stand amid the chaos of gear and stare at it. My eyes would wander through the counties and along their jagged boundaries until I knew how they all fit together and could visualize the country as a whole. I looked at the rivers and inland loughs, then followed the threads of blue rivers down to the sea.

The sea . . . my eyes always ended up on the coast. I would stare at a pencil-thick headland jutting out into the blue Atlantic and try to picture it as a two hundred–foot cliff pounded by ocean swells.

There was so much I didn't know; the map held its secrets locked away in the colors and flatness of the paper. I wanted to give it height and texture, enlarge it like a photo until I could read the details in the exploded grains. I wanted to feel the size of the waves and hear their thunder rumbling against the rocky shore.

I would walk my fingers along two inches of coast and cover a day's paddle—maybe twenty miles. I imagined westerly winds driving wave-covered swells, and squalls approaching from the distant horizon. With the pencil I would trace another twenty miles and tuck into the protection of a tiny hook of land, or slide in behind the lee of an island. On the map, it was easy. In a few weeks or maybe a month I would be there and I wondered how difficult it might be just to get around the headland, never mind finding the tiny cove that my pencil point sat in. That was the trouble with maps: they lured me into adventures by making it look so easy.

I spread my fingers like a chart compass and stepped off the distance to the offshore islands on the west coast. Five, seven, up to ten miles out into the pale blue of the map. The tip of my finger covered the islands and new questions flashed into my mind. Would there be any place to land? Does anybody live out there? Would the west coast weather and seas even allow me to make the crossings?

Slowly, as the weeks passed and the pile of gear grew more colorful and varied, the map began to fill with cryptic notes penciled along its blue margins. Tide notations, villages where I could restock the boat, and addresses that friends gave me were circled and underlined. The map was still just a piece of paper, a picture of an island country that I knew little about, but it was slowly becoming familiar.

The day before I left for Ireland, I folded the wall map into a waterproof chart case and packed it into an overstuffed canvas bag beside the back door. That map, with its four corners pierced and its border lined with penciled notes, was going to be my guide for the next three months. Almost everything that I knew about Ireland was on that map. If I was lucky enough to complete the circumnavigation, it would come home water-stained and torn, showing the wear of constant folding and unfolding. It was almost ridiculous to think how little I knew about what was in front of me, but maybe that was the very reason for going. Ten years of dreaming and anticipation had come down to a couple of canvas bags, an airline ticket, and a kayak that had been built in Nottingham England, and sat waiting to be picked up in Holyhead, Wales. From there I would catch the ferry to Dublin on the east coast of Ireland.

A week later, I was a mile into the trip, still trying to sort the memories and emotions rushing through my mind. The transition from my home on Washington State's Olympic Peninsula to Ireland had happened too fast. Through time zones and lost sleep I had arrived at the starting point of the trip groggy and trying to hold on to a place six thousand miles away. Two days before my flight to England, I had skied with a friend on the north-facing slopes of Olympic National Park. At five thousand feet above sea level we looked down on Port Angeles, my home, and north across the Straits of Juan de Fuca to Canada. At our backs was a maze of jagged peaks, snow fields, and glaciers protected by a roadless wilderness bigger than any in the lower forty-eight states. I had wanted to ski the ridges one last time before taking off for Ireland.

The next day I had taken my sea kayak out on the harbor, paddled a mile offshore, and sat looking at Port Angeles and the Olympic Mountains from another perspective. It was those memories that came to mind as I paddled out into the Liffey River and began my journey. From my other trips I remembered the same emotions; excitement about starting, yet wanting to cling to what was safe and familiar. My body was already into the rhythm of paddling, flowing smoothly with the lively sea, but my mind wasn't that easy to convince. It would be another week before the trip calmed the fears of the unknown. And even as those pre-trip jitters subsided, the longing for family, friends, and home would always be there.

A few inches in front of the cockpit, crossed bungee cords held the map case tightly against the front deck. Through the droplets of water splashed up on the clear plastic I could see the first one hundred miles of the trip. A thumb-width distance on the map represented about five miles. The island a half mile in front of me wasn't on the map. I didn't really expect it to be. The map was a small-scale Michelin road map that covered the entire country. I wouldn't have known the island was Dalkey Island except that I had talked with a fisherman just before leaving Dublin. He had warned me about the strong currents around the island and especially in the narrows separating it from the mainland. As I paddled closer, I could see the ruins of a small church tucked into the folds of a ravine. I wanted to land but the only place was in the narrows where the current was running the hardest. I paddled around the outside of the island, looking for the slacker water that I knew must be there. Waves rolled in and slapped against the larger rocks, sending white spray flying. The sound of the waves hitting the rock and the sight of the water being launched into the air set my heart beating faster.

I liked being in close and feeling the power of the waves. The boat shifted under me and I pulled it back on course after a rebounding wave set it too close to the tip of a rock barely showing through the clear water. The lower rocks were the ones I had to watch out for. The waves would cover them for a few seconds, then roll back and expose their sharp ridges that could rip into the thin layer of fiberglass beneath me. I watched strands of brown seaweed floating between the peaks of the half-submerged rocks. As the weed started to drift back with the receding swell, I let the boat drift off its course and follow the swell back into deeper water. It was a dance of hiding from the current in among the dangers of the rocks and having to play with the swirling waters.

A couple of seals appeared between two offshore rocks and watched as I worked the boat through the current. Their huge brown eyes and snub noses followed me through another maze of rocks. In front of me, a white mottled seal arched up on its belly, its tail and head silhouetted against the breaking waves slapping the rock it rested on. I swung the bow out into the tidal current and headed for the mainland around the back side of the island.

When I left Dublin a couple of hours earlier, I knew I wouldn't get far in the fading light of evening. I just wanted to make a break from the city and get on the water, if only for a few miles. Now as I approached the cobbled beach and spotted a likely site for the tent, I was just as excited about making the first night's camp.

All of the things that had been a part of those first three hours of paddling were going to be with me for the rest of the trip. The gannets, the waves rolling under the boat and washing up over the bow, the awareness of clouds and colors reflected off the sea, and the fluid movement of my body working in unison with the waves: all were constants.

As I slid out of the cockpit and pulled the boat up high onto the beach, I thought, "Oh yeah, this is the part of solo paddling that isn't fun." I had to get the boat and all my gear up a hundred yards of rocky beach to a small patch of level sand. The paddle, water bag, tent, and sleeping bag made the first trip across pancake-size slates layered perfectly atop each other. My feet found the larger slabs, and the stones settled beneath my weight with grinding crunching noises as I climbed the steep beach. Like a child on his first camping trip, I looked around at the different colors and shapes of rocks and made a game of finding the biggest stones to jump to. I hopped onto a large slab that tottered over at an angle. With my left leg thrust out in an ungainly counterbalance to the gear hanging off me like a Christmas tree, I hung there for seconds, laughing, before jumping down and continuing on. It was a sunny day and I had the leisure of setting up my first night's camp without the threat of rain.

An hour later I had the tent up and my gear neatly organized around me. The nearly empty boat was tied to the windward side of the tent and piles of stones held down the other two corners. Before I rolled out the sleeping bag and opened my journal, I took another walk around the tent to make sure it was set for the night. Satisfied, I settled down into the little slates in front of the tent and felt their gentle warmth radiate into the backs of my thighs and hips. The top of a full moon rose above a narrow stretch of clouds hanging on the horizon and slowly spread a band of yellow light across the sea. I wiggled deeper into the warmth of the rocks and watched the moon creep ever so slowly into the sky. Before this moment I hadn't even known what phase the moon was in. Its fullness explained the strong currents running in the narrows of Dalkey Island. Now in the bliss of evening, with the sound of the small surf tingling against the stones, I was reminded why I was there. This peaceful evening brought to mind so many other times, other travels. The tides, the moon, and the sense of my immediate environment all awakened a rhythm within me that had been drowned out by the noise of my regular life. As I sat on the beach and felt the first chill of the evening on the back of my neck, I knew the good fortune of being able to take the time and just be quiet for a few months. A proverb, "To be empty, in order to be full," came to mind. It said everything I was feeling. Long after the moon had risen overhead, I crawled into the sleeping bag and lay looking up at the stars through the tent opening. The trip felt as miraculous and as unknown as the night sky above, so many mysteries hidden right in front of my sleepy eyes. Tomorrow would be another day, but the simple cadence that had begun this day would roll on into the months ahead.

The first few days made me realize how important the calm waters of the east and south coasts were. It wasn't only my heart and emotions that were adjusting to the journey but also my body. I needed this time to work my muscles gradually into shape and get used to the daily routine.

I had planned for the first two hundred-fifty miles to be a breaking-in period, a time of training for the exposed west coast. I hadn't had time to train with a fully loaded boat, and after the first few days of paddling I awoke with shoulder muscles sore from the previous day's work. What a difference between an empty boat that responded so easily to a shift of weight and a subtle change in the angle of the paddle and the heavy, solid feel of the boat loaded with a hundred pounds of gear. I would be grateful for that weight and stability in the weeks ahead, but right now my body was fighting it.

My hands had begun to feel the strain of paddling after only the second day. Small, puffy white blisters formed on my palms and in the hollow between my thumb and index finger where the paddle sat cradled. I popped the blisters with a needle, then soaked my hands in the sea to soften the surrounding tissue. In the mornings, the seawater burned like fire for a few seconds, then eased off and I was able to grip the paddle shaft.

On the evening I left Dublin, I had called the Marine Emergency Service, which are responsible for tracking shipping and also coordinating search and rescue operations along the coast. I wanted to let them know about my plans just in case anyone spotted me offshore and reported my position to them. I had been surprised at how positive they were about my trip. After the fellow entered all of the information about departure time and destination, he signed off with a cheerful "Let us know how you're makin' out and all the very best of luck to you, lad."

Three days after leaving Dublin, I thought I had better check in again. A strong south wind had been building since early morning and the forecast was for Force 6 to 7 winds, twenty-five to thirty knots, by evening. The seas had been on the bow all day and I wasn't making much progress pounding into the short chop. I headed in behind the breakwater leading into Wicklow and paddled up to two yachts moored side by side to the inner wall. I could see a thin wire antenna on top of the aluminum mast on the outer boat, and an open hatchway leading below.

I called out, "Hello, anyone home?"

No answer. The wind was stronger than I thought. A little louder this time: "Hello, is there anyone home?"

The boat heeled over half a degree and a jolly round face appeared above the teak cowling, looking for the mysterious voice. He peered at the dock above, then fore and aft along the length of his boat, and started to tuck back into the warmth of the cabin.

"Hello," I sang out one more time. I didn't want to be the loud American but I really did want to use this fellow's radio.

Startled, he stepped higher out of the hatchway and leaned over the side of his boat. I sat looking up at him, chuckling from the shocked look on his face and enjoying the scene that had happened so many times on other journeys.

"I thought I heard someone out here, but ye had me guessing for a minute. Where in the hell have ye come from?" he asked.

"Oh, I started in Dublin a few days ago and . . ."

"You've come from Dublin in that?" he asked incredulously.

"Yeah."

"Ah, yer havin' me on now, aren't ye?"

"No, I really did. I saw your mast above the seawall and thought I'd come in and try to call the Marine Emergency Service and let them know I'm okay."

"All the way from Dublin in that wee little boat. Ye must be mad, but come aboard and meet the family. We're just having some chips and a pint before deciding what to do with this wind."

The thought of a warm cabin and something to eat sounded good. "Great, be right back." I paddled over to the ramp below the lifeboat station and pulled the boat above a line of green seaweed. A few minutes later I was crowded in around the cabin table of Barney's sailboat surrounded by his two teenage daughters, his wife Margaret, his buddy Gerry from the boat alongside, and Gerry's wife and two children. A pint of Guinness appeared from below a cushioned seat and a greasy brown paper bag filled with steaming, finger-thick potatoes was placed in front of me.

Barney opened a can of Budweiser for himself, and as if that was what everyone was waiting for, said, "Now, tell me again where it is that yer goin'?"

I had a feeling I was going to be telling this story many times in the next few months. I felt a little foolish because I had only come about thirty miles and the weather had already stopped me twice in those few days, but . . .

I outlined my plan for the summer to them and explained how I would be camping every night on whatever beach or island I found along the way. They wanted to know about my cookstove, how much food I had with me, and where it all fit inside the boat. Someone changed the subject from gear to sea conditions and the questions came at me faster than I could answer them: How big a sea had I been in? How far from shore would I paddle? What if I got knocked over? What was I going to do on the west coast where I would be exposed to the full power of the Atlantic? Had I ever done anything like this before?

I listened to myself answering all of their questions and thought how crazy the whole idea must sound to them. They had a thirty-five-foot sailboat that would sleep six and weather the worst of any storms, yet they had never dared to go around Mizen Head and face the open Atlantic. Here I was in a twenty-inch-wide, eighteen-foot-long kayak and I was going to paddle it all the way around Ireland—alone?

Margaret was scrunched in the corner seat beside her daughter and husband. She summed her feelings up firmly after the last of the chips had disappeared.

"I think yer mad," she announced.

31

That was the second time in less than a half hour someone had said that. Gerry chimed in as if I wasn't sitting there, "Oh he's mad for sure, but he'll be having a fine time of it."

I smiled, took a swallow of the thick frothy Guinness, and thought, "That's three, and I wonder what everyone else is thinking."

Eventually Barney showed me where the radio was neatly hidden under a cabinet above the chart table. He turned a tiny black knob and a series of red digits flashed across the narrow screen. Another dial was adjusted for squelch, then a dimpled button was pushed until channel 27 came up on the screen. It was set to transmit.

"Dublin Radio, Dublin Radio, this is the American Canoeist, the American Canoeist. Over."

The reply was almost instant, as though they had been waiting to hear from me. "American Canoeist, American Canoeist, this is Dublin. Come in."

"Roger, Dublin, I wanted to let you know that I am in Wicklow and that I'll be heading out tomorrow for Cahore Point. Over."

"Roger, be advised that Force seven southwesterlies are due by nightfall. Over."

Force 7? I paused a few seconds before keying the transmitter again. The cabin had gone silent and I could feel everyone's eyes on me. There was no way I wanted to be out in almost thirty-five mph winds. I'd have to find a place to hide from the approaching front and wait for calmer winds.

"Roger, Dublin. Be advised that I'll sit out the winds and proceed when the weather allows. Thanks for the report. I'll keep you posted. Over."

"Roger. Good luck. Dublin out."

I slid the mic into its holder on the side of the radio and looked down at the glass-covered chart, which showed the next thirty miles of coastline. Wicklow Head bulged out into the sea and would provide shelter from the forecasted winds. If I could get there before the winds picked up, I could camp and wait for the next calm.

Amid cheery "safe travels" and sincere calls of "God bless ye, lad," I climbed through the lifelines of the yacht and walked back to my boat. I looked down from the seawall to the small gravel beach where the boat rested. The tide was rising and wind-driven ripples slapped the stern and washed under the hull. A foolish thought drifted into my mind: I wondered if that beautiful boat with its graceful pointed bow and stern knew where it would be going in the next three months. It seemed to be waiting patiently for me to finish up with the silly things like radio calls, food, and weather reports. Maybe I was mad. Mad to think that my boat really wanted to be out on the open sea and that it was actually waiting for me to slide into the cockpit and continue the journey. Mad also to have dreamed up this journey in the first place; but it was a happy, carefree madness that felt right.

I settled into the boat, snapped the spray deck in place, and headed across the harbor. Gusts of wind curled over the seawall and scattered ripples across the smooth water. I watched these cat's-paws race toward me, then felt the wind catch the high paddle and gently try to twist it from my grip. I rounded the end of the rocks jutting into the sea and turned the bow into the increasing wind. A two-foot swell had developed and the boat sliced into each oncoming wave. In front of me, Wicklow Head dominated the skyline with its shadowy green flank rising above the surrounding bluffs. Further out to sea, beyond the headland, the waters were black and moving steadily northward. As I paddled, I watched the sea running before the winds. Steep-faced waves collapsed into leading troughs with bands of white broken water. Seconds would pass before the belly of the wave would rise again and the rhythm would continue. Not a single boat or ship floated between sea and horizon. I drove the boat into the wind and waves and in an hour I was in the shelter of the headland.

A bubbling stream followed the contours of two grassy hills folding into one another and eventually filtered through a steep gravel beach. I watched a few swells roll up over the rounded cobbles, then timed my landing in the lull between the sets. Somewhere beneath the tons of fine-grained gray stones, the stream gurgled and played before emptying itself into the sea. It was a good camp; high enough above the rising tide and building seas, yet sheltered from the winds that were ripping across the meadows above. I stomped the small stones into a level landing for my tent and settled into another camp.

It took me a week to cover the eighty miles from Dublin to Carnsore Point, which was the start of the south coast. That first week had been a windy one, with southeast winds cutting the paddling days short or blowing so strong that it wasn't worth the risk of being on the water at all. I was impatient. I wanted to be on the move, and the long days of sitting and waiting for the winds seemed to drag on forever. I would sit for hours in the doorway of the tent and watch the seas rolling steadily onward. Eat, read, sleep, and listen to the wind tearing at the tent fabric. That was the pattern of the day. I would walk the length of the beach, then turn and follow my tracks back as they slowly filled with wisps of drifting sand. The only company on the deserted beaches were the gulls standing with their necks pulled low into the protection of folded wings. As I walked by, bundled beneath layers of fleece and nylon, they wouldn't bother to fly but simply stepped to one side with a wary glance. We were all in the same situation, hunkering down and waiting for the winds to calm.

I was impatient, but at the same time knew that the waiting was as much a part of the trip as the paddling was. I knew it but still resisted it. The trip was young and there was six months of planning bottled up inside me. I didn't know it at the time but the wind was going to be with me for the next three months.

On June 8, I came around Carnsore Point against the last hour of the flooding tide. A member of the Rosslare Coast Guard had warned me against trying to get around the point before the ebb tide began. But he had also given me the wrong time for the tidal change. It wasn't until I paddled out from behind the last finger of rock jutting from the point that I felt the current grab the bow and swing it toward open water. Through the clear swells I watched the bottom sweep past as the boat carved a gentle arc back to the slack water behind the point again. I lined the bow up for another try and aimed for an eddy behind a large boulder. The sun glistened on the wave-washed rock. Tiny whirlpools cast off from the eddy, held miniature suns in their spirals that raced past me. Suddenly it didn't matter that the tide was against me. It was time to play and to enjoy this unexpected challenge; to dig into the ribbon of flowing water and feel its strength. From one partially submerged rock to the next I sprinted against the tide and rested in the quiet water behind each one. In front of me, long golden strands of beach disappeared into the distance and I knew that once around the point, I could slide in close to the sand and get out of the current. When the tide did turn, I could then move back offshore and ride the ebbing tide that flowed southwesterly.

The final push from the shelter of a ridge of slate to the beach was a heart-pounding workout. I watched a crab scurry away from the shadow of the boat, the outline of its shell dark against the rippled sandbottom. After a few seconds of watching it braced against the current, wary of this strange shadow from above, I realized I wasn't moving. The paddle's blades were spinning but I wasn't getting anywhere. Behind me I could hear the seas rushing through the slabs of upended rocks. I spun the blades as fast as I could and the crab scooted away as the boat's shadow moved across the bottom again. My shadow slowly crept across the sands, then picked up speed as I angled in toward the beach.

After struggling against the current, the boat seemed to glide effortlessly in the waters close to the beach. In the calm I was suddenly aware of the sound of my pulse in my ears, and my fingers throbbing to the same beat. I rested the paddle across the cockpit and let my hands trail in the water as the boat finished its glide into the protection of a shore eddy. I cupped my left hand against the numbing cold and slowly the boat swung around so I could look back at Carnsore Point, and the east coast I was leaving behind. Over the top of the rocks I had just come through was the white superstructure of a ferry headed for Wales. Above the rocky point, a green shamrock painted on the ship's stack floated across the blue sky as the ship slid out from behind the point.

Ten days earlier, I had pulled my boat off a similar ferry. In an indirect way the ferry was a connection to home; the last link in mechanized travel that had brought me to Ireland and, if the circumnavigation was completed, a reversal of those steps that would take me home. As it steamed away from land, the ship grew smaller with each minute. I sat and watched until it was nothing but a speck on the horizon. Then it was gone. With a sweep stroke on one side of my boat, and a back paddle on the other, I swung the bow back to the sandy beach tapering to a point in the distance. The tide was changing, pulling me west as certainly as the ferry was heading east. I was on the edge of another major step in this adventure. The pull of the paddles felt solid as each stroke slowly brought the boat back up to speed and I pulled away from Carnsore Point.

Awakening Rhythms

I want, in fact—to borrow from the language of the
saints—to live "in grace" as much of the time as possible. I
am not using this term in a strictly theological sense. By grace
I mean an inner harmony, essentially spiritual, which can be
translated into outward harmony. I am seeking what Socrates
asked for in the prayer from the Phaedrus when he said, "May
the outward and inward man be at one."

—Anne Morrow Lindbergh, *Gifts from the Sea*

The Saltee Islands lie three miles off the south coast, and at
dead low water an arched deposit of rocks connects the smaller of
the two islands to the mainland. Legend has it that St. Patrick
pelted the fleeing devil with the rocks as he tried to escape the wrath of
the holy man. Another legend tells of how Patrick borrowed a boat so as
to visit the islands. A few hundred yards from shore the boat began to sink
and the saint had to swim back. Angry and wet, St. Patrick cursed the
sinking boat and turned it into a granite boulder that sits in the tidal stream
to this day. The frustrated saint then built the causeway that I could see
as a dark shadow gracefully bending out toward the closest island. Geolo-
gists characterize the formation of the gravel bar as a glacial deposit. As I
floated across the causeway, bits of seaweed tumbled and raced over the
bottom. I liked the sound of the legend better than the cold facts of geology.

The Irish love to tell a tale, and if in the telling the story gets a bit grander with each recital, then it only makes for keener listening on a windy wet night beside a turf fire. Throughout Ireland there are legends such as the one about the Saltee Islands. Whether the legend is believed or not, it is still passed on. In a land of superstition it is easy to see how the tales would be repeated as they had been for the last five or six hundred years rather than risk the possibility of a curse for questioning their origin or truth. Who would question a legend connected with the patron saint of Ireland? Certainly not any man taking to the sea in a frail, tar-covered boat. Or perhaps even a tippy yellow kayak. When I hear the telling of a tale or legend, I never ask if the storyteller believes his or her story. I am not overly superstitious, but I like the idea of a world that straddles the gray area of fact and myth. In truth, I want to believe there is more to some of the myths and tales than merely age-old superstition.

I landed in Kilmore Quay for food and water before heading out for an overnight stay on Great Saltee, the bigger of the two islands. As I finished loading the last of the food on board, a middle-aged fellow walked over and watched me snap the black rubber hatches in place, then carefully double-check the seal on each one. With his hands jammed deep in his baggy trousers and his Irish cap set back on the crown of his head, he said, "She's a fine-looking boat, that one."

"Thank you. She's a fine boat, all right. Good in the rough water and fast enough when I need to cover some ground."

"You'd be headin' over to the islands, then, are ye?"

"Yeah, I thought I'd go over and check out the gannet colony on the big island. I want to take some pictures and if it's okay I'd like to camp overnight."

"Oh sure and why wouldn't it be okay? Ye can camp sure enough and no one will be bothering ye about it. There's a wee small beach on this side of the island that ye can see from here on a good day. Ye can pull the little lady right clear of high water and have a good look around. Ah, there's so many birds, ye won't be knowin' where to turn for a good picture."

The fellow's response to camping on the island was typical of the reception I had found along the way. There was always the initial curiosity, followed by advice on the weather, the seas, or maybe where I could get fresh supplies. As the afternoon sun reflected off the boat ramp and soaked into the stiff muscles of my back, I felt the ease of being a traveler in a friendly land. I never asked this fellow his name and he didn't ask me mine. It was enough to pass a few moments of the day, share a few thoughts, then bid each other a cheerful farewell. Before he walked up the ramp and out of sight, he told me he was a crew member of the RNLI, the Royal National Lifeboat Institute, and that he would keep an eye out for me on their training run later that afternoon. As he walked away, he paused, then said, "All the very best to ye, lad."

One of the challenges of sea kayaking is that every time the paddler snaps the spray deck in place and pushes off from shore, he or she is instantly in an environment that is potentially dangerous. Wind, tidal currents, reflecting waves, and water that is cold enough to lower the core temperature and kill by hypothermia are factors of the sea. On a calm day with flat water and sunshine, the smooth glide of the boat can lull a paddler into complacency and the warning signs of the surrounding environment can go unnoticed. A line of clouds on the horizon, a shift of wind from one quarter to the next, or whitecaps a mile offshore where an hour earlier there had been none, all paint a picture of the constant interplay of sea and sky. The freedom and ease of paddling on calm days can quickly become a battle of nerves and stamina when these signs are ignored or misinterpreted. It isn't the sea that takes lives and brings grief to shorebound families, it is the careless drift of the mind that accepts the moment of calm without looking beyond for what surely will be a change. The kayak allows the freedom of travel, but it also demands that the paddler be observant and have both skill and judgment to deal with the realities of the sea.

The three-mile paddle out to Great Saltee Island was not a long crossing. But it was one that I weighed with the same care as a fifteen- or twenty-mile crossing. The forecast was for increasing winds, gale force, forty miles per hour, by late afternoon. Banks of high clouds were building in the southwest and the wind was just strong enough to begin forming small breakers halfway to Little Saltee. Without the effect of a current against the wind, whitecaps will start to build at fifteen mph. It is a rough estimate that I use when contemplating a crossing. The paddle to Great Saltee would take less than an hour, but that didn't mean it wasn't without risk.

The tide was running half strength when I left Kilmore Quay. If I tried to shoot straight across, it would carry me beyond the west end of the island. I would have to head east of Little Saltee and let the current wash me into its lee. From there, I could cut across the "sound" between the two islands and deal with the steep, choppy seas that were funneled through the narrow opening. The lifeboat crew member had told me the channel had a bad reputation, as though it were temperamental and if provoked would stir up trouble. Local advice like that was something to listen to. The two mile crossing to the first island (Little Saltee) and the supposed rough water in the channel gave the landing on Great Saltee a different meaning: it wasn't only a destination but also a refuge if the wind and waves became too strong.

The low islands sat out on the edge of the immediate horizon: rounded humps of green, long and tapered as if drawn lower on one end by the tides that swept past them. From the mainland there was little detail other than shadow and sunlight drifting with the passage of clouds. As I drew closer, the base of rock that the islands sat upon rose out of the waves and took on the cracks and depth of ledges split in tumbled angles. Halfway to Little Saltee, the wind began to freshen and the waves curled over in white. By the time I had paddled into the lee of that island, the winds had increased to Force 4, twenty miles an hour. The waves were funneling through the passage of the two islands at a fast clip, tripping over each other as the wind rushed against the tide. I reached behind the cockpit for the nylon belt attached to the rear grab loop of the boat. I snapped the buckle around my waist and gave it a good tug. It was unlikely that I would get knocked over by the four-and five-footers, and just as unlikely that I would miss my roll and wind up swimming. But . . . I wanted to be prepared. These were conditions that I called my "double-tethered days": the paddle tethered to my wrist with a short piece of webbing, and me tied to the boat with the black nylon ribbon running aft.

The waves in the middle of the sound rose over my head and completely blocked out the view of Great Saltee a half mile away. The clouds had moved in from the west, and the seas no longer sparkled with the morning's sun. Now they were black faces with tops of breaking white that poured through the channel and occasionally buried the stern of the boat with a noisy shove to one side. A series of breaking waves lay between me and the relative calm in the shelter of Great Saltee. The RNLI boat was halfway out from Kilmore Quay, its bow splitting the waves in twin arcs of white that the winds carried away. I thought how impossible it would be for them or anyone else to spot me in the rough water. Another wave poured over the foredeck and washed my camera over the side. I reached for the tether strap and hauled the waterproof camera back on board.

If anyone could have seen me, the situation would probably look pretty hopeless: a strange-looking sliver of a boat being buried and tossed around like a cork on the sea. The difference was perspective. I had trained in waters rougher than these and knew what my abilities were. I was comfortable, alert, and enjoying the feel of the boat recovering from each rumbling wave and climbing up on the face of the next. The seas were big enough to test my skills but not so wild as to be threatening. They were perfect conditions for my first crossing of the trip. This was why I had come to Ireland; for the energy of open ocean paddling, to be washed by the salt spray and feel the boat driving toward an island filled with the mysteries of past ages. It was wild and romantic. A ten-year-old dream coming to life.

I had found a guidebook about the islands when I was in the small grocery store in town. As my bill for food was being totaled, I flipped through it and learned a little of the history of the islands. They had been inhabited since the Neolithic period, 3000–2500 B.C. The islands offered protection from bears, wolves, and wild boars, as well as other humans. There were plenty of fish, wild rabbits, and seabirds for food as well. Aerial photographs showed several large stone circles and what the archeologists thought was an Iron Age ring fort overlooking one end of the island. There is also a carved Ogham Stone in the county museum which originally came from the island. Like so many other things in Ireland, the origin of the stone was uncertain but similar stones date from the early Christian period A.D. 400–800, and usually marked the burial place of a chieftain or scribe. Stories of medieval abbeys, Viking raids, and pirates using the islands' sea caves to hide their loot became jumbled in my mind as I tried to comprehend five thousand years of history.

I paddled into the lee of the bigger island, landed, and slid the boat over a roll of storm-tossed kelp. A footpath cut through the thick barrier of head-high brush and briars above the beach. I left the *Little Lady* resting on the kelp above high water, stepped through the opening, and followed the mazelike path. Ruins of stone outbuildings seemed to be everywhere. Their crumbled walls were draped with vines, and tight clusters of grass grew in the empty spaces where mortar had long ago fallen out. A faint trail split from the main path and led to a single-roomed cottage surrounded by a tangle of underbrush. The half-opened door hung on one high rusty hinge. It felt spooky and friendly at the same time. The perfect place, I thought, for a gnome to live. Beneath the eaves and built into the corner of the foundation was a stone-lined well. A grotto of moss-softened stone with two steps led down to its dampness. A spider's web hung from the curved sides of the well, fine beads of dew clinging to the threads carefully woven across the arch. And overhead a domed ceiling of fitted stone. Tiny insects skated across the still pool. I cupped my hand and lifted a palm of pure cold water to my lips.

I returned to the main track and followed its curves toward a stone farmhouse, my head filled with the excitement of the sound crossing, the history of the island and the discovery of the well. Suddenly, a short, gray-bearded fellow dressed in frumpy clothes appeared around the bend. I almost jumped off the trail in fright. He was certainly too big to be a gnome and just as startled to see me as I was to see him.

After our mutual shock, we introduced ourselves. Oscar Merner worked for the Irish National Park Service. He was on the island with another ornithologist monitoring the various seabird colonies that nested on the cliffs. He told me where I could find the gannet, razorbill, and puffin colonies, and encouraged me to have a look around. Few people come out to the island and the birds are very tolerant of careful observation.

The footpath cut across the low rise of the island, disappearing amid purple heather stunted and sculpted by the winds. Tiny flowers grew in the protection of the heather, contrasting yellow against soft purple, while a thickening mist watered the island contours with drops that clung to the ferns, heather, and grass. A strong ocean wind carried the sound of crashing waves as I followed the winding trail to the cliff edge. Across the waves, black specks appeared out of the mist and flew hell-bent for the cliffs below me. Eye-watering winds tore past as I carefully made my way to the grassy lip; one foot forward, one back as I gazed down at the roiling seas below. Clear blue waves wrapped around pinnacles of rock, then rolled in and hit the island in a barrage of rumbling white water. Just beyond the reach of the flying spray were hundreds of razorbills and guillemots standing on ledges streaked with guano. They stood shoulder to shoulder, looking out to sea and shuffling to find better footing as the wind ripped past the cliff face. More birds appeared out of the mist, flew at wave height, then climbed suddenly and with a flare of wings somehow found a foothold on the crowded ledges. Neighbors moved over, craning their necks to look down at the waves or up to the clifftop. Several others chose to launch into the winds and soar away, or drop into waves below and disappear beneath the surface in search of food. Cormorants, shags, fulmars, kittiwakes, and huge black-backed gulls were everywhere. Fifty feet of bird-filled air separated me from the waves below. Outstretched wings swept by in a blur as I tried to identify the individuals flying past. A curious fulmar flew in close, then circled back into the wind and hovered motionless twenty feet away, its crystal black eyes set so elegantly within a snowy white head.

In a hushed voice that came from a place deep within, I said: "You are so beautiful, my friend. What have you seen and where have you been today?"

Gusts of wind lifted and buffeted the fulmar as it struggled to hold its position. Thirty or forty seconds passed, each of us studying the other, until with a dip of a wing the fulmar tore away. I pulled the fleece collar tighter around my neck, zipped into the hood of my raincoat, and continued along the cliff. The trail cut through tangles of wildflowers and grass, and at each point where it met the cliff edge, I could look down on rockfaces crowded with hundreds of seabirds.

Oscar had told me the main gannet colony nested on the southern, most exposed tip of the island. The trail dropped into a shallow ravine, then climbed back into the noise of the wind. Across a chasm filled with raging broken waves was a jumble of blocks and ledges that climbed a hundred feet out of the sea. There wasn't a single blade of grass or vegetation on the small mountain of rock and every square foot of space was covered with nesting gannets. The guidebook said there were one thousand five hundred pairs of these golden-faced birds with seven-foot wingspans, but I had no way of understanding that number until I had crested that last rise and saw the colony.

I leaned into the powerful gusts and crept from one rock to the next until I was at the edge of the chasm. A flat-sided boulder offered some protection from the blasts of wind. Twenty feet to the left and slightly below me was a subcolony of two hundred gannets that ignored me as I sat huddled against the rain-splattered rock. On every ledge or flat rock was a nest: seaweed, bits of rope, discarded feathers—and an adult gannet protecting its domain with stabs of its beak. On the crowded nesting rocks there was a constant testing of boundaries as individuals reached cautiously for a stray piece of seaweed or pulled a piece of orange netting from a neighbor's nest. Half-grown chicks with black heads would appear from under their parents. The young birds grew fast on a steady diet of fish and they looked like teenagers literally afraid to leave the nest. After a quick look, the chick would retreat under the warmth of folded wings and the parent would attempt to cover the young bird again.

Gannets returning from fishing or carrying nesting materials would suddenly appear from below the cliff in front of me. They would bank into the wind, break their forty-mile-an-hour airspeed with cupped wings and flared tail feathers, then somehow find their mate amid all of the upturned bills. From where I sat, I could see the fine overlapping feathers on the gannets' breasts and the long flight feathers of their wings rippled by the wind. A second or two of stalled air time and each big bird would settle down on the nest and join in a gentle duel of beaks with its mate. Again and again the pattern repeated itself throughout the colony, while all around the space between cliff and sea was filled with every species of bird on the island tearing along on the winds.

For the moment, my life consisted of only what was immediately in front of me—a world of screaming winds, flaring wings a dozen feet away, and the marvel of so much life and energy. Another fulmar soared up the face of the cliff and purposefully stalled right in front of my perch. That brilliant crystal eye stared into mine as if it could read my thoughts. I could feel the wind buffeting its body and passing beneath the short, rounded wings as if I was part of the flight. A puffin came in for a controlled crash landing onto a rocky ledge. Once safe on land, it tucked its wings and waddled into a sheltered corner of rock to stand at attention and look out over the cliff.

As I sat there I was aware of how still I had become, and how insignificant I was compared to everything around me. The air was filled with the noise of the wind, the waves washing powerfully against the rocks below, and the helter-skelter flight of seabirds whipping past on the gusts. I was surrounded by all this energy and activity, yet inside there was only silence, an overwhelming sense of awe.

As the sky threatened heavier rain, I stretched my cramped legs out of a crouched position and slowly moved away from the colony. I followed the path along the sheltered side of the island back to the farmhouse and the beach, where my boat sat waiting. Darkness had settled in as I pulled my sleeping bag and thermarest from the front compartment and followed the trail back to the overgrown cottage. Inside, a rickety ladder led from the damp stone of the main floor to a low-roofed loft above. In the dark I spread the sleeping bag on the wooden floor and listened to the rush of wind battering the cottage. My body was tired but my mind was filled with memories of the day and imaginings of what was ahead. In the morning I would head back to the mainland on a ten-mile diagonal crossing to Hook Head, then on toward the west coast. The gale-force winds that had been forecast howled against the stone cottage and whirled around dreams of seabirds, rocks, and waves.

The south coast unfolded before me in a series of cloudless days and blue seas gently lapping against the cliffs and sea caves along the way. I spent part of each day three or four miles offshore, cutting across shallow bays between headlands. The hours slipped by as I steadily pushed into the southwesterly swells. My eyes and mind were free to wander as my body slipped into automatic and flowed with the rise and fall of the seas. Tiny jellyfish, the size of my thumb, floated by with their translucent sails set to catch the faintest breeze. Dozens of equally small moths stood on the surface of the ripple-free swells and only took to the air when my bow wake disturbed their rest.

After a two- or three-hour crossing, I would look forward to the change of scenery and watch as the approaching headland began to take on details. Dark fissures that I had at first thought to be separate cliffs became simply the play of sunlight and shadow. The golden reflected light at the base of the cliff turned into a crescent of unmarked sands. In the calm, the tingle of gentle surf floated across the waters like a welcome. I would land, strip naked, and walk slowly back into the sea, feeling the cold water wash over me with gentle hands. With the sea flooding my ears, I would listen as small waves broke with a little rumble, then receded in a fine whisper. Later, with the heat of the sand soaking into muscles that welcomed the rest, I would feel the salt drying on my skin and offer a wordless prayer of thanks for this life. It was at times like this that I was aware how little I spoke, yet how filled my mind was with images and feelings. I breathed, ate, slept, and lived with the sea and the tides. Within that physical world of listening and patiently watching there was a growing spiritual connection that went beyond spoken words. The paddling life quieted me and the exposure, both physically and emotionally, made the entire day an ongoing form of prayer.

On days when the sea was more like the calm of a pond, I would detour off course to explore the entrance of a sea cave. As I paddled toward the dark, jagged openings, there was time to watch the swell rise against the surrounding cliffs and decide if I wanted to risk entering. If it felt right and looked as if there was enough ceiling height, I would backpaddle at the entrance, slowing the boat, and slip wide-eyed into the darkness. A cool damp would sweep across my face like the touch of a spider's web, silent and sticky in the blackness of dripping walls. Gone were the open horizons and the vast sea. Now I felt like a giant enclosed in a tiny, mysterious world. Sounds of the swell flooding the cavern echoed back from the ceiling somewhere above. Crevices filled and blowholes hissed as the swell lifted the boat and compressed both air and sea in rising notes. Neptune's flute played a melody in the echoing chamber of darkness. Beyond the light of the entrance I drifted blind, every pore of my skin and effort of my senses probing the void and struggling to measure each drip that defined walls, tapered ceiling, and width of passage. After a swell passed, it met the sloping rock somewhere in the blindness ahead and with a rumble, ended half of its cycle. Seconds later the waters flowed back, some of their energy lost in the depth of the cave but enough left to repeat the melody of their retreat.

By twisting in the cockpit, I could see behind me the ragged opening and the shiny wet walls of the entrance. Framed within that opening was a world of blue sky and sparkling waters. Two worlds, one of light and one of darkness, connected by a tunnel filled with the sounds and smells of the sea. I would sit through three or four cycles of swells, then carefully back out of the cave and into the glare of sun.

By the third week in June I was almost two hundred miles into the trip and enjoying what would be the best weather of the entire journey. Moderate east winds brought dry air from the continent and pushed me along the cliff faces and across the open bays. Beneath towering headlands jutting into the sea I paddled on water that rarely broke over the bow. For some reason, the winds and the tides were cooperating and seemed anxious to push me westward. The east and south coasts had been surprisingly easy. With the exception of a few windy days at the start, the weather had been stable. From salmon fishermen, pub owners, and shopkeepers I kept hearing how unusual the weather was and how maybe it would be a repeat of last summer, the best they had seen in twenty years. Each evening I would listen to the marine reports on the radio. While the rest of Ireland was lashed by high winds and rain, a high-pressure system sat over the south and brought sunny days and a gentle southeast breeze.

On June 20, I camped opposite a small island near Glandore, twenty miles from the start of the west coast. It was late evening, the sun resting on the edge of a grassy hill overlooking my campsite, the channel in front of me as smooth as glass. Across the narrow waterway two stone house ruins stood bathed in the last rays of sun. The island, radiant in the evening light, looked as if it was an enchanted fairy-tale land. Shadows of stone walls divided green meadows, and the cap of rock that broke through at the top of the island looked like a place where the fairies might dance.

I spread the sleeping bag out on the thick grass above the beach and watched the sky fade to a soft blue, then gradually deeper shades of purple until the first star appeared. One by one, points of light flickered in the gathering darkness and I struggled to keep my eyes open. A moonless, star-filled night and the black silhouette of the island were my companions. The warmth of the bag and the smell of the grass with tiny yellow flowers inches from my face invited sleep. I thought about the ruins across the channel, then curled up in the fragrance of the night and slept.

By dawn, the earth had flown through the galaxy and the island was now silhouetted against the white-blue of the morning sky. A heavy dew bent the tips of the grass and soaked my feet as I walked down to the boat, then back to the knoll with my breakfast. With the warmth of the bag around my shoulders, I sat and ate as the sun peaked over the top of the island and slowly moved down my body. What a privilege, I thought, to see both the setting and rising of the sun and to have the time to sit and watch the shadows change. Such an ordinary thing—and yet so extraordinary.

I paddled over to the island and the two ruins silently standing watch above a natural landing. Low tide had exposed a ridge of algae-covered rock on both sides of the cobbles. The rich smells of the exposed tidelands hung in the air. I let the boat drift to within a few inches of the beach, then stepped into the chill of the water. A tongue of stones reached into the slope of the island and led to a break in the rock bluff where a trail climbed gently up to level ground. On this shelf the two roofless houses looked out across the channel to the mainland.

Nettles and briars crowded the outside walls and orange lichens grew in brilliant contrast on the gray stones around the window openings. I circled the first house, avoiding the nettles that guarded a walkway leading to the low door. Between gable ends angling into a blue sky were walls that once would have supported rafters and thatch.

A sheep trail led twenty yards through the nettles and thistles to the second ruin, behind and slightly higher on the landing. The house had been built into the slope of the hill, the shallow soil pulling back, revealing island bedrock that seemed to give birth to the walls nestled against it. Ledge and walls of stone became one. A cluster of sea pinks, a low bouquet of green with four long stems supporting cloverlike flowers, swayed gently, touched by a breath of wind I could not feel. Pink flowers splashed against gray stone as if a spirit of the ruins had planted it and could watch from afar the fragile flowers by the cottage doorway.

I walked through the doorway into a single room with a rubble-filled hearth at the gable end. The foot-and-a-half-thick walls were less than my height and I would have had to stoop to enter if the roof had been in place. On the far wall, two openings, window-size, looked out onto the channel and the rock-guarded coast of the mainland rolling away in overlapping meadows. I stepped across the width of the room, then lengthwise to the fireplace. Between the silhouetted gables the sun poured into the room, flooding it with light and warmth. I leaned against one wall, felt the stones against my shoulder blades, and let my mind wander freely through the past.

I imagined the smell of a peat fire and the sound of children's voices. A thatched roof. The barking of a dog. I wondered who had lived in the cottage a stone's throw away and if they had been related. For some reason that was important. I wanted to know the people's names, not just their family name but their first names. The children must have run in and out of this doorway, at times laughing, at other times crying for the attention of a weary mother. Maybe the father was a fisherman, maybe not, but there would have been a currach pulled up on the beach where my boat now sat. Children would have been born on this island, and no doubt the old ones—and probably some young ones as well—would have died here. In the quiet, the spirit of the stones reached deep inside and touched me. I wanted to know more.

I looked for some broken pottery or a piece of furniture, some glass from the windows or even a rusting chunk of farming tool. Something that I could hold in my hands, something that these people had touched. But there was nothing except the stones and the dirt floor that had soaked up the lives and passions of these people. I wanted to squeeze from the rock and the packed earth beneath my feet the voices and lives of whoever had existed within these thick walls crumbling with time.

Who were these people and why did I feel this ache for them? What was it about the silence that was so haunting? There was a strange contrast of peace and also loneliness amid the stones. These people had a life here as real as my own and yet nothing so much as a dinner plate or fragment of glass remained.

The call of a gull and the song of a warbler in the briars floated in the air as my thoughts reached back. They must have longed for days like this; days of sunshine and calm winds when windows and doors would have been thrown open to invite the sun in and drive the dampness out. Days when an old man would have sat against the sun-warmed wall of the cottage and enjoyed the sounds and smells of spring.

I left the house and followed a sheep path to the far side of the island. I wanted to walk, to feel the land and connect it with the ruins. The trail cut through several stone walls and meandered through fields, cresting the island and dropping to the rocks of the outer shore. I followed its path and on the way stopped to look at a long, low ridge running up one side of a hill and down the other like a bulging vein rippling beneath the meadow. I walked over and gazed at its length winding across the field. In some places, it looked as if it had melted into the earth; in others, it pushed a grazed felt of shorn grass into a gentle rise. After a moment of wonder I suddenly realized what I was looking at: It was the top of an ancient stone wall, settled with the ages and buried beneath centuries of sod and grasses. It was indeed a vein and it pulsed with the lifeblood of a people so long ago that I felt I was standing on sacred ground. I thought of a time when oak forests covered Ireland thousands of years ago. A time of Druids and holy wells. Time so distant that myths, legends, and stones are its sole remains. A breeze, soft as velvet, drifted over the island, touched my face with its gentleness, then faded.

I continued along the path, dipping into shallow ravines, then climbing to the top of the next hillock and gazing out at the neighboring islands, mounds of rock, and greenery surrounded by blue seas. My mind was back on the recent history of the ruins and thoughts of children herding sheep through these fields, maybe running to the cliff edge to spot the familiar shape of a sail or color of a boat returning to the cobbled beach.

As I stepped up on a rock and looked back at the roofless cottages, I suddenly knew what was so disturbing about the island's ruins. Their haunting emptiness was an echo of how little I knew of my own Irish ancestry and I was jolted by that awakening. It wasn't that the cottage dwellers would have been related to me but rather they were in some way a connection to who my ancestors might have been. I hadn't come to Ireland looking for my roots. I had come to paddle its seas, explore its coast and meet the people, but not in the sense of reaching back four generations. During the past ten years, every time I had heard the name "Ireland," it struck a mysterious chord, as if in the name there had been a calling. Now I understood. It was this genetic memory; a feeling of familiarity for a place I knew nothing about. Perhaps it was the emptiness of the ruins, the absence of anything other than the stones that had jogged this sixth sense of awareness. I had to look deeper, to pull from the earth, the fields, and the stones past generations that had left only doorways and walls to wander through. It was as if the ruins had been an invitation to another era, a place to stand and look back. Perhaps it was no surprise that they should speak so deeply to me or that I should feel the power of the wall running beneath the pasture. The island's history was part of me just as certainly as the sound of my heart beating in my ears. For the first time, a sense of belonging, of identifying an origin that I could believe was unique to me, was defined and important.

I wandered over the island again, looking out from its low cliff and feeling a comfort settle within me. The day was still young, as was this journey, which was stirring deeper feelings for the land and its people. The island had cast a spell on me, luring me for a visit with the previous evening's light, then touching me with the spirit of a past people where time did not exist as a barrier but as an invitation. The physical journey of paddling around Ireland seemed to have split into two parallel routes: one of the paddle and one of the heart.

I remembered that my uncle had traveled around Ireland and knew some of the family history. This island spell had awakened an interest in that history. I decided to write to him and ask him to send me whatever information he had. I wanted more than a circumnavigation of Ireland; I wanted a spiraling back in time, a burrowing in to where my roots lay entwined around the rocks of this island country. Somewhere in the passage of time and the stones of many ruins were my own beginnings.

Almost a thousand miles of paddling lay in front of me. Twenty miles away was the beginning of the west coast, with all of its challenges and unknowns. I paddled from behind the island and felt the familiar lift of the swell. The waves felt larger than before but maybe it was just knowing I was so close to Mizen Head and the Atlantic. Thoughts of the island mingled with concerns of what was ahead as the pieces of the Celtic puzzle began to fit together. I looked back at the ruins one last time, another perspective of sunlight on stone. The tide was pulling at the boat, the walls of the cottages disappearing behind the rise of the island. I drifted lazily with the tide until the gabled end of the ruins slipped out of sight, setting me on course for the west coast.

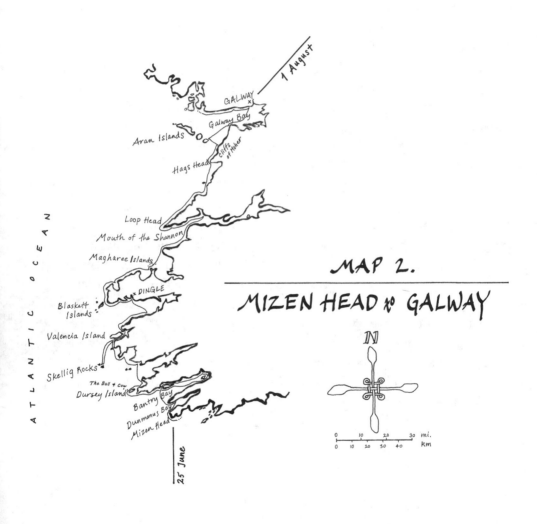

1 August

GALWAY x

Galway Bay

Aran Islands

Cliffs of Moher

Hags Head

Loop Head

Mouth of the Shannon

Magharee Islands

x DINGLE

Blasket Islands

Valencia Island

Skellig Rocks

The Bull & Cow

Dursey Island

Bantry Bay

Dunmanus Bay

Mizen Head

25 June

ATLANTIC OCEAN

MAP 2.

MIZEN HEAD to GALWAY

N

0   10   20   30 mi.

0 10 20 30 40 km

West Coast Beginnings

Hitherto shalt thou come, but no further:
and here shall thy proud waves be stayed?

—Job 38:11

The sea, like any expanse of nature, is a great teacher of humility. It strips away the nonessentials: the ego, the place in society we fill, and the clutter of busy lives. Swells stirred to life by mid-ocean storms radiate outward, losing little of their power until they steepen in shallow waters or crash with relentless hammerings against cliffs rising straight from the depths. At times it seems that the oceans, with their ruthless power of destruction, would be better left alone. They care nothing for human fear, misjudgment, fatigue, and whatever strength or fragility the human visitor brings to their shores.

Wind, waves, cold water, and the exposure of miles of endless cliff can bare the soul as any desert experience might. All the insecurities of society—the stress of success or fear of failure—suddenly seem inconsequential. What is left is the stripped-down reality of purposeful, passionate living in an environment that tolerates nothing less. It is a great and continual cleansing, at first shockingly cold; but like the initial plunge into a mountain stream, it refreshes and wakes the body and mind to new life.

I arrived on the southwest tip of Ireland wondering if I was ready for that plunge, if I could handle what the Atlantic continually throws against the west-facing cliffs of Ireland. I had thousands of miles of sea-paddling experience, yet I was still intimidated by the power of the open Atlantic that was literally around the next corner. The first two hundred fifty miles had been easy, with nothing that had challenged or tested me for what was certainly ahead. In my mind were images of west coast headlands that I had seen in large-format photos, pictures taken from the safety of land that showed the seas lifting and meeting a line of coastal cliff in violent explosions of thundering spray. Against blue sky and impenetrable rock, the photographer had captured the power and drama of ocean meeting land. Thoughts of those images filled my stomach with flutters and at the same time drew me in with their power and beauty.

Coastal photos are often taken from the perspective of the land, from the eye of an observer looking outward, the perpetual draw of the sea pulling at the imagination and heart of the landbound. Being a paddler, I have often wanted to turn the page and see the same photo from the other perspective: that of the sea, looking inward toward the land. From the land, the sea is a place of departure: from the sea, a place of arrival. To a coastal paddler, the corridor of ocean meeting land is a place of both departing and arriving. A time of looking out as well as inward. A place and time of self-discovery.

I had refolded the map, and now the fingers of Counties Cork and Kerry, which reached into the Atlantic Ocean, showed through the clear plastic chart case. The east and south coasts lay hidden in the folds of the map just as their memories lay within my mind. In the lower-left corner of the map was Mizen Head, the start of the west coast. In front of me, ten miles across the mouth of Roaringwater Bay, was the vague outline of the same headland. I had left the village of Baltimore that morning and paddled in the lee of Sherkin and Clear Island to a point beneath the cliffs on the west end of Clear Island. It would be two days before I would attempt to get around the Mizen, but this paddle out to Cape Clear would give me a feeling for the mood of the Atlantic. What I saw was encouraging. Aside from a low easy swell, the seas were perfectly calm; not a breath of wind moved across the water. Four miles to the west was Fastnet Rock, the lighthouse of the south coast. Beyond was the flat horizon of the Atlantic.

The horizon: three thousand miles of nothing but ocean. It looked the same as the east and south coast, an empty line of sky meeting sea. The difference was the threat of winds and of storm-powered waves meeting the first landfall of Europe. Hundreds of miles beyond the horizon was

Iceland, a land that bred low-pressure systems that tracked southward and hit Ireland with their fury. South winds would bring moisture, north winds would bring the cold. Both would produce the waves and heavy surf that the fishermen along my route had warned me of. I had a feeling that calm days like this were going to be rare.

Six months earlier, I had looked at this point on the map and tried to imagine what the exposure would feel like. Today, despite the calm, I could not have known this feeling of being so vulnerable. This was the leg of the trip that had intrigued me during the planning stages. It was the reason for coming to Ireland, to know the wildness of this coast. In front of me were four hundred miles and two months of living on the edge of the Atlantic.

I was intimidated by the exposure but also felt the thrill of being poised to turn this corner and see for myself the power and the beauty of the west coast.

A swell broke with a rumble near the base of the cliff. The tide was pulling me in closer to the island and I thought about the two-hour paddle back to camp. It was time to leave. I paddled around the south side of Clear Island, then across a half mile of cauliflower boils and small whirl-pools in the crossing to Sherkin. The tide had turned and was running like a river through this shallow passage. Thoughts of the Mizen mixed with the currents that grabbed the bow and pulled it toward an exposed reef, then just as quickly released it to a counterflow that set me back on course. I pulled the boat from one current to the next, changing partners as if in a dance with each swirling eddy and back current. I was lost, playing in the sunshine and the tide, and had all but forgotten the concerns of an hour ago. They had melted away as soon as I saw the tide rushing between the islands.

On the way back to camp, I stopped on Sherkin Island and walked through a fifteenth-century priory that was under restoration. The iron gates had been locked two days earlier when I had beached the boat and walked up the narrow road leading to the belltower. This time the lead mason was struggling to unload a cement mixer. I offered to help with the mortar-covered beast and in return I learned the history behind the gates and the five-foot thick walls.

The mason told me how the priory was built by Franciscan monks in 1460 as a center for learning. We stood in the courtyard, surrounded by the four walls and the square tower standing against the sky. He showed me sections of carved sandstone arches that had risen between the pillars of stone in the cloister. The kitchen was through a low doorway off to one side and down into a room with a massive arched ceiling like a baker's oven. The only light came through two doors on opposite ends of the room and barely lit the corners where I imagined a cat curled on the top of a barrel of flour or grain. One floor above was a large room, windows running the length of both sides. Students from all over Ireland and Europe studied Latin, philosophy, and math in this simple room of slate floors and high windows. I walked alone through low doorways and narrow halls, some returning to the dazzling light of the courtyard, others connecting to yet another room within the maze.

The doorway to the belltower was half filled with the accumulation of centuries of earth and rubble that had yet to be excavated. I ducked low beneath the opening and stood within the shaft, looking up at a square of blue. An arched doorway no wider than my shoulders showed the first three stones of a spiraling stairway. In the dark, my feet felt for the wedges of stone as I climbed in a tight circle within the wall of the tower. Sixty feet up, the spiraling steps abruptly ended at another doorway leading to the collapsed top floor. Beyond the glare of sun was a fatal drop to the rubble below. I found a foothold, stepped across the corner of the drop, and hopped up on the wall for a rest. Below me the walls of the priory lay exposed like cells of a honeycomb, and I thought about a tragic story that the mason had told me.

In 1537, all the surrounding lands had been under the control of the O'Driscoll Clan. The clan stronghold was just beyond view of the priory. As the story goes, the master of the castle offered refuge to a storm-damaged ship within the shelter of the harbor. When it was discovered that the ship's hold was filled with casks of wine, the ship's status as visitor suddenly changed to that of captured vessel. Eventually the owners in Waterford learned where their ship and its valuable cargo were being held and launched a punitive raid against all of Sherkin Island. The inhabitants' houses and boats were burned and the castle and priory were reduced to ruins. During an archaeological dig, the results of the raid were uncovered. Below the centuries of rubble, the English roof tiles and fragments of Italian glass, were the bones of a number of men, all around thirty years old. All hastily buried. The resting place of the murdered monks.

I looked down on the clean lines of the restored courtyard and the gravel path beneath which the graves had been uncovered. On the day of the raid it must have been a scene from hell. This view of peace and order would have been filled with smoke and the terror of violence. The raiders would have left, taking with them the ship that had been the cause of death and destruction. Those villagers who fled to the protection of the hills and ravines must have returned in shock to bury the dead.

The priory was rebuilt and continued as a learning center until 1766, when it was deserted and then slowly deteriorated with the years. The mason told me that beneath the grasses surrounding the walls of the priory were more clues to the history of the ruins. Vague outlines of walls and depressions in the rich green field hinted at what lay waiting for the archaeologists' skills.

A billowy white cloud stole the warmth of the sun, and I retreated from the wind into the spirals of the tower. On the ground again, I wandered along the rear wall of the chapel and remembered the mason telling me where his crew had removed some plaster to reveal the lepers' entrance. The outline of a dismantled stairwell climbed the exterior wall of the chapel, then abruptly stopped in the face of the filled-in entrance. Why had it been blocked off? Were there no more lepers at the time? Or maybe there was a shift in attitudes? The mason had asked the same questions and arrived at the same wall of rock. This labyrinth of passages, spiraling stone steps, and low-arched doorways held such secrets securely in their mortar.

I left the priory and followed the lane back down to the water, my mind filled with robed monks, sculptured stone, and the imaginings of stone halls echoing Latin, Greek, and the teachings of the Gospels. Behind me, the belltower, arched windows, and crumbling walls stood bathed in sunlight against the green meadow and blue sky. Everywhere I looked and walked, I felt the history of Ireland walking with me. The overgrown stone walls, the thicket of green that covered all but a corner of laid-up stone on a tiny roofless house. I thought of the people who must have walked this road linking the height of land to the beach—the path taken by the villagers, monks, and raiders of the sixteenth century. No doubt there had been others much earlier who knew of the safe landing and the notch in the hills that led to the inner island. I was learning that Ireland was a living history book. One had only to turn a corner and see remnants of the past poking through the turf and tangle of vegetation. I had only to pull back the thicket of growth and there in front of my eyes would be another story of the past.

The paddle from Roaringwater Bay to the Mizen was a rite-of-passage. The protection of the south coast fell behind me like a cloak being pulled from my shoulders. I moved two miles offshore to get a broad view of the land fading into the haze of the east and felt like I was saying good-bye. To the west, the land that had stood between me and the Atlantic was gradually narrowing; it ended at the cliffs dropping into the sea.

Great volumes of low ocean swells lifted the boat for what seemed an impossibly long time, then slowly rolled away with the same long decline into the next trough. In the distance, the land tapered to a finger pointing to the Atlantic like some kind of prophet warning of what was beyond. At the tip of that finger, just out of view, was the Mizen. Silent eruptions of white broke over the reef that extended out from the cliff, then raced onward to try to scale the vertical walls. Six months of preparation had brought me to this southwest corner of Ireland. Now it was time to wait for the right moment and attempt to get around this first headland of many in the next two months.

The skies had filled from the west with a thickening cover of dirty, layered sheets. The forecast was for a strengthening low-pressure system, followed by north winds and rain. I slipped into the calm of a narrow inlet, the last protection before the headland. I was close and feeling impatient, torn between chancing an attempt and realizing that the weather was changing by the minute. A powerful gust of wind whipped across the inlet and raced away with the texture of cat's-paws. It was late evening, a time when the winds usually calmed. The cat's-paws were a warning of what lay beyond the cliffs to the north, the predicted north winds. The Mizen would have to wait one more day.

I paddled past the pier at Crookhaven, and the cluster of buildings that huddled together as if remembering the winter gales. In the low light, everything looked bleak. No trees or shrubbery, just rock ledges, the short grasses bent in waves of wind, and the seagulls sitting on the village pier, heads tucked into folded wings or hunched low and staring into the increasing wind. When the gulls aren't flying it's a sure sign that bad weather is on the way. I paddled a mile into the inlet, where the rock finally gave way to a sloping meadow, and set up my camp.

The next morning, I paddled back out to the mouth of the inlet and spotted a fishing boat tucked in the lee of the rocks. Beyond the boat a black rolling sea reflected an equally sinister sky. I paddled up to the fisherman as the netting of a lobster pot broke clear of the water. A line ran taut from the ribs of the pot, around a shoulder-high pulley on the side of the boat, then down to a winch on the deck. The lobsterman reached for a lever just as the pot came even with the gunwale. One orange-gloved hand hit the lever as the other reached smoothly for the weighted pot and swung it aboard. Dressed in dirty yellow oilskins, the guy seemed oblivious to the raw cold and the pitching of the boat. His thick, curly black hair was wet either from sea spray or the squall that had come through a half hour earlier. He looked a little older than me, heavier and toughened by the conditions I watched him working in.

" 'Morning," I called out.

With a little shake of his head and a faint smile, as if I was the tenth mad kayaker he had seen that day, he replied, " 'Mornin' to ye."

His hands gripped the sides of the pot resting on the gunwale as his eyes ran the length of my boat. He didn't say anything, just stood there solid and seasoned from years of working on the sea as his boat pitched and rolled in the four-footers coming around the headland. He looked every bit the seasoned fisherman, confident, tough, and quiet. His eyes told me more than any words could have. To him I was a damn fool sitting in a twenty-inch-wide boat that looked like a toy.

"I was hoping to get around the Mizen and was wondering what it would be like today."

Another knowing toss of his head in the direction of the cliffs.

"Aye, she's a boiling cauldron today. I was out earlier. Ye wouldn't make it round Brow Head, that's the worst, but ye still have a ways to go before the Mizen. Where is it yer thinkin' a' goin'?" His voice was friendlier than I expected.

"Well, I'm actually paddling around Ireland."

The smile was replaced with a look of stunned disbelief. He asked, "In that?" and pointed to my boat.

"That" was my boat and my boat was a part of me. The anxiety of what was literally around the corner had made me edgy, and I immediately felt defensive.

"Yeah, she's a fine boat and she'll do all right." My response came out quicker than I had wanted and spoke more of the tension I was feeling than an abundance of confidence.

I had been primed for the headland ever since rolling up the bivy bag at dawn and now I felt the high of anticipation fading as the first raindrops hit my face. I understood this fellow's disbelief. I also respected his knowledge of the headland that he fished daily. His description of a "boiling cauldron" wasn't something I wanted to experience. I wasn't going anywhere but back to a place where I could find shelter from the increasing wind and driving rain. I thanked him for his help. He nodded, rebaited the lobster trap, and tossed it back into the water. I let a wave surf me away from his stern and paddled back into the inlet.

The next day, June 26th, under a clear sky, I came under Brow Head just as the same lobsterman was returning from his morning of fishing. High on the crests I could see the waves overtake his boat, then we would both drop into a trough. The only things visible were the cliff to my right and a sloping wall of blue water all around. I reached the bottom of the trough, then felt the lift and the heavy weight of my stomach as the boat surged upward. The lobster boat was gone! The ocean was as barren as the dunes in a desert, one rolling wave after the other reaching out to the horizon. Suddenly the boat reappeared, popping into view on the crest of another wave, much closer than I expected, and looking helplessly small amid the seas. The rising tide was pushing me around the first of the three headlands that made up the bulk of the Mizen. We passed within a hundred yards of each other. He stepped out from the pilothouse and raised his hand, open palm to the sky, as if to say, this is what we live for; a salute to the sun, the towering cliff that dwarfed both of us, and the hearty thunder of waves against rock. The sunshine seemed to have helped both our spirits. I returned the salute with a raised paddle, then dropped out of sight into another trough. Two cycles of trough to crest and I caught a glimpse of his stern disappearing around the rocks where we had met yesterday.

I was so focused on the size and power of the oncoming waves that I didn't realize how fast the tide was pushing me. Brow Head was looming larger by the minute and I remembered the fisherman's warning that this would be the worst point of the three. In front of me, the flooding tide veered off the rocks beneath the cliff and ran straight into the northerly swells. A rolling mass of dark-faced waves with breaking tops defined their convergence. Gone was the rhythm of swell followed by trough then swell again. Like white-eyed horses in the starting gate, the seas were bunching together and kicking out in the confines of tide and cliff.

Rogue waves that broke loose from the band seemed to race toward me, anxious to throw themselves onto the bow and wash over the foredeck. The bow dove into these waves, then rose to the surface with water cascading off the curve of the deck. Front hatch, compass, and camera reappeared. Another wave lifted the bow in a steep climb. The impact of the first wave and the climb up the face of the next slowed the boat to a crawl. It was stalling and still not over the next crest, which looked ready to break. Three or four adrenaline-packed strokes in as many seconds and the wave passed under the cockpit with the bow hanging in midair. Another second and we dropped into the trough: three feet of air, then the shock of the hull slamming into the water that rose to meet the boat. My upper body folded onto the front deck as the boat was jerked skyward again. The paddle shaft hit the crown of the deck. I pushed myself upright, tried to focus through the saltwater running from my eyes, and reached forward for the next stroke.

The gap was closing rapidly and I decided to paddle in closer to the cliff base where the waves weren't as big. I watched a couple of boomers fold over a submerged rock, waited for the tide to pull me beyond their threat, then angled in toward the cliff. To seaward the waves seemed to stand still; tide against storm swell, a battle of moon and earth, with neither one willing to let the other run free. Two hundred feet to my right I felt the mass of Brow Head watching over the struggle. Between cliffs and standing waves, the tide carried me through the narrow slot.

The waters beyond Brow Head were deeper and the waves had the feel of the ocean. Long rising slopes of indigo lifted me into the sky, then gently slipped away, lowering me into the next valley. Sitting in the bottom of the trough, I realized how big these gentle giants were as sunlight-dappled water rose all around me. The troughs were wide and flat-bottomed, the length of three or four boats, then a long climb up the enormous volume of water rising in front of me. A steady climb, eight to ten paddle strokes, the body of the wave rising and lifting the boat gently into the air until suddenly the world was all sky, horizon, and distant cliff. Atop the back of this mountainous wave the ocean was a continuum of crest, trough, and rolling energy moving ever southward.

A fulmar swept in from the west, following crest and trough, appearing and disappearing, drawing closer with each second as it honed in on my bow. I paddled across the top of a wave, feeling a mix of awe and fear at the power and volume I sat upon. These were the biggest waves I had paddled in and I wasn't sure if the crests were any less scary than the troughs. The fulmar floated out of the depression in front of me, flying with the waves and finding lift on the face that I was starting down. Blunted round wings, high forehead, and brilliant glistening eye. We passed midway on my descent, ten feet apart, the yellow hull knifing into the sea while the fulmar's snow-white plumage floated across a solid blue sky. I followed his flight, twisting in the cockpit while the paddle rested on the face of the swell and gave me a reference to hold the boat upright. It was a foolish move, to take my eyes off the seas, but the fulmar's flight is like that of a Siren: men will do careless things in the face of such graceful beauty. Just before the swell took him from view, he banked into a turn.

I remembered the ever present fulmars on my paddle around Great Britain. How they kept me company in all kinds of winds and weather for the five-and-a-half-month journey. I would talk to them, sing my highs and lows to them, and wait for their long sweeping turns to bring them around for a second look at this splinter of a boat so far from land. For me, the flight of the fulmars embodied the spirit of the open sea.

Trough rising to crest, up and over the top, and there was the fulmar again, this time to starboard, gliding in for a low pass over the bow, then back out to sea.

Swept with the poetry of the fulmar's flight, my body suddenly was not big enough to hold my spirit. I was part fulmar touching the rise and fall of the waves with my wingtips; part driftwood cast upon the waves. Fragile and adrift one second, then gliding free and unencumbered the next, confident and certain of my place in this world of cliff, ocean, and cloudless sky. I called out a loud "Yes!", dug the paddle into the sea, and threw a bladeful of sparkling water into the air. I was home, riding the power and lift of giant seas again. This was what I had come to experience. Big water, fulmars, and the wild feeling of deep ocean swells that washed through me and raised my spirits. The bow buried into the bottom of the swell, shed the waters, and started climbing again.

Up ahead were the toylike structures of the Mizen lighthouse perched two hundred feet above the waves. Red roofs and white walls surrounded by ledges of rock watching over tides and sea. On this, the first great headland of the west coast, broad and rugged as a fist shoved out into the Atlantic by the forces of geology and erosion, the buildings looked so small. They seemed to cower in the protection of crevice and rock, a human fingerprint of impermanence set against the colossal forces of nature.

If the buildings looked that insignificant from the sea, I wondered what I must look like, or if anyone could even find the glint of yellow and see the rhythmic dipping of paddles as I moved amid the waves. I imagined visitors marveling at the expanse of horizon, then gazing northward and picking out points of land that reached out into the sea one after the other until the last one was more hazy sky than land. Part of me wanted to be able to see that same view, to set in my mind a route along this coast of cliffs and indented bays. Yet another part of me was satisfied with seeing this coast as only a paddler could: from three feet above the seas and one measured paddle stroke at a time.

I remembered paddling around Lands' End, the southwest tip of England. Like the Mizen, it had a similar feeling of exposure, a place of powerful tides and huge waves. I had rounded that point singing, rejoicing in the wildness. A mile to the north, I landed on a beach and ran back to the clifftop to gaze down on where I had paddled. From the height of the cliffs, the waves had looked almost flat, no reverberating echo of wave against rock or dampness of mist-filled air. I could see fifty miles up the coast, but I couldn't feel what was three hundred feet below me. It had been a good lesson in perspective.

There is nothing so humbling as to sit beneath these headlands, to feel their power and to know that for thousands of years they have weathered the storms and the tides that tear at their bases. In one day out of hundreds of millions, I am blessed to slip cautiously past these cliffed headlands that will stand against the seas long after human beings have vanished from the earth. To live that moment and to hold it in that perspective is to know fragility and full humanity. Maybe a view from the heights of the Mizen lighthouse would show me where I was heading, but I realized I didn't need that view; in front of me was more than I could absorb in a lifetime.

I sat beneath the cliffs of Mizen Head wanting to soak up these feelings. Two hours earlier, I had been in the relative safety of the sheltered south coast, and now I sat at a point that I had dreamed about for many months. I had made a choice to come here, to be this speck on waves that could swallow a thirty-foot boat in their troughs. I had come here for this moment, this beginning and this sense of awe that reached deep inside me and struck a note that I knew would be there. I was living the moment half in my head and half in my heart, humbled and speechless.

As I sat surrounded by breaking waves, noise, mist, and the booming rhythm of folding swells collapsing on a submerged ledge, a sadness made my eyes sting with tears. Out of nowhere, awe was suddenly replaced by fear. Not fear of the sea or the power that exploded on the rocks and climbed twenty feet up the glistening black walls, but fear for the safety of this little corner of the world. And how many others? What I was looking at was the raw perfection of the earth and sea as it should be. I suddenly wanted to gather it all in and somehow protect it. I looked to my right, then to my left and back again. Overhead, to the cliffs and out to the sea behind me. Sun and shadow on vertical rock, the blur of guillemots flashing by, the purity of blue ocean meeting cliff and filling the air with white fingers reaching upward and dissolving into mist that fell back to the sea. The frightening thing was that I felt so powerless. Not against the sea but against my own species and the madness that seemed bent on destroying the elements all around me. The paradox was absurd. One frail human sitting in an eggshell of a boat and crying for the beauty and fragility of something that could crush me like an empty crab shell against the rocks.

I wanted to tell the headland, the waves, and the limpets clinging to the rocks, running white with the retreating waters, that I cared. It sounded so foolish. Speaking my heart to a rock, to the sea. But it was more than talk; it was a prayer. I thought about an image that I had—actually, a nightmare—of the possibility of a single second when not one human being on earth gazed in wonder and awe at the night sky and the miracle of the stars. I imagined that if that second ever came to pass, the world would suddenly cease to exist. Amid the beauty and wildy choreographed chaos around me, I offered a prayer of silent emptiness. Saying nothing,

just sitting amid the thunder of crashing waves and acknowledging its perfection, allowing it all to be wild and sacred, and thanking God for the
privilege of being there.

There have been times in my travels where I have felt touched by a
feeling of being fully alive physically, emotionally, and spiritually. These
are moments of true harmony, places of prayer and mystery that do not
necessarily answer questions but allow my mind or soul to dwell briefly in
another realm. These places to which I travel are always wild and require
great effort to reach. They are places where I can only stay a short while
before retreating from the exposure, both physical and emotional. I always
leave with a mixed feeling of having been blessed and at the same time
heavy with a sadness that is half in the rising and falling of my chest, and
then somewhere much deeper. I know I will never return to many of these
places, though they will live forever as feeling and emotions and snapshots
of memory.

The Mizen was such a place. I reminded myself that this was a point of
beginning, that ahead of me was the entire west coast. I wanted to linger,
but the impact of a huge swell folding over the reef and collapsing with
the rumble of thunder convinced me it was time to leave.

I lost sight of the lighthouse as I followed the cliff toward Three Castle
Head. The ruins of one of the castle towers rose into the sky atop the cliff
and looked down on both the sea and the land beyond the cliffs. The
green of the meadows gave way to eroded rock and fingers of land that
reached westward into the ocean. I paddled close to the fingers, wanting
to feel this place of land meeting sea. These cliffs, like those of the Mizen,
had been pounded by millions of years of winter gales, had felt the fires of
Neolithic villages, heard the music of Celtic migrations, and watched the
passage of Viking ships and modern oil tankers. It wasn't only the exposure
of the coast that made me feel so small, it was also this awareness of time;
a reminder that brought about an awareness of how brief my own visit was.

It was amazing how easily I could get lost in my thoughts. The steady
rhythm of paddling was like a mantra, a constant that the body unconsciously maintained while the mind was free to wander with the unfolding
images. In the middle of a thought that was winding back thousands of
years or exploring some esoteric idea, I would suddenly remember that my
body had been reaching and pulling, balancing the twenty-inch-wide boat
beneath me. I would joke with myself and tell the physical me to wake up

and pay attention, and then almost immediately drift back to my daydreaming of castles, harp music, and times when the land must have known the scent of wolves, bears, and nomadic peoples.

The physical moment was a gift of the present that I wanted to live fully. But I also wanted to acknowledge the past. I wanted to be sure that there was at least one human being who either gazed at the night sky in complete awe or wandered back through the ages with that same sense of wonder. Both worlds were essential to me, the physical and the spiritual, and I moved from one to the other, bringing them to life and finding a balance between the two.

I left Three Castle Head behind and pointed the bow across Dunmanus Bay. Three, maybe four miles away, another headland met the oncoming waves. Somewhere on that far shore I would need to find a safe landing, but for the moment I wanted to feel the open ocean free of rebounding waves.

Two miles from shore I stopped and looked down the length of the bay, to a place where the land converged in a hazy meeting of low hills. I liked the feeling of being in the middle of something so big. I swung the boat so my back was to the open Atlantic and the bow was pointing into the bay. In front of me the land disappeared behind a rolling mountain of water that moved eastward and lowered me into its belly. The volume in each smooth-faced wave astounded me. On top of the wave I would sit, for what seemed like an incredibly long time, the warmth of the sun soaking through the layers of drytop and fleece, warming my back as I looked across the length of the waves running into the bay. Thirty, forty yards across, was it possible for the waves to be that thick? The long backward slide down into the trough would begin and suddenly the view of the distant hills was gone again. All around me was blue-green water.

It had been four hours since breakfast and I was a long way from land, rest, and food. It was time to think about where I was going. The next wave lifted the stern and swung the bow in a gentle arc back to the north shore.

A mile to the north a fishing boat powered slowly through the waves toward me. As we closed the gap, I watched the antennas and radar unit above the pilothouse swing in a wide arc as the trawler rolled in the swells. I altered course a little and came as close as I dared, then hollered up to a deckhand who was hosing down the foredeck.

"Hello, can you tell me where a safe harbor is?"

My voice sounded thin against the vibrations of the engines and the slap and hiss of the waves split by the trawler's bow. The deckhand, dressed in yellow bib oilskins, and lost in the chore of hosing down the foredeck, jumped at the sound of my voice, and a silver stream of water ran wild from the hose over the gunwale and into the sea.

I called out again, "Where's the nearest harbor?" worried that the boat would pass before I could get an idea of where they had come from.

The fellow called out something and pointed north. I couldn't hear him. The trawler rolled in the swell and when the exhaust stack dipped toward me, the rumble of the engines drowned out all other sound. The boat looked big and powerful, plowing through the broadside swells and rolling over to expose the black bottom paint of the planked hull. I was quickly drifting aft. Two steel cables stretched over the stern and ran straight into the seas, boiling from the thrust of the propellers. They had a net out and couldn't slow or stop, but I could see the astonished look on the faces of the deckhand and the captain who had dropped the pilothouse window to stare down at me. I waved as the trawler rolled into the next trough and left me behind, alone again on the sea. The only sign of its passing was a mushrooming billow of water that hit my bow and shifted the boat sideways like a feather caught in a whirlpool. I still didn't know where I was going to land, but that brief contact with the fishing boat had been worth the slight detour. I liked being close to another boat on the heavy seas. There was that brotherhood that I had wanted to feel, that sense of sharing the ocean with another human being and just having someone know that I was out there. The trawler was rapidly pulling away, looking small against the cliffs of Three Castle Head and the Mizen.

Approaching Sheeps Head on the north side of the bay, I was worried. It didn't look like there was any place to land, nothing but rock pouring off the heights into the sea. I was running out of energy. With every paddle stroke the land seemed to move further away. What a strange thing to be paddling toward a headland of rock that offered nothing of what I needed in the way of rest and a place to haul out. Yet it was a point of reference, something solid to focus on. Somewhere along its length there had to be an indentation, a little protection for a safe landing. The high of two hours ago, of feeling so small beneath the cliffs and experiencing the swells thunder against the rock, had melted with the uncertainty of where I was going.

The closer I got to the headland, the more worried I became. Even if it had been flat calm I couldn't have landed on the near-vertical rocks. I was down to the last bite of a candy bar that lay pinched under the bungee cord on the front deck. I was saving it. For what? A little reserve for the next hour or more of paddling? It was a small comfort in the face of un-certainty.

I needed to make a decision: Do I run with the seas down this shoreline and hope for a landing, or do I round Sheeps Head and turn into Bantry Bay? I wanted to believe that just around the headland in front of me would be a sheltered beach tucked in behind a curve of rock that would break the power of the waves. A beach that would face the setting sun, a place I could drag the boat from the water and collapse on firm ground. In reality, I knew I would find more steep-sided rock and broken waves.

I turned into Dunmanus Bay and paddled wearily along the base of the rocky hillside. Above, stone walls climbed from the last rock at the edge of the sea and snaked their way upward, trying to run a straight line to the crest of the hill. A land of sloping green divided by walls of stone and colored with the shade of passing clouds. Shadows and light. Rock ledges breaking through the softness of pasture; grazing sheep and a trickle of reflected sun in a ravine halfway to the summit of the hill. The roll of the sea was fatiguing. I wanted to reach out and touch the land, feel it under my feet, sink into its grass, and stretch out flat on its firmness. It was so close, yet unapproachable, the two worlds separated by rock and churning water.

An hour later, I literally fell out of my boat when I mistimed a wave and tried to slide out of the cockpit with cramped legs. Suddenly I was in the water. My fingers raked over coarse rock as I tried to get my feet under me and stand in the surge behind a long-abandoned stone pier. It wasn't graceful but at least I was ashore, waist-deep in cold Atlantic waters and happy to be out of the boat.

Later that evening I was writing in my journal, my back cradled by a sun-warmed rock. A couple appeared from behind a ledge where a single-track road led from the pier upward through a gully. The yellow boat and my clothes spread out on the rocks caught their attention. They walked toward me, the woman's hands resting easily in the pockets of her quilted jacket, the man dressed in a worn, thick sweater, their easy gait suggesting this was a familiar evening pastime; a walk down to the pier, then back home before the sun set.

I greeted them with a soft "Good evening."

The woman was the first to speak. She smiled gently. "Good evening to you."

The man sort of nodded, his face relaxed, his eyes moving over the boat, the cookstove, the half-filled pot of pasta, and the gear lying in the last rays of the sun.

"It's a fine evening," he said.

"Yes, it is. The end of a fine day."

"And where have you come from?"

"Well, today I came around the Mizen, and Three Castle Head. This was the first place I could find to land."

There was a pause as the man pulled his head back a little, looked straight at the boat, then back to me.

"You've come around the Mizen in that?"

"That" seemed to be the operative Irish word for disbelief.

I smiled and answered, "Yes."

"And Three Castle Head?"

"Yes."

"I've never heard of anyone doin' that before."

I felt like a schoolboy pulling off a grand prank, then being caught by the principal and having to explain what it was that I had done. I didn't want this Irishman, this block of a man who stood in front of me with hands half again as big as my own to think that I was some sort of a fool playing on the ocean; his ocean, in the sense that he knew it from season to season and no doubt had memories of storms and tragedies that I knew nothing of. I didn't have time to respond to his disbelief. The woman beside him had picked up on my vague answer as to where I had come from. In the same gentle voice she asked, "You said you've come around the Mizen today, but that isn't where you, started, is it?"

I didn't try to hide the smile that spread across my face.

"Well, no. Actually, I started in Dublin."

"Dublin," the fellow almost shouted.

I jumped and replied, "Yes."

"You started in Dublin?"

"Yes."

"You're havin' us on, now, aren't ye?"

"No, I'm serious. I really did start in Dublin. It's taken me three weeks to get here."

The woman asked, "Are you alone?"

"Yes, I am."

"And does anyone know where you are?"

"Well, no, except for you folks."

She looked at the boat again, then over to the man, and said, "I don't believe this."

The big man held out his hand as if it were time for an overdue introduction.

"My name is James O'Mahoney and this is my wife, Eileen. We own the farm at the top of the road." He went on to explain that the area surrounding the cove and pier was part of land he had inherited from his father.

Eileen and James were curious about the boat, the compartments packed with clothing, camping gear, and food, the camera and map strapped beneath the bungies on the front deck, and the feather-light paddle that looked like a toy in James's hands. I showed him how to reach forward with each blade and roll his wrist back so that the high blade sliced into the air with its edge rather than with the flat of the blade.

The sun had settled behind the hillside above as we sat on the warm rocks and talked. I told them about the swells and the currents that played around the base of these headlands and how the fulmars, gannets, and seals were my companions on the sea. They wanted to know about the waves, the places I had camped, where I was going from here, and when I might finish back in Dublin. What struck me was this wonderfully innocent enthusiasm that they had for my travels.

The conversation turned to the history of the area, to the little cove and the hills that folded around it on three sides. Eileen told how there had been a shipwreck many years ago. The story had been handed down through the years though the details were few. The bodies had either been washed into the cove or maybe the fisherman had found them out in the bay, she didn't know. James sat and listened, nodded his head in agreement as Eileen told how the bodies had been brought ashore and buried in the field behind the pier.

James then told me that the tower I had seen on Three Castle Head had been the O'Mahoney Clan stronghold in the twelfth century, and he could trace his family history back to those days. All of the lands that we looked at across the bay had belonged to his people. I was amazed that he could look around and be aware that for eight hundred years his family had known these hills and headlands. He told me his father and grandfather had farmed this land and that on the far side of the cove there was a circle of stones in the middle of the field. He explained how the circle had never been disturbed, the lands around it being turned over and planted but the rocks left untouched. It was the remains of an ancient ring fort, a village site where a cluster of stick and mud huts would have been encircled by timbers and the stones that remained. Eileen said that there was another ring in the field above this one and a third in the neighbor's field.

"The old people believed the fairies, the Little People, lived there. That's why they never disturbed the rocks. It was bad luck if ye did," James explained.

He then recalled how, as a child of ten, his father had shown him an underground tunnel in a nearby field. "It was just a slab of stone, mostly covered in weed. My father pulled it up and we looked inside. It was big enough to crawl into an' maybe thirty, forty feet long. It was as old as the ring fort. Probably used as a place to hide during a raid or to store food or valuables. Eileen and I want to go back and look for it this winter." Almost as an afterthought he said, "There's plenty of time in the winter for that sort of thing."

In the damp of the evening my mind was filled with the images of this cove and surrounding hills blanketed in layers of time. I inhaled and breathed in more than just air. In the stillness a wave broke against the outer rocks of the pier and I imagined the glow of fires burning within the stone-circled villages on the surrounding hills. Somewhere between my stomach and my heart there was a pulsing warmth, a stirring of my soul. I remembered long hikes in the islands of Scotland that had led me to remote hillsides covered in purple heather. Places where the stones had been piled high in burial cairns and others where a single massive pillar stood in solitude against the rise of empty lands. I remembered the feelings of mystery, the silence that had settled over me. Once again I experienced those same feelings of wonder and soul silence.

"How old is it?" I asked.

With a shake of his head and a raised eyebrow, he answered, "Two thousand, maybe twenty-five hundred B.C."

Twenty-five hundred B.C.? For over four thousand years people had lived on these hills overlooking this cove. With only the sound of an occasional wave against the rocks, I felt myself being quieted. I wanted to go deeper into that quiet, deeper into the stillness of the night, to smell the fires and hear the voices of the people who had lived on these hills. I felt close to them, yet knew nothing of them. What did they wear? What language did they speak? Were they strong and independent, a force moving inland with the generations, or had they been pushed off better lands?

The cove also intrigued me and connected me to the hill people. What role did the sheltered water play in the settlement of the hills? Could the people have arrived as I did, by chance and the necessity of searching the shoreline for a safe landing?

My mind floated from one thought to the next, asking questions and making connections as different images played out. There was a strange familiarity to the evening and to the quiet of the cove.

James stood and stretched. It was getting late and there were still chores to be done. I walked with him and Eileen up the track and asked if they could point out the ring fort. A few hundred yards along the steep narrow road, James pointed across the long shadows of the hills. Across a gully facing us in the gathering dusk was a tangle of briars and brush ringed by a mound of earth and rock. It looked like a land from another time, a hillside framed by the sea with no sign of modern man. We said good night, and in the gathering darkness I found my way down into the gully, then up again and across to the middle of the field.

I stopped below the ring and turned to look at the surrounding land, the setting for this ancient fort. There was one light off in the distance and nothing else—just fields, the soft sounds of the sea, and a slight chill of evening air. I approached the ring, then slowly circled it, listening and feeling the history that I walked around, aware of the noise my sandaled feet made in the dry stubble of cut hay. Halfway around, I felt a slight breeze on my face and thought of the fairies.

In the eastern sky the first stars appeared, but only when I didn't look directly at them. In front of me was the wall of stones, tightly pushed together in a ring that held four thousand years of history in a tangle of nettles and brush. It was only by looking away from it, by holding it in the corner of my eye and taking in the rest of the hillside, that I could imagine it alive with movement and sound. I closed my eyes and listened to the night, felt it closing in around me with its shadows. The air brushed across my hands and face, the mass of circled rocks in front of me. In the darkened field, touched by the mystery of the village site, I was drawn deeper into the quiet of my heart. For the moment there were no questions, only awe.

Later, as I lay in the bivy bag, my eyes playing in a dome of stars, I felt a glow from the day's blessings. My mind was calmly awake, my body tired, eyes closing longer with each heavy-lidded blink. Somewhere in the warmth of drowsiness I thought how very long the day had been. Was it only this morning that I had started around the Mizen? Towering headlands, my conversation with James and Eileen, and the wonder of the ring fort filtered through the excitement of finally being on the west coast. Tomorrow I would retrace my route out to the open water and across Bantry Bay. I didn't know where tomorrow's camp would be or what I might find along the way. Those thoughts were better left for the morning. I half-sat up in the bag and checked the boat one last time. It sat waiting above the high tide mark, a shadow of graceful lines illuminated by moonlight.

Abbey Refuge

Give me the benefit of your convictions, if you have any,
But keep your doubts to yourself, for I have enough of my own.

—Johann Wolfgang von Goethe

A half mile in front of me a cliff rose out of the sea into a gray, overcast sky. Without sunshine and shadow the wall was flat black, no detail or texture, just two hundred feet of vertical rock separating the two worlds. According to the map this was Crow Head, the western tip of mainland County Cork. Three miles behind me was Black Ball Head, where the Martello Tower, Britain's response to the fear of a Napoleonic invasion, stood on top of the cliff breaking the smooth line of sky meeting land. The night before, I had camped in the safety of a narrow lough beneath the tower and sat watching the reflection of brightly colored fishing boats floating on a mirror of green fields and blue skies.

Today the ocean was in a different mood, an oily smoothness that wasn't friendly, but neither was it hostile, at least not in the lee of Crow Head. Two miles beyond the headland I could see the tip of Dursey Island, occasional white breakers washing over the rocks along its base. According to the map, there was a channel at the head of the island, a sheltered, direct passage north that would save me from going around the outside; but I wasn't paddling for that point. I wanted to go on the outside, around the tip where the waves were breaking white. I had spent four days trapped by winds that funneled into Bantry Bay and held me tentbound on its south shore. After sitting, writing, going for walks, and impatiently waiting, the winds had shifted from west to north, the close-packed whitecaps laid down to a deeper swell and finally let me out of the bay.

I crossed to the island and paddled close beneath the fields and rock that blocked the winds. It was beginning to rain, and a shiver ran down between my shoulder blades. The north side of the island was breaking most of the swells, but as I drew closer to Dursey Head, at the western tip, the waves wrapped around the point and the boat began the familiar rise and fall of the swells. The outside was going to be a push. Another hundred yards and I was losing the protection of the land. The high paddle fluttered in the wind, a wave broke over the bow and rolled halfway to the cockpit. With the wind howling in my ears, the sea grew boisterous and lively, my senses filled with the sights of cresting waves and glistening rock. I felt as if I was moving with an orchestra, listening to the subtle changes of rhythm and tone, and being drawn with the music toward a grand crescendo.

I pulled out from behind the last rock into the wildness of a stormy ocean. The calm of just moments before was blown away with the winds and replaced with a splash of cold spray that hit me in the face and ran into my eyes. I felt the rush of commitment, the exposure fueling me with energy and pulling me out beyond the rocks. Six-footers with occasional eight's sinking me into their troughs, then rising above in green blackness. A wave in front of me peaked, the top three feet crumbling with a sound that I had heard too often: a hiss, raspy at first, then growling deeper as it collected momentum and tumbled onto itself, a warning. I leaned into the paddles and moved into deeper water.

Off to my left was a towering thimble-shaped island; bare rock, proud and seeming to dare the winds and sea to throw what they might against its strength. Walls of gray-white, a solidness that looked out of place rising from the sea and thrusting into the air. The island was two miles away but looked much closer, bathed in sunlight by a single shaft breaking through a Kansas tornado sky. A lighthouse, stark white in the sun, so small against the mass of rock it sat upon, tiny dots of circling birds that must be gannets. The island was Bull Rock, and the smaller island a mile closer must be the Calf. Their names fit the image perfectly, one massive and formidable while the other sat within its protective lee, as if it had broken away but was hesitant to venture far from the larger island's protection. Drifting sheets of rain moved with the squalls across the horizon and moments later the islands looked distant and less dramatic in the absent light.

Between the wave crests and out beyond the Bull and Calf I saw a sharp-peaked island on the northern horizon, then quickly lost it again as I dropped into a trough. A rebounding wave off Dursey Island hit the stern and swung the boat back toward the rocks. A corrective stroke on the crest of another wave and I was back on course, and searching the horizon. Two crests later I saw it again, plus a smaller island a little to the east. The Skelligs? I didn't think they were that close, but there was no mistaking the silhouette of the larger island for anything else on this stretch of the coast. Even from a distance and through the squalls that obscured any detail, the island seemed to leap out of the ocean, pushing skyward not with the gentleness of rounded islands but with harsh lines that shot straight into the low clouds. The larger of the two barren rocks had to be Skellig Michael. I remembered seeing pictures of sixth-century monastic ruins clinging to its side, massive slate steps rising to a shelf of rock, and a cluster of finely built stone beehive huts. Seeing the islands through the squalls and rolling black waters added to their mystique. In a week I might be close enough to attempt a crossing, but I wondered if the seas would allow it. I couldn't imagine a ten-mile paddle in seas like these. I lost sight of the islands again and concentrated on just staying upright.

After an hour of getting tossed around like a cork, I entered the narrows between Dursey Island and the mainland. I was drained and it felt good to close my eyes and let the current gently spin me in a circle. Rough water paddling was exhausting. The physical exposure seemed to strip away all the protective emotional layers, and I felt as worn as the rocks on the outer coast. In the thick of big breaking waves, it was a constant measure of controlling the flight or fight instinct: too little adrenaline and I won't be aggressive enough, too much and I'll burn up energy too fast. The inclination is to pour on the power and try to get through the rough stuff fast. It doesn't work. The boat charges ahead, then plows into the oncoming wave or crashes into a trough. The only way is to slip into low gear and grind it out. Slow and steady, not fighting the power of the waves but letting them set the pace and hopefully missing the ones that fold over and break on themselves. Dig in, a brace or back stroke here or there, then dig in again. It can be frustratingly slow and fatiguing.

After a brief rest in the channel, I turned and headed back out. Moments after leaving the calm, I almost went over. An inflamed tendon in my right wrist made gripping the paddle shaft with my thumb impossible and I couldn't control the angle of the blade. I had ignored the pain in the rough waters on the outside of the island. Now, without the distraction of breaking waves and a pitching boat, I was keenly aware of it. A wave tossed the boat over on its side and I sliced the edge of the paddle, rather than the back of it, into the water. A last-second hip flick with my right knee jammed against the inside of the cockpit kept me from going over. Despite the tendinitis and the near capsize, I was encouraged by my reaction time. It was instant and automatic, the way it had to be.

Getting thrown over and hanging for that millisecond on the edge of the boat was a reminder of just how tenuous my grasp on the trip was. I had to be "on" one hundred percent of the time and it was wearing me down. It hadn't been a massive wave that had almost upended me. In fact, it had been a ridiculously small one that I hadn't been paying attention to. I had come down off the adrenaline high of an hour earlier and was focused on a cove a quarter mile in front of me, looking forward to getting out of the boat, into warm clothes, and already thinking about how much food and water I had in the rear compartment. I hadn't been attentive to the moment—the worst mistake I could make. It wouldn't have been a big deal to have gone over, but it was a reminder of how a month of paddling had both honed my reactions and also begun to take its toll.

I paddled into the tiny harbor of Garnish, a naturally protected cove that looked as if it would dry out at low water. A couple of thirty-foot fishing boats were anchored at the mouth, their lines hanging loose between bow and buoy. Next to the government pier was a boat ramp piled high with lobster traps and three dinghies pulled above the highest line of seaweed. I landed and walked up to the bigger of two buildings near the water's edge. In the corner of one window was a post office emblem and a stained piece of cardboard with STORE hand-lettered on it. I needed bread and jam, the basics for lunch, and knocked on the open door. An Irish lass with a tangle of red hair, a baby in her arms and another at her feet, greeted me with a smile.

"Hi," I said. "I saw the sign and was hoping to buy some soda bread, if you have any."

"Oh, that's an old sign," she answered. "My mum has some sweets for the kids but I wouldn't know about any bread. Come inside and I'll ask her."

She disappeared into the house, the little guy at her feet hesitating, struggling to keep his balance and staring up at me with huge blue eyes and a dirty, chubby face. We looked at each other for a few seconds, me the giant in the doorway, he the little Irish cherub. I waved my fingers at him and he bolted.

From the doorway and in through another that led to the kitchen, I followed the bare feet and fat little legs. At the far end of the kitchen was a simple table, chairs pulled out as if everyone had just gotten up, and a picture of Jesus on the wall above. A sea breeze ruffled the curtains over the sink and a lady looking just old enough to be a grandmother was stirring something on the stove. "If it's soda bread you're looking for, I haven't got any. But come in and sit down. I'll make ye a sandwich. There's salmon in the fridge and it'll take only a minute." Then as if everything was decided she said, "Yer from America, are ye?"

"Yes, from Washington, on the West Coast."

"And ye here on holiday, are ye?"

"Well, it's a sort of holiday. I left Dublin a month ago and I'm trying to paddle a kayak around the coast. I should be back in Dublin . . ."

The stirring of the pot stopped. She turned, looked me over head to toe, then straight in my eyes, and said, "Ye mean to be telling me ye rowing a canoe right round Ireland?"

"Well, we call them kayaks, but, yes, that's what I'm hoping to do."

The pretty lady with the flaming copper hair came through another doorway with her husband, the babe still in her arms, the toddler clinging to her leg and staring at my feet. The dad, in his mid-twenties, smiled, nodded, and shyly said hello. I suddenly felt like I was on stage, everyone looking at me with expectation. It felt awkward. These people not believing what they were hearing and me still feeling the rush of the morning paddle and the salt drying stiffly on my face.

It was the little guy in diapers who broke the spell and made me smile. I wondered why it was always children that saw the obvious. He didn't care where I had come from or where it was I was going. He was staring at my sandaled feet, my toes covered in sand.

"And are ye alone?" His mother's puzzled question brought me back to the world of adults.

"Yes."

"Ye came through the channel and not the outside, I hope," the older lady scolded.

The spoon was poised over whatever was in the pot and no one moved an inch. Oh boy, I knew where this was going, but there was no backing out of the kitchen, especially since there was the offer of a salmon sandwich.

"No, I wanted to see what the outside looked like." Then, as a quick diversionary tactic, I said, "But I did paddle into the narrows and saw the cable car over the channel." As if that would somehow excuse me from being a fool and paddling around an island with an easy inside passage. My diversionary tactic didn't have the effect I had hoped. In fact, it sounded pretty weak under the scrutiny of her gaze.

"Ye come around Dursey Head on a day the likes of this?" She paused a second, then pronounced the verdict, "Ye must be mad!"

There it was again. I knew it was coming and thought how I should be counting the number of times I had heard it. The salmon fisherman pulling nets, the shopowners adding sums of penciled figures, the fellow in the pub pulling a pint of Guinness. They each had the same reaction: a look of disbelief, hands frozen in space, and when they saw I wasn't "having them on," the inevitable: "Yer mad. Ye know that, don't ye?"

I had little defense to fall back on. I was hoping the baby might cry or the pot boil over, anything to release me from center stage. But no such luck. The verdict was in and I had the right to a final word.

I nodded and with resignation admitted, "Yes, I've actually heard that before."

The woman shook her head, stirred the contents of the pot once again, then dried her hands on her apron. "Ye must be hungry after such a foolish thing. Pull up a chair and I'll make you a sandwich."

In her eyes maybe I was mad, but if it's one thing the Irish are famous for, it's their hospitality—even to madmen. Despite my obvious instability, everyone I met wanted to help in whatever way they could. This time it was salmon, mayonnaise, and lettuce. A sandwich and strong tea heavily sweetened never tasted so good. We sat and talked. Mostly about fishing: lobster, mackerel, and of course the weather. I heard again how the summer before had been the finest in twenty years. Seven weeks and not a day of rain. The seas smooth as glass and everyone had color in their faces. The little beach had been filled with locals and tourists alike. A Dutch couple, or maybe they were German, were cycling through Ireland and camped on the knoll above the pier. Good thick grass—I could stay there if I wanted to. The older lady's brother owned the lot.

"He wouldn't mind if I camped there?" I asked.

"And why would he mind? He lives in Allihies and only comes over to fish. Ye might hear the boats goin' out in the mornin' but no one'll bother ye. If anyone asks, tell 'em ye talked with me."

Two or three cups of tea, maybe an hour of sitting and chatting. An old dog wandered in through the open door, took a look at the stranger, and stiffly walked out again. Life was slow and easy when the road ended at the lobster pots sitting idle on the pier.

I was beginning to like the lazy pace. The sea could wait for tomorrow. I needed a day to rest my arm and the offer of the grassy knoll sounded like a good place to hang out. I camped that evening above the quiet of the moored boats. The smell of the sea, a pile of nets outside the tent opening, and the grass beneath my head assured me that all was right in this little corner of the world.

The next morning, I set out with the wind raising whitecaps on the open water. Looking back at the protected cove, I could see someone standing on the knoll, hands held to their eyes. I remembered seeing an old pair of binoculars sitting on the windowsill near the kitchen sink. I held the paddle on end and waved an arc of farewell, then let the seas surf me over to Allihies—a wild ride across three miles of dancing waters. To the north was Cod's Head, then five miles of open water that was too rough for a safe crossing. The mouth of the Kenmare River would have to wait for calmer winds. I decided to land and walk into the village of Allihies.

I left the boat upside down on the beach and headed up the one-lane road. Out of the wind the sun was warm and there wasn't anyone in sight. A perfect day for a walk. Halfway to town, I passed a gray burro sleepily walking in the opposite direction. He stopped, let me scratch him between the ears, then continued on his way.

A whitewashed cottage with a sign on the stone wall offered tea and scones and a place to sit in the sun. I stepped through the low door and asked for a pot of tea and two scones, lots of butter, then returned to the courtyard to chat with an old man leaning against the warm rock of the house. He must have been at least eighty, tall even in his old age, big hands slightly trembling and folded half on his lap. He wore a dark suit jacket, buttoned and covering shoulders that were still wide but stooped. A white shirt and tie, and eyes that closed in warm, safe sleep in the middle of a sentence. He would awaken and ask if I was staying in town. I would explain again that, no, I was just traveling through. Just in town for the day. And again he would doze off.

I wondered who he was. How he had spent his life and what I would be like when I reached his age. Was I his past and was he my future? In that courtyard the same sun warmed us both and so little time separated our ages. I wanted to know him. I drank my tea while he slept.

When he awakened again, I gently asked, "Have you lived here all of your life?"

There was a pause and he answered, "No, no."

I could see his eyes trying to reach back through either sleep or confusion of time, maybe both.

"Where did you live?"

He turned his head slowly to the west and pointed a shaking hand in the general direction of where I had paddled from that morning. Toward the hills that climbed above the bay and looked down on the single lane coast road.

"Three miles from here. A little farm." His hand came down, found its folded position on his lap, and his eyes closed again.

The day before, I had spent a few hours following the road that cut over the headland and looked down on the island narrows. I thought of the crumbling buildings I had seen. Four walls open to the sky, doorway and windows filling with brambles and making a home for the birds singing in the safety of wild roses and bracken. Maybe one of those houses had been his? Where I had spent a few hours, he had lived most of his life. One old man had lived his life above a small bay looking out on the sea. A young man travels the world looking for adventure and maybe the sense of place that the old one has known. I paid for the tea and scones and left him sleeping in the sun.

The day I crossed the mouth of the Kenmare River, I felt crummy—a headcold, chills, and muscles that felt like they had already paddled fifty miles. For three days the weather had been dark, cold and wet—pretty miserable for midsummer and a mirror of how I felt emotionally and physically. I couldn't stand another day in the tent and had opted for the dubious benefit of exercise over more rest. Two miles into the day I had regretted leaving the warmth of the bag, but it was just as easy to continue as it was to turn back.

Kenmare River is actually a bay, longer and wider than both Bantry and Dunmanus, but for some reason, certainly Irish, it had been given a river status. I had wanted to paddle into the town of Kenmare, twenty-five miles up the bay, but after my experience with Bantry Bay and the westerly winds, I changed plans. It was almost mid-July. I had lost a lot of time sitting out bad weather and was less than a third of the way into the trip. Clearly this wasn't going to be a repeat of the previous summer, and I couldn't afford to get trapped by the winds again.

That was the trouble with big trips and exposed waters; so many miles and so much to see, but the weather always dictated the pace. If I explored every bay and island along the way, I could find myself a month behind schedule and running into bad weather on the last leg into Dublin. On the other hand, the fall could be fine and I would be kicking myself for not taking more time early in the trip. Time and weather were a gamble.

As I paddled across the Kenmare River, I had plenty of time to think of the demands of the journey. The sky felt like a wet gray sponge waiting for a shift of wind to wring out its weight of trapped moisture. An easy four-foot swell did nothing to pull me out of the low that had crept up and hung like a shadow over my emotions. My mind and body felt disconnected, out of harmony with each other, for the first time in weeks. I was two or three miles from land and wanting desperately to crawl into the warmth of the bag, somewhere out of the wind, and just sleep off the physical and emotional drain. I wanted to be warm and dry. I wanted to eat the breakfasts that I dreamed about and see things familiar. I missed home and was tired of being on guard, of constantly worrying: food, water, tides, the weather reports three times a day, summer slipping by and still eight hundred miles to go. Four miles per hour if the seas were flat. The trip suddenly felt too big.

I remembered a retired lighthouse keeper warning me about the waters around Malin Head, some three hundred miles to the north. An Irish banker I had met two days ago in Allihies had told me how rough the seas were in County Sligo and how the winds were always so cold.

Why did people always do that? Why did they tell me of a fisherman who had drowned just two weeks earlier, or of waves bigger than any I had seen so far? Were they trying to distance themselves from something they did not understand? I had heard the same warnings when I paddled up the Mississippi River, and in Nova Scotia's Bay of Fundy, in the Bristol Channel, and the Pentland Firth in northern Scotland. People were always quick to point out the hazards and just as quick to label me mad for attempting something they did not understand. Most days I could handle the doubts that people so freely shared, but on days when the trip had worn me down, their disbelief burrowed inside and undermined my confidence. People didn't realize that what I needed to hear was encouragement not stories of an impenetrable coastline or severe weather a hundred miles to the north. They had the comfort of returning to a warm, safe house after telling their tales, while I was left with the task of sorting out what I had been told. The irony was that I couldn't cut short these stories people wanted to tell me, because hidden in the telling there might be a bit of truth that I needed to hear. The trick was to separate the truth from the teller's emotions and balance that with my own knowledge and abilities. When I was low, the deciphering didn't work as well.

Where were the highs that I had felt just last week? The glistening white-capped seas and the cliffs spotted with fulmars soaring halfway to the summits two hundred feet above? The reality was that I had been riding the momentum of the trip and the combination of bad weather and being worn down had caught up with me. What I needed was rest. Do nothing, think nothing. Turn my brain off and let my body get well again.

What I found was a refuge called Abbey Island—a place of misty serenity cut off from the mainland at high tide and connected by a sandbar at low. The island sat off Derrynane National Park, on the north side of the Kenmare River, and was a welcome sight after the hour-and-a-half crossing. A stone wall followed the contours of the land, circling the abbey ruins and burial stones silhouetted against the moody sky. The shoreline completed one arc of the circle, the wall of the abbey rising from the very rock that seemed to hold the island out of the sea. I slid across the smooth water of the cove just as a bank of fog moved in from the west and settled on the hills I had seen from the middle of the crossing. Long tendrils of clouds reached down to the sea with the gentlest of mists settling over the island.

I landed and dragged the boat to high ground. With a piece of driftwood

I leveled a place, between two sand dunes, big enough for the tent. I worked slowly and carefully, settled in the tranquility that felt so welcoming. Despite the fatigue and weight of being sick, my mind was clear. I was aware of the abbey fifty feet above me, some seven or eight hundred years old, and how generations had walked past the place where my boat sat on the packed sand. When the tent was set and the gear transferred from the boat to the dripping nylon, I walked, hooded in raingear, amid the gravestones. I saw the hollows in the soil by each headstone, then crouched through the doorways of the abbey that had half filled with the centuries. Through the mist and the waters that wrapped the island in a hush, I could feel the people of the past walking out to the abbey: a line of black coming along the beach from the mainland. Generations carrying the weight of prayers or that of a loved one along the sands, then retracing their footsteps that the next tide would erase.

I felt again my own genetic memory stirred by the ghosts of the island's past. If I had wanted I could not have ignored the presence of something on the winds of that misty day. Not when the protected veneer of emotions had been worn away from over a month of exposure and left my soul seeking the comfort of an island sanctuary.

For a little while longer sleep could wait. I walked over the island, small, gently crowned, entangled with weeds and grasses. A sheep path led to the top, where the west winds came off the sea with the promise of rain. I had felt the highs of the trip, the elation and the adrenaline of adventure; now I wanted to feel the emptiness that my fatigue filled me with. What a precious gift to be too tired to think. I simply stood and felt the wind, the mist and age of the island. Then let it be still.

I followed the sheep trails in a meandering circle above the rocks, returning through a small bog to the abbey, then over the last knoll to where my tent sat cradled in the dunes. A warm bag, the boat tethered to the tent. The camp was sheltered from the winds and only a strong southerly swell would make the launch, whenever that happened, a risk. Another gamble I could accept. Now I could sleep as long as I needed. The last thing I remembered was the sound of mist whispering against the tent.

Skellig Spirits

I go out there so I can look into myself,
and when I'm there I can see myself standing still,
and the rest of the world going mad.

—Des Lavelle, *The Skellig Story*

In the past week, I had paddled only twenty miles. I went to sleep with the winds, heard them buffet the tent in my dreams, and felt them in the chill of the wet mornings. I remembered days of sun, warm sandy beaches, and smooth, wind-free swells. It was a memory from a month ago. Was that possible—only a month? Time was a strange thing when it slid past at the length of a paddle stroke. So many headlands. So many emotions and memories, countless thousands of waves that boat and paddle sliced through, then left behind. Time was a heart that sang, muscles that pulled, and eyes that took in details of rock, bird, water, and sky. If it was only a month, then it was a lifetime lived in that brief period.

Time was indeed strange. Now it was weather: sitting and waiting, praying for the rush of the wind to be silent, then listening to the stillness of fog and hearing nothing but my own breath. I sat in the opening of the tent and thought about the days slipping past and how summer should have already been here. When I was tentbound, the hours dragged by and the long northern days teased me with daylight until eleven o'clock. And still I sat.

I was in Ballinskelligs, three miles from Bolus Head, then another nine or ten miles out to the islands I had seen from Dursey Head, the Skelligs.

87

They had become my primary focus. I had been determined to wait out the unstable weather, but after three days I was running out of time and patience. When the winds left the bay free of whitecaps and swells, the fog moved in and cut visibility to a half mile. I knew the landing on Skellig Michael was risky in anything but calm seas, and I wasn't going to do the crossing on a compass bearing in low visibility. I had to wait.

As I sat writing these thoughts in my journal, I heard the laughter of children, then the sound of running feet. I knew who it was. I had met two families from Dublin, the O'Sheas, who were camped over the knoll. Two brothers that had married sisters. There was another sister visiting from Canada with her husband and children and it was impossible to re-member everyone's name. And so many kids! Laughing, running, screaming with the delight of the boys teasing the girls. Sandcastles, water fights, wet sandy towels, and best of all, the American in the tent and his funny-looking boat. The edge of the floorless tent lifted and two giggling Irish faces poked up from the grass. I closed the journal.

"Dad says to come for lunch. An' maybe we can go out in yer boat afta."

"Donall, my mum said not to ask him."

There was silence and a glance up to me to make sure he hadn't just blown the carefully laid plan to get a ride.

"I didn't really ask him." Donall sounded defensive. Diplomacy doesn't come easily to a seven-year-old boy.

"Oh, don't worry. If the winds stay calm, I'll let you have a ride this afternoon," I said.

The faces disappeared and all I could hear were screams of "We're going in the kayak!"

"I'm going first."

"No, yer not, I asked him and he was talkin' to me."

"Yea, and Mum told ye not to ask."

I left the quiet of the tent and was instantly surrounded by kids pouring out of the caravan like chickens on the run for scattered corn. Sand-covered little hands reached up to grab mine, the theory being whoever made contact got the first ride. More screaming. More darting wet heads; some running to the boat and making plans, others rushing ahead and confirming with an uncle or parent that they had the first ride.

The caravan, Irish for car trailer, was pure chaos. A dozen bodies packed into a space too small for six and everyone yelling for someone's attention. Food, plates, towels, and toys. An eleven-year-old boy chasing his cousin with a water pistol missed and squirted me.

Con, the father of two, or was it three of the kids, pleaded for some order. "Kids, kids. Quiet! Settle down! Chris isn't used to this. He'll get in his boat and leave if you don't sit and eat your lunch." It was a nice try but it didn't work. Either no one heard, or they knew Con wasn't the disciplinarian. He was the dad who would swim, play hurly or soccer, and sit with them on his lap and tell them a story. In truth, the pandemonium didn't bother him. He was happy in all of the confusion, as likely to be telling a story of the ancient history of Ireland as he was to argue about the latest hurly match between Munster and Leinster.

Con was an athlete like his brother Patrick and a lover of all things Irish. The spoken and written word was the joy of his life. In the past three days I had sat and listened to his stories of ancient Ireland, stories that were thousands of years old and ones that the kids knew and would add details that Con left out. Tales from the "Annals of the Four Masters"—a compilation of ancient manuscripts that four monks in the seventeenth century had the wisdom to preserve. He talked and I listened with thirst.

I had read a book about a tenth-century giant of a man who briefly united all of Ireland. Con and I talked about this near-mythical warrior, a man whose family had been slaughtered during a Viking raid and who rose to unite a tribal people against their common enemy. Eleven-year-old John knew who Brian Boru was and that he had been killed not at the Battle of Clontarf, but in a cottage at the battle's edge. He had interrupted Con's explanation of where the battle had been fought, and while his cousin Donall and the other kids listened to the legendary tale (as if it was the first time they had heard it), John finished telling the story that we all knew. How Boru had stayed out of the final battle, an old man, still strong but convinced by his son that his reflexes were too slow; the people needed a king, not a dead warrior. Boru, the Lion King of Ireland, the *Ard Ri*, ruler of all the land, had been praying in a cottage for the victory of his army. A Norseman, retreating from the battle that had turned in favor of the united tribes of Ireland, stumbled on the cottage and fought the aged King Boru to the death.

"The Viking had a battleax and Brian only had his sword." John finished the story as any eleven-year-old would: He raised his hands over his head and brought the imagined ax down. "He buried the ax in his head."

In the corner of that crowded trailer I had witnessed what Ireland was all about: the telling of stories. Surrounded by noise and confusion, the stories had been told in pubs and in castles. Warmed by mead and the glow of peat fires, this story of an Irish hero had survived over nine hundred years and had now been retold by a young boy, retold to a stranger, a traveler who would take it with him and tell it in some distant land. The legend of Brian Boru would live on.

It wasn't one of the kids who got the first ride in the boat. It was Con. I gave him a few tips, suggested that he stay close to shore, then stepped out of the water and watched. For the first few minutes he looked awkward, his upper body rigid and the boat responding like a nervous horse with a rider who had never sat in a saddle. I remembered my first time. The boat had felt claustrophobic. If I tipped over, I was certain I would be trapped in the cockpit, unable to get to the surface for a breath. The narrow hull mirrored my anxiety and tension, quivering and responding to every twitch of muscle. Paddling is like riding a bike, you have to be half removed from it before it begins to feel natural. After a half hour Con had relaxed, his shoulders had dropped, and the boat glided smoothly with each stroke. Occasionally he would lean too far to one side and the boat would hang on its edge, threatening to capsize, but giving Con a few seconds to again find his balance. He paddled it one way, tenderly eased it in a broad turn, and paddled it back, then around a little faster and back again.

When the pleading and pacing of the kids in knee-deep water got to be too much, Con eased the bow onto the sand and it was Donall's turn. I watched him sink into the cockpit that seemed to swallow his seven-year-old body. No fear or anxiety, just the thrill of the moment engulfing him. Con held the stern and gently pushed him around in waist-deep water while Donall dipped the blades, laughed, and pretended to paddle. I returned to the tent for a few minutes of quiet while everyone else played on the beach.

I had picked up the journal again when suddenly I heard cries of alarm. I looked up to see the boat drifting away from Con's outstretched hands and a look of panic on his face. A sudden offshore wind had caught him off guard and was blowing Donall out to sea. He yelled for someone to get the lifeguard and started to swim after Donall.

I ran to the water's edge and dove in. The frigid water hit my inner ear and eyesockets with such pain that I felt nauseated. *"Forget it. Swim! Get to Donall."* I came up on Con, then pulled past him. On a breathing stroke I caught sight of the lifeguard hitting the water on the run and a crowd of people gathering on the beach. Straight ahead I could see the stern of the boat but I wasn't gaining on it. The wind was picking up, the water getting choppy, and I started to pray, "Please God, don't let him go over. Stay calm, Donall, stay calm."

I could feel the cold locking my chest and arm muscles in spasms. Every fourth or fifth stroke I would look up, but the boat, wasn't getting any closer. Through the cold I tried to concentrate, ignoring the nausea and focusing on pulling through the water. I had done a lot of long-distance swimming, but not in fifty-degree water. My arms felt as heavy as water-logged stumps and I couldn't get a full breath of air. With every stroke I wondered if I was chasing a boat I couldn't catch, and if not, would I have the strength to make it back to land? On and on. Desperately looking up and still the boat drifting ahead of me. Maybe a little closer but so little. How long could I keep going? I lowered my head again, the waves catching my arms in their forward arc and blocking them in mid-stroke.

I stopped and yelled out to Donall: "Just sit there. Don't move. Just sit."

He looked scared, the land getting more distant by the second and me taking so long to reach him. He was crying. I was almost there but I couldn't close the last ten yards. Damn the wind! With every stroke I gained a foot. I was at my limit, my breath gone and my body beginning to shake from the cold and exertion. Finally, I reached out to grab the stern, missed it, and grabbed again. On the third try I got it and hung on, sucking in lungfuls of air. My head felt like it was being split open by the cold slicing into my eyesockets. I tried to focus on the stern of the boat, looking at the yellow of the hull, anything to get my mind away from the nausea and pain as I slowly regained control of my breathing.

I tried to reassure Donall, told him everything was going to be all right even though I couldn't feel my legs and didn't think I could tow the boat the half mile back to shore. Tears ran down his face and he was shivering. He nodded, his entire body shaking from the cold wind. I started towing the boat, stern-first, back to the beach. My one thought was, "Gotta get out of the water." The lifeguard was still swimming out, raising his head out of the water more often than keeping it down. He was obviously near his limits, but towing a rescue buoy that I watched like a desperate man. I prayed that he wouldn't turn back when he saw us struggling back toward the beach. "Come on. Come on. Don't turn back. We need that buoy."

We closed the gap and he finally reached out for the boat. He was wiped out, his breath as ragged as mine had been. We lowered Donall onto the buoy—his legs dangling in the water, his upper body draped over the bow, white fingertips clinging to the boat. I pulled myself over the rear deck and into the cockpit. With Donall shivering on the front deck and the lifeguard hanging on the rear toggle, we headed for shore. Donall was one brave boy. Cold and scared but staying low on the deck like I told him, even as the waves washed over the bow and soaked him. He didn't say a word but I could hear the gasps as the waves hit him and the shivering shook his little body.

The paddle back took as long as the swim out. The lifeguard was so cold he just hung there. I kept calling back, encouraging him to hang on and that it wouldn't be long. If it was me being towed, I would have been finished. The cold would have drained all muscle control from me. Thankfully, he had more body fat. He was shaking but still coherent.

As we got within yards of the shore, Con waded out and reached for Donall, the lifeguard let go, and strong welcoming hands pulled us from the water. There were tears of relief, hugs and handshakes as we landed and were hurried to the warmth of the caravan. For an hour we sat wrapped in blankets clutching hot-water bottles to our chests and drinking hot tea. I kept spilling mine, my hands and body shaking uncontrollably from the cold. I looked over at Donall, wrapped in a blanket on Con's lap. He was safe in his dad's arms but very quiet. He would look over at me with huge eyes, smile softly, and bury his head in the warmth of the blanket again. Someone asked him what he had thought while he was drifting away. With a lisp he said quietly, "I was afraid I would capsize." Such a big word for such a little fellow. Con kissed him on the forehead and he snuggled in closer. I thought how brave he was and thanked God that we had both made it back to the beach. In an hour Donall was asleep on the couch. Con came over and sat beside me. "Thank God you're a good swimmer or we would have lost Donall. I don't know what I would have done." His voice had an edge to it that brought tears to my eyes. I was still shivering. Con got up, brought me another blanket, and filled my cup with more tea.

On the morning I left Ballinskelligs, all the O'Sheas stood on the beach and watched the preparations. Donall was in front. I snapped the spray deck in place, fastened the belt around my waist, checked the camera and hatches, then turned for a last good-bye. I hated this part. I no longer could hide behind the preparations. I sat and looked at all the faces staring at me a moment before I would take that first stroke of the paddle. The traveler is always saying good-bye. To some it may sound adventurous, romantic, but for me it is a lonely feeling that I never get used to. It was another paradox of the trip, the excitement of moving on and the reality that I might not see these people who had befriended me ever again.

"Be careful on the seas, Chris."

"God bless and safe travels."

"Have fun and say hi to Fungie the dolphin."

The blessings and farewells mingled with the sound of tiny waves curling onto the beach. Con leaned over the water, the solid warmth of his hand closing over mine and holding it for a long time. Donall stepped into the bay next and mimicked his dad. His hand so small and his voice just loud enough for the two of us: "Thanks for rescuing me."

My voice cracked as I said, "Thanks for being so brave."

I pushed off the sandbottom and slowly turned the weighted boat toward open water. Fifty yards out, I turned and looked again. Everyone was standing there beneath the moody skies, just standing and watching. I waved again. Hands stretched into the sky and farewells floated across the water. I was off. The kids ran down the beach to get a last parting wave before I rounded the castle ruins on the point.

Suddenly I was alone.

I had an hour of paddling before I reached Bolus Head. An hour of settling into the quiet of myself, of feeling the sea again and letting images of the past few days float through my mind. It was a transition time and I was glad for it. I wanted that time to set the memories of names and faces. The sound of voices and the feel of emotions. By the time I reached the headland and the bigger waves working their way around the point, I was ready to tuck the images away and focus on what was in front of me.

Four-to six-foot swells, nothing breaking, a soft breeze from the north. Familiar conditions. I was calm but alert, ears and eyes searching the winds and water surface for clues of what was around the corner. I was two hundred yards offshore, pulling away from the last of the protection of land and wondering if each view of cliff ahead was the actual headland or another mountaineer's false summit. Not that it mattered. Beyond a certain point the safety of a landing two miles back becomes a moot point. The commitment to rounding the headland was already made.

I wasn't completely around Bolus Head when suddenly the Skelligs appeared. One minute there was only gray sky and a horizon that changed with each swell. The next minute Bolus Head was forgotten, and in front of me, impossibly close, were the two islands. I knew Skellig Michael, the sharp-peaked bigger island, was two miles further out than Little Skellig. Yet they looked as though they were on top of one another. Nine miles to Skellig Michael. It couldn't be that far. Could it?

Nine miles. In these seas, it would take a minimum of two and a half hours. And what about the landing? Could I haul the loaded boat out of the water once I got there? A fisherman had told me there were concrete steps on the side of the pier but no easy way to land a small boat. What if I got out there and couldn't land? That's another two and half hours back, with no food and the possibility of the weather deteriorating. They looked so close.

I knew it was foolish to think about attempting the crossing, but this was the best weather in over a week. What if this was the only chance I had? Was the risk worth it? If the winds increased as little as ten miles per hour, the seas would be dangerous. Anything more and the risk would be tenfold.

Half my attention was on the Skelligs, the other half on the buffer of seas between me and Bolus Head. I was being driven closer to the rocks. I had to make a decision and move in one direction or another. I watched the swells for another minute, then decided.

On the crest of a wave I turned the boat north and headed for the shelter of Puffin Island, four miles further along the coast. It wasn't worth the risk, not alone. The Skelligs would have to wait. I stopped a dozen times in the next hour to look at the islands and wondered if that was as close as I was going to get to them.

I waited two days for another break in the weather. Camped in a field above a cobbled beach, I sat, watched, and waited. The first day, the swells battered the outer islets and rolled over the ledges extending like wings on either side of my protected cove. I was safe but taunted by the islands on the horizon.

The second morning, I awoke to dead silence and the tent fabric dripping with condensation. The world had changed overnight and now mist collected in fine droplets on my beard. Out of the filtered light that hurt my eyes the islands would appear like an apparition and then mysteriously fade away in thickening fog that blanketed the ocean and muffled all sound. Gulls sat on the islets as if the weight of the fog held them against the rocks, their heads tucked in the folds of wings. An occasional cormorant would break through the fog, flying low to or from its nest site along the coast, then quickly disappear again. There was nothing to do but wait.

I paddled two miles into Portmagee, bought some fish and chips in a pub, and watched the news on a thirty-six-inch TV screen. The transition between my reflective life on the coast and the sudden flickering image of the news report left me empty of the appetite I had walked in with.

There was renewed violence in the North. Police were dragging peaceful demonstrators out of the path of a marching band that wanted to go through a Catholic neighborhood. Batons were crashing down on people's heads and four police half-carried a bloodied man from the tangle of bodies. There was no fight, maybe no life left in him. A bishop was pleading for peace and more troops in armored vehicles were moving in, cutting people off from their own houses.

I had stepped out of the fog of innocence into a part of Ireland I knew nothing about. The violence stunned me and I couldn't comprehend it. I could hardly believe that just a few hundred miles away there was such twisted political and religious anger. I might expect it in some corrupt corner of the world, but not in Ireland. Not in the Ireland that I knew.

In that moment I felt more alone than at any time on the trip. I walked out of the pub into the rain. My idealistic world of seabirds, cliffs, and blue ocean had been violated by the cruelties of the conflict in the North. I wanted to leave the memories of the news report behind the door that shut with a click. I needed to talk to someone, to family. I called my parents' number and listened to the repeated rings. Hung up and dialed the number of a friend in Port Angeles. I just wanted to hear a familiar voice, something reassuring that I could hang my emotions on. Candace answered. Six thousand miles melted away in a blur of friends' names and stories of what everyone was doing. Summer had arrived. They had gotten the postcards I had sent and were all concerned for my safety. My spirits lifted.

Candace said her mom wanted to talk to me.

Irene had cancer. In the time I had been gone, the cancer had spread and she no longer got out of bed. She asked how I was doing and if everything was going well. She wanted to know all about the trip. Briefly, I told her of the kindness of the people, the beauty and the peace that I was finding on the sea. She sounded tired. Her voice was weak and she cried when she said good-bye.

Candace was back on the line. She was crying. Through the tears I heard her say, "You're an inspiration and we all love you."

I watched the rain drip down the glass of the phone booth and felt my own tears run over my cheeks. The fragility of two worlds, thousands of miles apart, washed through me, and I let the tears flow. It was my own confusion and probably the weight of the trip that let me feel so deeply the pain of my friends. How was I an inspiration? I wasn't the one caring for a dying mother. I was out on an adventure, exploring a country both beautiful and broken, while Candace nursed her mother through her illness. We said good-bye, and this time it was the click of the phone that left me alone in the rain.

In the gray of late evening, I got back into the boat and paddled back toward camp, then kept paddling around the islets, not ready to land. I wanted to sink into my feelings for a while. To sort them out and let them find a place of rest. For a long time no thoughts came. Just sorrow and an emotional fog. The violence up north and the weakness in Irene's voice seemed to echo in my heart and the stillness of the night. The day was gone, a few stars flickering between the parting clouds. I floated between heaven and earth, between sky and sea, and struggled to hold both the weight of an imperfect world and the beauty and promise of an evening sky that was rapidly clearing. I wished my heart and mind were as bright as the stars that shone overhead. How could there be such pain in some people's lives and such beauty and promise in mine? It seemed a cruel contrast. I took a few strokes, let the boat drift like my feelings, and slowly surrendered them to the night sky. There were no answers. I could not understand the conflicts of the North, the violence, the killing and the blood. Neither could I accept, with any comfort, the pain in my friend's voice.

The news from both within Ireland and back home in America re-minded me that this adventure was not a solo journey. John Donne wrote, "No man is an island." The truth is that solitude draws us closer to those we love and allows us to feel their joy and their pain in greater measure. Perhaps the trip, with its shifting winds and tides, was a mirror of life itself. One day the seas would be calm, filled with sunlight and blue energy, the next a raging fury that only a fool would venture out on. Harmony and chaos existed side by side and seemed carelessly to sweep lives into either path. There was no understanding it. There was only acceptance.

When I had come to that place of acceptance, I turned the boat in the blackness and eventually found the cove where my tent waited. I carried the boat above a line of wet seaweed, looked again at the stars, and crawled into the sleeping bag.

It must have been the stillness that awakened me the next morning, or maybe the drier air. After a week of waiting, I had become sensitized to every change in the weather. I unzipped the tent and listened. In the halflight of predawn, I couldn't see the water, but I didn't need to. Beyond the shadows of the islets, a rhythm of surf told me this was the day I had been waiting for. No time to snuggle back into the warmth of the bag. It was time to move.

By the light of the headlamp I pulled most of the remaining gear from the compartments of the boat and stowed it in the tent. The boat would be skittish without the ballast of weight, but I needed it empty for the haul-out on the island. I stuffed the sleeping bag and bivy sack in the forward compartment, insurance against getting caught on the island by a weather change. Food and water in the middle hatch, and by dawn I was a half mile from land. To my left was Puffin Island; rebounding waves broke the smoothness of the swell and made me nervous in the empty boat. It was two miles before I was beyond the confused chop, and I settled into the rise and fall of the five-foot swells.

In the first rays of light, the sea and air were filled with birds. Puffins, razorbills, fulmars, shearwaters, and gannets were everywhere. The shear-waters circled the boat, their wingtips seeming to read the height of each swell with a gentle touch of wing to water. Effortless, perfect harmony.

Twenty feet in front of me, a puffin broke the surface of the water, its orange beak full of tiny silver fish. With a startled flutter it was gone as quickly as it appeared. The water closed over wings and webbed feet, and a swell erased the concentric circles of its dive.

Overhead, gannets were heading to Little Skellig while others altered course or just glided and turned their heads in my direction as they flew past.

I kept checking the compass. A steady two hundred and forty degrees as the bow rose and fell in line with the peak of Skellig Michael. Over my shoulder Puffin Island was losing the detail of rock cleft and grassy ravine. Lemon Rock, a half mile in front, was my next reference point, then an-other three miles to Little Skellig. Two miles beyond Little Skellig and an hour and a half from where I sat so insignificant in the swells was Skellig Michael.

I was a mile from Little Skellig when the first gannets began circling. There were a few dozen at first, scouts from the colony of over forty thousand on the island. The closer I got to the island, the more gannets joined the flight, until the air was solid with birds turning in a vast wheel of black-tipped wings and golden heads. I was the hub, the focal point of this massive spiral. The only sound was the whir of hundreds of wings slicing through the air fifty feet over my head. I forgot how vulnerable I had been feeling in the tippy boat and was drawn into the circular flight turning above me.

I paddled below this dizzying umbrella of life, pulling it slowly through the sky as I closed the distance between the two islands. Slowly the circle began to break apart as I drew closer to the pinnacle of Skellig Michael. I had been escorted across the final two miles of my pilgrimage, then left to stare, overwhelmed, at the mountain island towering over me. It seemed to erupt out of the swells, splitting the seas and standing with undeniable power and certainty against the clear sky.

Somewhere on that seven hundred feet of near-vertical rock were the ruins of the sixth-century monastery. I could see a track that led from the pier and gradually circled out of sight to where I knew the lighthouse stood a hundred feet above the waves. From the track, my eyes wandered over the crags and patches of green searching for any sign of the beehive huts that I knew were there. In the interplay of shadow and sunlight, I could see only walls of rock dotted with the white of soaring gulls. I wanted to land, to get out of the boat and begin the climb. But I also wanted to just sit in the relative calm of the island and savor the moment.

The approach had taken two hours. Two hours of slowly drawing closer and feeling the anticipation building with each new detail of the island. The seabirds, the feeling of being dwarfed by the expanse of ocean, and the awareness of moving away from the safety of the mainland were all part of the crossing. All of the waiting; the glimpses of the island through fog and rain, and the memory of that first sighting as I came around Dursey Head two weeks earlier added to the emotions of arriving.

I paddled around to the pier and made a difficult landing on the steps formed into the concrete. I sat on the rear deck of the boat and clung to the concrete as the swells dropped out from under me. I timed the swells and launched myself onto the steps, then waited in waist-deep water for the final move. The swells washed over my waist, then dropped again as I lifted the boat and struggled up the steps. Fiberglass scratching against stone, my back and arms straining against the weight of the boat, and my feet feeling blindly for the next step, I finally stood on the pier and gently set my scarred boat on the rocks. Then I sat down and rested.

The air was filled with the noise of waves and the screams of a colony of kittiwakes nesting in the cliff above the track.

Skellig Michael: named for the sighting of the Archangel by fishermen tossed on a stormy sea. Gannets, gulls, sunlight, and the solid warmth of rock beneath my legs. Straight above, an overhanging cliff darkened by shadow hid the sun-bathed flanks of the island.

I started up the paved stones of the track clinging to the side of the island, climbing higher with every blind turn leading to another view of the waves and rocks below. I walked slowly, quietly, letting a calm settle over me after the rush of the landing.

I walked within ten feet of a puffin standing on a rock at the track's edge. With mournful glistening eyes, heavy orange bill, and tuxedo jacket, he stood at attention: A jester greeting the traveler on his pilgrimage. He shuffled on his perch, uncertain of this stranger. I turned my eyes deliberately away and stepped wide around his rock. The nervous shuffling and turning of the head stopped and he watched me continue on.

Further along, more puffins dropped from hidden perches, catching the updraft of air currents and disappearing in a blur of orange and black. From around a turn in the track other puffins appeared and flew straight toward the rocks above and below me. At the last second, wings would flare and bright red feet would pop out of white-feathered bellies. Suddenly there would be another puffin comically standing where there had been only rock.

After a few hundred yards the track leveled out and to my right a set of massive steps rose through dense ground cover, climbing steeply into the rocks above. The steps disappeared amid the outcroppings and hollows, then reappeared a hundred feet higher, steadily climbing until they melted into the confusion of ledge and protruding angles of rock. Six hundred steps—quarried, dragged into place, and leveled by monks fourteen hundred years ago—rose in switchbacked silence.

One ancient step at a time slowly took me higher and higher above the sea. The sound of wave against rock grew faint and the ocean never looked so vast.

Hundreds of puffins were everywhere, flying, standing, waddling, and growling from burrows that reached under tufts of grass. Some stood on the same steps as I did, staring out with teary eyes toward the sea.

My pace was slow and gentle. Two or three steps. Then a long pause to try and grasp some sense of the time I was walking through.

I tried to imagine the early Christian monks, working in leather sandals, clothed in coarse robes, lifting and struggling with the hundreds of pounds of each rock.

I was alone. Free to wander back through more time than I could understand. In that solitude and silence, with only the sound of a gentle breeze in my ears, I sat on the steps and listened. Just listened. Then stood and continued.

I reached a sloping ridge between the two summits of the island—Christ's Saddle—turned right, and climbed another hundred feet. Around a corner, the steps ended on a level dirt path. In front of me was a beautiful rock wall, the joints free of mortar, each stone locked in place by another. The contrast couldn't have been greater: the crude heaviness of the steps suddenly replaced by the order and graceful beauty of this wall gently following the curve of hill. It felt like an invitation, a hint of what was ahead. The wall ended at the junction of another, the outer wall of the enclosure, this one having a heavy rock lintel above an opening that I crouched low to pass through.

I stood up and froze, unable to move for fear the scene in front of me might vanish. It was as if a curtain had been drawn back to reveal the sudden beauty of the pilgrims' quest.

Six domed beehive huts, a small graveyard dominated by a standing stone cross, and the walls of an eleventh-century church stood huddled together on a narrow shelf of land. The graceful curve of the far hut was framed by the sea and the green mainland nine miles away.

The paddle out to the island and the slow, reflective climb had deepened a quietness within me. In that silence I stood and let my eyes wander over the holy ground I was about to enter.

The stone huts were built above one side of a sunken courtyard. A rock-lined burial plot with a massive stone cross, a domed oratory, and a later tiny eleventh-century church comprised the lower level of the ruins. The beehive huts seemed to huddle protectively over the courtyard and cross silhouetted against the sea below. Finely built walls, tight passages, and the soothing curve of the domed cells interlocked with simple beauty and purpose. This was indeed holy ground, somehow still very alive with the spirit of five hundred years of continuous monastic life.

I lowered the pack and camera to the ground and walked empty-handed into the courtyard. Within and around me everything was still. Peacefully, willingly empty, all was wrapped in a cloak of mystery and reverence.

I stood in the center of the courtyard and listened, the only sound a gentle touch of breeze brushing stone. I reached out in my own silence and let my fingers lightly touch the stone of the oratory.

A few feet away was the graveyard. The cross, crudely chipped out of thick stone, stood higher than my head. Smaller crosses, a foot high, picketed the raised ground that held the dust of the long dead within the rubble of earth and fill.

I turned and walked up four or five steps leading to the first hut, crouched low, and crawled through the four-foot thickness of rock wall. Inside, there was only dampness, a vacuum of light and sound. In the darkness I sat on my heels, my back following the curve of the dome, my eyes shut, listening to the whisper of wind against stone. No sound other than the softness of my own breath. Inhaling, exhaling. Feeling the dampness of the rock surrounding me and moving back through fourteen hundred years of time.

I tried to feel the fatigue of the monk who lived there. I imagined his hands: dirty, sore, and callused. Silent and in prayer, he must have felt the pulsing of blood in his fingers, the ache of muscles in back and arms. I thought of his clothing, a coarse woven fabric that he worked, slept, and prayed in. I imagined the simplicity, the prayers, the singular devotion of the man. For the briefest second I felt the monk beside me. Felt him still and silent in prayer. At the same time I could hear my own distant breathing feeding a stillness and mystery deeper than any I had known.

A tingling in my cramped legs brought me back to the present. I shifted position, then tried to settle back into that moment of stillness. But it was gone.

Who was that monk and what was it I had really felt?

Whatever it was had faded like a dream. There was only the sound of my breathing and the low whistle of wind through stone.

I opened my eyes, looked around for a moment, then crawled out and stood blinking in the glare of day.

I ducked low into the next dome, a smaller, much lower roof. Maybe a sleeping space but barely wide enough for me to stretch out full length.

The "Annals of Ulster" and the "Annals of Innisfallen," ancient manuscripts that have survived the ages, shed some light on the history of "Sceilig Mhichi'l." The annals recorded that in the year 812, the first Viking raids plundered the monastery. The Vikings landed on the rocky pinnacle again in 823, this time taking Etgal, the abbot of Skellig, and starving him to death. In 833 and 839, Turgesius, sovereign of the Danes, raided again. The last reference to the inhabitants of Skellig Michael was in 1044, when the "Annals of the Four Masters" simply states: "Aodh of Skellig died."

Again I walked around the tight cluster of buildings, my eye drawn to the artistry of stone, my mind halfway between the past and present. Intellectually, I could not understand fourteen hundred years of time. It was easier, somehow, to imagine the labor of the monks rather than the passing of the ages.

I let go of the struggle to understand and finally retrieved the camera to try to capture some of the beauty around me.

I retraced my steps back to Christ's Saddle, then began the climb to the seven hundred–foot summit of the island. High overhead, like the Anasazi ruins of the American Southwest, I could see the regular lines of laid-up stone against the vertical face of a cliff. But how to get there? The trail climbed and wrapped around the pinnacle of the summit. I would have to climb above the ruins and find a way to drop down to them.

The faint trail followed a ledge of rock clinging threadlike to the cliff face. To my left, the ground fell away in a mix of scree and a few tufts of grass; then nothing but five hundred feet of air to the jagged rocks silently buried by breaking waves. I kicked a rock over the ledge and watched it take two bounces, then free-fall out of sight.

Around a corner, the trail came to an abrupt end. I cautiously peered over the edge. It was undercut with the same drop as before, but this time there was nothing for the eye to focus on and my head began to spin. I pulled back and explored a couple of dead ends, gingerly returning to the grass ledge, frustrated that the summit seemed impossible to reach.

I looked again at the wall of rock to my right, and then I saw it: a shallow gouge a foot above my head and another near my hip. Could it be? I eased my sandaled toe into the carved step, pushed up, and settled my hand into the first gouge. My heels hung in the air, my weight on fingertips and toes. With every reach I found a hand-or foothold where I needed it and didn't stop until I reached a narrow chimney of rock that I wedged myself into. I remembered Con telling me of a German student who fell to his death last year on this same climb. One slip and I could see how it would happen. I shuddered with the thought of that first impact and tried to forget the story.

I moved up through the narrow chimney, then out on a ledge that ran like a grassy tightrope between the safety of two rock pillars. I rested on the far side, then found a way down to the single ruins I had seen from below.

Only the base of the hermitage remained. It was ten feet across and covered all of the level ground on the tiny landing it was built on. Against the cliff the hermitage leaned on was a shallow double basin cut out of solid rock. Rainwater half filled the algae-covered sides and bottom. Far below, across Christ's Saddle, then up on the other summit, I could see the beehive huts clinging impossibly to the slant of the island. Their exposure seemed greater from this height. Small, terribly vulnerable against a backdrop of ocean and distant mainland, I wondered how they had stood for fourteen centuries.

I thought of winter gales, of bitter-cold winds laced with freezing rains, of a small community of men surviving on seabirds, a few goats, and whatever could be gleaned from the garden plot below the ledge they lived on. I remembered a poem written by one of the monks:

> Bitter is the wind this night
> Which tosses up the ocean's hair so white.
> Merciless men I need not fear
> Who cross from Lothland on an ocean clear.

Lothland was the land of the Vikings, and the poem spoke of the peace a winter gale afforded the defenseless monks. Isolated by the fury of the storm they could sleep safe, for no man, including the fearsome raiders from the north, would dare take to the sea on such a night.

Five hundred years of prayers had drifted up over this peak; prayers, poems, and the sounds of men working stone. Five hundred years of spring flowers, of long summer days, then dwindling hours as the autumns approached. Sometime in the eleventh century, the island monastery was abandoned.

Now, except for the winds, the island was silent.

I finished the climb to the summit and sat for a long time lost in the flood of views that stretched out before me. I could see Dursey Head, the Bull and Calf, Kenmare Bay, and Bolus Head. I tried to imagine a kayak moving around or across each point. It seemed impossible, yet I knew that I had paddled and lived each one of those places and had memories of each. To the north was Dingle Bay and the Blasket Islands. Soon I would know them as well.

As I sat perched atop one of the westernmost points of Europe, my back to the expanse of the Atlantic, I thought, as I had done so many other times, how blessed my life has been. So much beauty—magnificent soul-moving beauty. Why was I lucky enough to sit on that peak and know all of the freedom and wonder of my life? I didn't have an answer, just a powerful feeling of humility.

I returned to the single ruins below the peak, curled up on the grass, and shut my eyes. I would climb down later, deal with the toeholds, the ledges, and eventually the nine-mile paddle back to the mainland. But for now I just wanted to feel this moment: the silence, rest, and warmth of the sun. On the edge of the known world of the sixth century, I drifted into sleep.

The Pipes and the Bodhran

Hands of invisible spirits touch the strings
of that mysterious instrument, the soul,
and play the prelude of our fate.
We hear the voice prophetic and are not alone.

—Longfellow, *The Spanish Student*,
Act II Sc. 37

As I paddled away from Skellig Michael, its spire of rock reaching into the sky behind and the lush hills of the mainland tantalizingly close, I understood why Ireland has been called the Land of Saints and Scholars. Who would not be inspired in either prayer or prose, or feel the need to express in music or hospitality the blessings of such beauty ringed by the ocean's white? Viewed from a distance, the land, sea, and sky seem to be in constant flux, one moment allowing the heart to be stilled in wonder, and the next, stirring it with passion as clouds sweep over islands, coastal castles, and hues of blue water. The passions of the observer rise and fall with the sea and follow the rapid wingbeats of the puffin or the folded wings of the gannet as it drops spearlike a hundred feet into the waves. Waterfalls, cascading freshwater into salt, the brilliance of sunlight, squalls of wet winds, mountains rising from the sea, trapping clouds in heights that squeeze the rains from their gray blankets. All of this and a coastline that offers, in its convoluted shores, refuge for the traveler of the heart as well as the heel. Ireland is a land of contradictions and inspiration, fertile soil for the soul and mind. Scholars and saints, musicians and storytellers, peasants and kings all have found a place on its shores and islands.

When I began this journey I knew so little about Ireland, and that only from what I had read. As the sea and winds allowed, I moved along the coast, and through the weeks and months began to know Ireland as a sum of my own experiences. The Skelligs had added another perspective to the journey, a window into the time of Ireland's monastic history when these centers were places of learning and reflection. Returning to the mainland, I realized that the ruins and indeed much of coastal Ireland offers today what they have for hundreds of years: the breath and time of inspiration.

As I continued north, I thought of the wall map that not long ago seemed so foreign to me. It now lay damp and beginning to tear along the edges, but a penned line of blue ink starting in Dublin led south, then southwest, and now north with a twenty-mile round-trip loop to a tiny island. With luck, the penned line of blue would thread a continued course north along the coast and eventually over the top of Ireland and back to Dublin. If that line had a voice, it would have sung of all the beauty and wonder along its course and joined with the praises of the saints and scholars. With each passing week, I would add more verses to that song, more lines of poetry, and a better understanding of both myself and Ireland.

I turned in behind Valencia Island, using the compression of tide to slingshot me past Portmagee and the memory of the newscast warning of what lay north of the border. The tide carried me swiftly over sandy shallows, through the channel, and out toward Dingle Bay. A cloud of sand billowed up as a skate, startled by the boat's shadow, headed for deeper water. With a flash of tail and graceful flight of wings, it skimmed inches over the bottom, then disappeared into the depths. Fine ends of floating kelp gently swayed side to side, and assured me I still had the current with me. In another hour the tide would shift, but by then I would be in open water and it wouldn't matter.

It had been weeks since I had paddled on calm water. The bow split the reflection of clouds and blue sky, rippling the fields mirrored between the sandy bottom and the water's surface. Each paddle stroke left tiny whirlpools of spinning bubbles that trailed past the stern and got lost in the turbulence of the boat's wake. For a few miles, the island blocked all trace of swell and wave and I became aware again of the subtleties of flat water paddling, the reflections, the surge of the bow wake with each stroke, and the fluidity of muscles. No wind or pitching and twisting of the boat, no worries of changing weather or breaking seas, just a steady reach and pull with each blade slicing into a mirrored sky.

With eyes closed I could feel the sun's glare reflected off the water. Warm and soothing, I paddled into it and let its comfort soak into me. As though stripping off clothes at the edge of a lake and diving in, I wanted to leave the concerns of the trip behind for a moment and just enjoy the ease.

Beyond the narrows of the island was Doulus Head, the southerly headland of Dingle Bay. Part of me wanted to stay in the warmth and safety of the island channel. Another part was already drawing the bow on a course that ignored the shelter and headed across the bay for the headland. The calm water had provided a few miles of rest, but it didn't feed me as the energy of the ocean did.

I came around Doulus Head with the winds spilling off the cliff and catching the paddles in bursts of cat's-paws that fanned out around the boat. On a dark day, the winds would have felt threatening, but in the warmth and sun, the waves sparkling with thousands of carelessly tossed diamonds, it felt playful. I paddled close to the rocks, half hiding from the winds, almost daring them to find me sneaking past their guard into Dingle Bay. An east wind. I knew I'd have it straight on the bow as I turned the final corner, but until then I wanted to play this cat-and-mouse game.

Into the bay, the first blast was stronger than expected. My body acted like a sail that almost stopped the boat, the same gust carrying off the top of a wave that broke on the bow. In front of me were lines of white-capped dancers heading out to sea. Not all in perfect step, some breaking while others were just forming, but all steadily moving seaward. Now there was no hiding from the winds.

Knocknadobar Mountain shouldered its way between lower hills and rose two thousand feet above the waves. Shadows of clouds raced over its ravines, missing the summit by a few hundred feet and leaving the mountain massive and green against the sky. The winds seemed to curl off the top of the mountain and gather momentum as they raced between folds of hills and tumbled like great volumes of water into the bay. Ahead, the shoreline curved out of sight, the glare of white-tipped waves on deep blue to the left and a towering slope of green to the right.

A mile into the bay I saw two streams, ribbons of silver running through heather and ferns and falling twenty feet over a ledge into the sea. It was an invitation I couldn't pass up. I paddled over to the biggest and surprised a seal rolling beneath the falls. We both had the same idea, a freshwater bath on a sunny day. He slipped out of sight and it was my turn.

I coasted under the deluge of boggy brown water and felt its weight pound my shoulders in a massage that almost drove the breath from my lungs. Salt ran from my face and beard and was replaced with the taste of earthy waters. With back, arms, and hands tingling, I retreated, got a breath, and glided in for another drumming. One more time, then back out in the sun and moving along the base of the mountain again.

For ten miles there wasn't a break in the shoreline, the hills rose against each other side by side and straight up from the rocks that made landing impossible. I was headed for Kells Bay, a point on my map where the cliffs ended and I could spend the night before crossing to the town of Dingle.

I was content to watch the beauty of the hills and try to angle the bow into the steeper waves. When I didn't get it right the bow would dive, load up with the weight of the breaking wave, and the boat would slow to a crawl. I would have to work harder to get it back up to speed before the next wave stole the remaining momentum. This was the other part of sea kayaking: no great drama unfolding, just the reality of finding a pace that I could hold for a couple of hours and settle into. Mile after mile I worked the boat into the winds, tasting the dried salt on my lips and feeling the healthy strain of muscles against waves.

That evening, I lay beside a stream that gurgled out of a tree-lined glen. A blood red sun, filtered and no longer glaring, settled into the ocean, its rich light bathing the hill behind the glen. As I lay in the bivy bag, my head cradled in a soft bundle of clothes, I could still feel the sea rolling under me. My eyes were heavy and the weight of my body resting on the sand was a gift; the reward of peaceful rest after the day of sunshine and glistening waves. In those moments before sleep, when the sky was a veil of the softest blue, I knew I was a blessed man. There would be light in the sky for a long time, but I was content to let sleep overtake me.

It was a ten-mile crossing to the break in the cliffs that led into Dingle. Halfway across the bay I still wasn't sure what shadow of rock to head for. The shoreline looked like solid cliff, shadowed here and there by coves, but nothing that looked like the passage I knew had to be there. I kept checking the map, wiping the bubbled water off the plastic and peering over my shoulder at the cleft in the far shore that marked Kells Bay. I was on course, but it wasn't until I was a mile from the north shore that I spotted the break in the cliff, and the boats that were circling in the narrow opening. It was the boats that had caught my eye.

One of the O'Shea children had told me about a dolphin that had shown up at the mouth of Dingle Harbor twelve years earlier. Each morning the dolphin would wait in the narrows for the fishing boats to come out of the inner harbor, then play in their wake as they headed out to sea. Someone had named him Fungie; the name stuck, and twelve years later he was the star of daily boat excursions filled with tourists.

The circling boats and the wakes they carved in white marked where Fungie was leaping and rolling in the waters. Tourists with video cameras and binoculars crowded the sides of the boats and screamed with delight every time he surfaced. Apparently, Fungie loved the attention and raced from one boat to another, free to leave any time he wanted but happy to play for a few hours each day. I was afraid I'd get run over by a throttle-happy boater. I skirted the frenzied chaos and headed for the marina at the back of the harbor.

I paddled into the finger docks that were filled with fishing and sailboats and met John, the dock maintenance man. He was stripped to the waist in the sunshine, nut brown skin, tattoos covering his forearms and a gray ponytail hanging between his shoulders. He was probably fifty but moved with the ease of a man half that age. He watched me climb from the boat, then came over and noticed the ROUND IRELAND '96 decal on the bow.

"You're goin' right round, are ye?" His voice had a different ring to it than others who had asked me that same question.

"With luck I am," I answered. "I need to restock some food and want to have a look around town. Maybe spend the night if it's all right."

"It'll be fine," he said. "I've done a fair bit of sea traveling myself and know how it is to find a harbor to rest in."

I liked John instantly. There was the connection of the sea, but it was more than that. While I sat on the dock, gripping the boat with my toes and pulling things from the rear cockpit, we talked. Amid the flutter of pennants hanging from the expensive yachts, we both knew we were out of our element. He pointed to his boat anchored offshore, an old wooden-hulled sloop, aged but obviously loved. It would cost half his monthly salary to keep her berthed at the dock. In the winter he hauled her out on the mudflats across the harbor. A stand of gnarled pines planted on Lord Ventry's estate decades ago sheltered him from the winds and provided a free place to live. He spoke of the herons that nested in the trees, the curlews and oystercatchers feeding on the flats, and how they all needed a place to live.

On the surface he looked like such a tough guy, the tattoos on his hands not helping the image that I had of him as a young man, a rebel, questioning all authority and running wild. But as we talked, I heard the voice of a gentle person beneath the veneer.

John checked with the harbormaster, then told me it would be fine to tie the boat where the dinghies were. It would be out of the way and he would keep an eye on it while I got a shower at the hostel and did my shopping.

Later that evening, I wandered the sloping streets of Dingle. Narrow and lined with shops and pubs, the streets were lit with a softness spilling out of open doorways as small groups of people went in search of music. A door would open and the melodies would pour out with the light and mix with the sounds of a fiddle coming from down the street. In one pub after another I watched the people and listened to folk tunes, ballads, and songs of the 1921 uprising.

On the way back to the boat, I passed a low doorway, then stopped when I heard the throbbing of a drum accompanied by the drone of pipes floating into the damp air. Two steps down led to a dimly lit room that looked as if it might once have been a warehouse selling sailcloth and fishing nets. Against one wall was a bar, and in the far corner a group of people gathered around a drummer and piper. Through the smoke and clutter of noise and people, I found a place against the stone wall and watched. Watched and listened.

The piper began a tune. Fine notes, clear and singular, rose into the air and seemed to fill the low-ceilinged room, notes that hung for an eternity with a sorrow that words could not have expressed. A lament.

The piper's gaze, his fingers, and the way he occasionally sat straighter, sighed, then settled deeper into the music spoke of the feelings he was swept with. As one note ended and another trembled into the air, he shifted in his seat as if the emotion was too much, and settled his gaze on a point far beyond the confines of the room. When I was certain the lamentation couldn't reach further into my heart, I heard the first gentle beating of the bodhran. Slow and deep, like a sigh that comes unannounced, it began to fill the spaces between the soft tears of the pipes.

The piper softened the trill of his music, then faded to a lover's whisper as the beat of the drum echoed through me. For a few moments there was only the drummer, her hand floating and striking the goat skin with a rhythm that stripped away the last emotional protection. I let go of my heart, freed it completely to feel the pain and beauty of the lament. Broken wide open, it floated with the resonating throb of drum and distant pipes.

I was drawn in by the beauty of this drummer. Eyes closed, body folding over the curve of the drum and leaning into the rhythm of her music, she played that ancient instrument as though it was a part of her own heart. Beautiful in a way that was more than physical. I didn't know the story of the lament, but I didn't have to. In her swaying movements, the tilt of her head, and the smile that began to pull at the corners of her mouth, I knew she had weathered the anguish of the lament and now the pain had passed.

There was a new tempo, a growing freedom as the pipes came in with a flurry of quivering notes. The double-ended beater was a blur of back-handed wrist snapping, flying over the face of the drum, mixing the haunting bass of the center with the light tapping of the wood rim. The staccato of drum and trill of pipes intertwined and climbed to a new height, finally united in complete abandonment. Heads held high and faces glowing with a warmth that radiated from the love of their music, the piper's and drummer's eyes finally met. Through the ripping finale, their smiles and eyes glowed as brilliantly as their music.

In the space of a few moments my heart had been torn apart by the terrible pain of the lament, then miraculously sewn together by the love the music blossomed with. I wanted it to go on forever, but neither the players nor the listeners could have sustained that passion. It was too painful yet too joyous, fully Irish in its extremes. It had to end.

When the last note faded into the rock walls of the room and the softness of each of our hearts, the silence broke in a flood of emotions. I looked around and saw people smiling and applauding as tears rolled freely down their faces.

Glasses were refilled with the rich darkness of Murphys and Guinness as I stepped back into the night and wandered toward the sound of halyards clinking against masts. There might have been more music that night but none that could have been better.

As I walked through the quiet, I knew the comfort of my own company and I liked it. I was still feeling the emotions of the music and wanted to walk with them beneath the stars of the Milky Way. They invited other feelings that washed through me: contented aloneness, wonder at the stars overhead, and awareness of my own breathing. I embraced this sudden quiet, the touch of sea air on my face and the feeling of walking down the middle of a narrow street in Ireland. Alone, at peace with my surroundings and myself, wasn't this what the journey was about? Taking the time to feel the exposure, not only to the sea but also to the heart.

The day didn't seem real. Was it just this morning that I had left the shadows of the glen and felt the first rays of sun on my back? It was long ago but really just ten miles across the blackness of the bay. There was the memory of the crossing and the brilliant cliffs guarding the harbor entrance. There had been the long, easy conversation with John, and later the taste of Guinness and the gift of the music. Now there was fullness and fatigue and I realized how long a day it had been. Long but well lived. I wanted to do that with every day of my life: to live it consciously, aware of all the blessings.

The wonder was that none of this day had been planned. Like the rest of the trip, it had been simply a matter of waking up, checking the weather, and setting out. Everything else was chance and serendipity.

I walked between the stars and the blackened streets of Dingle. In a few hours, the eastern sky would brighten, another day would begin, and I would follow the ebb tide through the cliff passage out to open waters and whatever lay beyond.

Between Slea Head and the strand of beach on Blasket Island was a two-mile channel of eddies and currents confused by shallow waters. John and a fisherman in Dingle had both warned me about the sound, it was an area they knew well and treated with caution. As I started across, I could see the flooding tide sweeping through the channel like a great river. I lined the bow up with a rock that broke through the swirls, and the beach on the island, then watched how quickly their relative positions changed. Not alarming but pretty fast. It was my way of figuring the speed of the tide and setting an angle for the crossing. I could have waited for slack water, but then maybe the winds would change and who knows what the seas would do? I pointed the bow to the south end of the island, making adjustments as tide and counter tide shifted beneath me. Halfway across there was a band of small waves leaping into the air, nowhere to go but straight up in the confusion of currents. Like a hundred salmon desperately fleeing a feeding orca, the water was a panic of heaving waves catching the sun for a second, then melting back into the melee. They slapped the sides of the boat as the paddles dipped into the strength of the current and felt the ripple of its muscle.

After a half hour of working the tide, using it when I could and fighting it when I had to, I paddled into the slack water in front of the beach. Sunlight reached through the shallows and reflected off the sandbottom, turning the water an aqua green, fading to deeper blue as the bottom dropped away.

Above the beach, the island rose in squares of stone-lined fields that looked over the crescent of sand and Blasket Sound. Stone walls still divided the fields but now ran like fingers beneath the carpet of green that covered everything from the beach to the island summit. I could see four or five house ruins up on the hill and an old path leading down to a scattering of tiny cottages, some of their roofs gone, windows and doors open to the elements.

In 1953, the last of the islanders had left. After hundreds of years the island's peat supply was nearly exhausted. Emigration, dwindling fish stocks, and the hope for an easier life elsewhere contributed to the empty windows staring out across the sound. Dingle had been the nearest town, a day's travel either by tide, or cart along the coast road. Now, like the houses, the beach was empty. The currachs and the willow lobster traps were gone with the fishermen who had lifted their catch from the seas.

The only thing that remained was stone: the houses and the rock walls that climbed the gentle rise of the island's fields.

I beached the boat through two-foot surf and left it cradled in the sands while I wandered up to the old village site. Rabbit and sheep trails skirted thickets of brambles and avoided ravines too deep to climb down into. There was an unhurried air about the island that even the trails seemed to obey.

I followed a path to a cottage, its back wall settled into the slope of the hill, the front yard falling away to another level and looking down on the roof of a neighbor. Above, below, or just over a grassy rise were other small houses that were settling into the land. There didn't seem to be a pattern either in the style or in how they were laid out. Angles and spacing were as random as the web of footpaths that connected neighbor to neighbor.

I wandered around the village site, sometimes taking the paths, other times following rabbit tracks that crested the hills and disappeared in the next gully. Bits of rusted metal—the bail of a bucket, a shovel, or part of an old plow—lay in the grass beside some of the houses. As neighbors, the cottages still seemed tied to one another; tied now with the loneliness of age and the memory of another time: voices, young and old, that spoke of the weather, the state of the sea, and the prices they might get for their fish in Dingle. Voices that blessed God and neighbor and were ever hopeful for a better harvest of fish or potatoes.

From any point in the village, I could see the beach and the sound. A practiced eye could know the tidal strength by the swirls around the rocks. Another glance toward the summit of land behind the village could predict the day's weather. Life must have been simple. Harsh in the long, wet winters, but slow and predictable like the tides that continually swept past the island.

I left the village and followed a cart track that climbed slowly along the south slope. My mind was easy with the imagined creaking of wood axles, thoughts of donkeys, a few cows, small stone houses, and the Gaelic-speaking people who had lived here and built the road that my feet followed. Across the sunlit waters were other islands, smaller and steeper, standing like sentries around the perimeter of Great Blasket. I sat on a cushion of grass, ate my lunch looking out to sea, and thought of nothing, my mind emptied for the moment by the tranquility and warmth. The day mellowed in the growing shadows of hill over ravine. I walked around the island, then back to the beach for a swim that stole my breath and left my skin tingling and pink.

Toward evening, as the grass-covered stone walls cast their shadows, I climbed to the summit and walked the undulating ridge. On the first peak were the remains of a Martello tower, shattered not by the weapons of war but by a bolt of lightning. In a single explosion the upper portion of the tower had been reduced to chunks of rock and mortar that now lay scattered about the tower's base.

Around this summit were the outlines of other buildings, the highest stone no more than a few inches above the grass, some round, some rectangular, but all set within the broken circumference of a larger circle. A book I had picked up in Dingle shed some light on their origins, possibly pre-Celtic and maybe a monastic community much later. All was speculation. If it was pre-Celtic, I wondered what the people had looked like, what clothes they had worn and what language they had spoken. The circle of stone suggested a fort. Protection from whom? And was it ever tested by an enemy that would have landed on the same beach and perhaps crouched low in the grasses, climbing the same slope that I had? If there had been such a raid, what was the outcome? A violent end for the islanders trapped within their own walls or a panicked retreat of the raiders where height could have been the deciding advantage?

Before I paddled out of Dublin, I had spent a day absorbed by the treasures and artifacts in the National Museum. Crude stone axes, bronze weapons, iron swords, and fine Celtic gold were displayed in glass cases. Some had been found while digging roads, or foundations for houses. Some of the gold—finely tooled earrings, brooches, and heavy crescent neck ornaments called torques—had been unearthed in pits as though hastily buried before an attack. Irish mythology tells of the Firbolgs, the first people of Ireland, and the Tuatha de Danaan, the people of the gods of Dana, who came from the north and fought with the Firbolgs for a share of the island. The myths are full of accounts of battles, of Druids casting spells, and of peoples coming from beyond the sea and challenging each successive ruling tribe. Irish myth has it that the Tuatha de Danaan were eventually overrun by the children of Gael. They became invisible and lived in the hills and hollows of the land, becoming the Little-People of Irish fame.

How much is factual and how much is mere imagination? It would take an anthropologist to unravel the intricacies of Irish history and folklore, but some of the ancient history I understood.

It is thought that the Celts landed on both the north and south coasts of Ireland somewhere around 600 B.C. They arrived in waves of expansion from Central and Eastern Europe. They were not the first people of Ireland, as the myths imply, but instead were preceded thousands of years earlier by a people who made stone tools. The Irish myths were based on these later inhabitants, the Celts, people skilled in the ways of war, as well as the arts of metallurgy. The torques that were uncovered in pits and now rest in the National Museum were the coveted neck ornaments of Celtic warriors. These were the people that had left behind not only the buried caches of fine jewelry and tales of great battles, but also one of the oldest languages in the world, Gaelic, the language of the west coast of Ireland.

Beneath my feet the outline of a circle remained, but the stones of the fort were scattered, swept away with time like the lives of the people who had lived there. That wind-blown summit held the tales of more ages than anyone would ever know or could accurately date. The stone that now barely broke the surface of the ground had felt the touch of human hands thousands of years ago on a day maybe similar to this. I stood in the ring, the highest point of land on the island, and thought of the people of the past.

What was it about these stones and others that I had found along this journey that spoke so strongly to me? They were nothing but rocks, and yet I either gave them a life and spirit of their own or they already had it and I was just stumbling upon it.

I was half afraid of denying the Christian faith that I believed in and acknowledging a world of spirits that might still be somehow in the ground and air around the stones where I walked. I was confused by my own learnings and the intuitive feeling of something that was more than just a circle of stones on the earth. Why did this place, like so many others I had found in Scotland and now Ireland, feel sacred and holy?

Maybe the man or woman who had built the base of that circle was in attendance, silent and watching as I struggled to understand the over-lapping history of the people who had stood on that summit. Their spirit could not have just vanished, here one moment as a living, thinking being and the next moment gone. Or could it?

Maybe I was feeling something that wasn't there, something that was only in my head. But, no—though I couldn't understand, neither could I deny that there was something on this height of land that looked out over the waters and mainland below. If there was a connection to the people of the past, then maybe it was that my eyes saw the same folds of coastline stretching into a fading blur of greens and blues, that my skin felt the same warmth of sun, and my mind held the same memory of cold winds and soaking days. It was the physical world that connected these ages. But there had to be more to this life than merely what the senses revealed. It was a strange thought, but I knew it was only time—in this case more than two thousand years, but still only time that separated me from the people who had stood and gazed out on the same ocean I did. I became convinced that somewhere in the stones was the spirit of those people.

In their primitive ways they would not have had the knowledge of the world that we have. The vagaries of nature would have been seen as the work of the gods and prayers would have been petitioned for everything from a good year for the crops to the return of the summer sun. Perhaps there are still cultures that believe in the deities of the heavens to bring them good fortune. Some would say this is heresy. I wonder how prayers offered to a divine being, one that a people stood in awe before, could be any more heretic than the absolute power we, as a Western society, have given to technology. While we race toward an ever more complicated future, it is said that the world will become smaller and communication faster and more important. I wonder when, in that future, there will be time to stand silently and let the mind wander back to a time when the stars were still a mystery that people stared at in wonder. Not in scientific wonder but in spiritual awe. And where in that promised land of rapid communication will there be the rich, empty time to look, not forward into an age of promises built on technology, but back in the direction of our ancestors, whose value may be measured in spirituality rather than in technology. I didn't come to Ireland with this perspective. It came to me, in the form of a circle, a circle of stone barely visible in the grass; a gift of my solitude and that of a people whose origins are as vague as the outline of a ring fort. Science has usurped some of the gods of old, but I hope that it will not replace the mystery of the divine that the Celts revered.

On the way down, I walked more slowly, pausing so often that I knew it would be dark long before I reached my boat. It didn't matter. I carried my sandals and felt the coolness of the grass in the arch of each foot, picking my way along a path I hoped would lead back to the beach. I sat on my heels and watched from the corner of my eye as the sun touched the sea and slowly gave up its light and warmth. Now there was a chill in the air.

I thought about how many sunsets I had ignored, not missed, but ignored because of something that was more important. I breathed in deeply, then let it out slowly, more of a sigh than a breath. A silent prayer of thanks for the sunset reaching toward me from across the ocean.

In the dark I found my way down the bluffs and eventually to my boat, the drag mark of its keel erased by the darkness and maybe the high tide that had come and gone.

I slept on the sand that night, my body resting in its warmth, my back gently touching the hull of the boat. Out of a peaceful sleep, I awoke several times, eyes suddenly open and wandering through the constellations: Pleiades—the Seven Sisters; Ursa Major and Minor—the Big and Little Dipper—and Cassiopeia, wife of Cepheus. Others that I recognized but didn't know the names of. So many pinpoints of flickering light. Beneath the vastness of the heavens I felt small, fragile, and yet utterly peaceful. Sleep came again and it wasn't until the soft light of morning that a breaking wave awakened me.

Peat Fires and New Friends

If a man be gracious to strangers,
it shows that he is a citizen of the world,
and his heart is no island, cut off from other islands,
but a continent that joins them.

—Francis Bacon

In a kayak, the paddler sits facing forward and must turn around to gaze back at where he has been. In a currach, the oarsmen face the stern and watch their wake as they pull on the long, bladeless oars. I turned and looked back at Great Blasket Island and thought how painful it must have been to have the island houses continually in sight as the last currachs pulled away from the beach. It was hard enough for me to leave after only two days of the island's antiquity soaking into me like a balm. I could not imagine the wrenching heartbreak of the last villagers as they either rowed or sat in the hulls of the currachs that carried them to the mainland for the last time.

I left the Blaskets on a morning of flat, calm water and hazy light. It was one of those rare days when the winds left the water surface untroubled and the swells were long and low. What little tide there was carried me swiftly across the sound to the mainland and along the cliffs that ran like a fortress wall for fifteen miles.

A series of headlands stood close-shouldered to each other. Looking down the coast, they lined up like siblings, identicle in form but varying in sizes. Born of the same cliff, they seemed to have matured into their own boldness, united in their stance between sea and sky, but separated by steep slopes of green dotted with specks of sheep. They were the Three Sisters. Further north was Brandon Head, distant but dominating the coast. A mile or two inland, Brandon Mountain stood almost three thousand feet high and looked out over the tops of the coastal heights. The morning haze that made distances hard to judge added to the drama of the mountains rising from the sea.

On a stormy day this coast would have been a different scene, one of wildness, of winds pouring out of those mountains and of swells driven by distant storms. I would not have the ease of sitting a half mile offshore, the paddle resting across the cockpit while I soaked in the peace and beauty of the moment. I was lucky to see it on a calm day.

I stayed offshore, far enough to take in the grandeur but close enough to feel I could reach out and touch the mountains. The buzz of an outboard motor, like that of a bee somewhere in a thicket of lavender, distracted my mind. Searching, I spotted the boat, probably a lobster fisherman, moving along the base of the cliff. I took my eye off the speck of white and couldn't find it again. Maybe he had turned toward me, the engine out of gear while he pulled buoy, line, and finally pot over the gunwale. I thought how small he had looked against the hundreds of feet of cliff and not-so-distant mountains. Then I thought how I must look floating on the sea and the unbroken horizon. It was a little disconcerting.

How strange the perception of danger is. When the sea is rough and the boat pitches and rolls through the waves like a piece of flotsam, I am too busy trying to stay upright to think of how vulnerable I am. It is only with the leisure of flat water that I can look around and remember that I am a mile or more from land and sitting in a boat whose deck is more often awash than not.

I paddled past a feather, its downy upswept ends catching the faintest drift of air and turning it in a tiny circle. It stopped spinning, frozen for a second on its reflection, then slowly turned again. Perfectly balanced, it floated with grace and beauty: a lesson of Zen on the open sea. Suddenly I didn't feel so alone.

Two days after leaving the Blaskets, I crossed the mouth of Brandon Bay, the compass pointing due east. In the middle of the dead calm crossing there was nothing to concentrate on but the needle that seemed frozen on ninety degrees. I swung the boat a little to the north and settled the needle on a group of low islands a mile off the point in front of me.

The island group had two names: the Seven Hogs or the Magharees. How they got either, I didn't know. I paddled past a couple of smaller islands that looked as if a good storm would almost wash over them. Further out, another looked too steep and rockbound to land on; I headed for the middle island, its southern tip tapering to the sea with some sort of rock structure silhouetted against the sky.

As I paddled closer, the island seemed to grow. I played the game of looking away for as long as I could, then back again to see what new details had come to life.

The rocks on the end of the island were definitely a ruin, but of what? It looked like a wall built on the last solid ground above a small beach. The swells steepened as they rolled toward the shallows, gradually losing their grace, and spilling on the sands with a whoosh. An oystercatcher, with its long orange beak and piercing whistle, veered into flight as I surfed the last fifty feet of a swell that left me sitting high and dry. I popped the spray deck, slid out of the boat, and grabbed the bow before the next wave could pull it back into the surf.

Above the waveline, the sand was dry; my feet sank deep into the warmth and doubled the effort of dragging the boat to higher ground. Another dozen feet and the texture changed again, softer, almost powdery, sands that even the highest tides had not touched. I let the bow toggle slip out of my fingers and flexed the joints as I walked to the upper edge of the beach. A couple of Hereford cows stood dangerously close above the undercut bank. Trickles of sand rained down in tiny avalanches as they watched my approach. White-faced and brown-bodied, they stared with forgotten mouthfuls of half-eaten grass until I was within a paddle length of their treelike legs. Then, bored or maybe slightly alarmed, they ambled away a few yards, stopped, and watched as I climbed over the low bank.

As my eyes came even with the surface of the pasture, a stone wall curved away in a perfect arc of gray rock planted in the middle of a freshly mown field. Smells of cut hay filled my head and mixed with the subtler smell of the sea. The rest of the island rolled away in hummocks and dips, the only other structure a cottage on the far side of the island.

I walked over to the wall and stepped up on a fallen stone, peering over the wall of the enclosure. Eight feet thick and running as true to a circle as anything that massive could, the wall encompassed three beehive huts, two piles of stone that may have once been huts themselves, and several mounds and depressions that a thousand years or more had softened into the earth. Across the greatest width of the circle was a break in the wall. I stepped down and followed the curve of rock to the entrance.

The cry of kittiwakes and the distant rumble of surf on the ocean side of the island accompanied me on my walk through the monastic ruins. I looked and listened, felt the mystery and the beauty, pondered the ages, and thought of the men buried beneath the crudely cut stones standing in the shadow of the wall. The twenty-odd gravestones gave the surrounding wall and beehive huts a purpose, a connection of flesh and bone.

Within the main enclosure of rock was another lower circle, more of a sod-covered mound than a wall. It mirrored the outer circumference for a short distance, then melted into the relative flatness of the inner grounds. A wall-within-a-wall? What added to the puzzle was the stone-lined en-trance of a tunnel that burrowed under the mound and surfaced still within the confines of the outer wall.

I crawled into the dampness, felt the earth touch my back and shoulders. As I inched forward in the blackness, the ground pitched downward for fifteen or twenty feet. All light, all sound was gone. I stopped midway, heard my breath echo against stone and earth. I wondered who had crawled into this passage in the last thousand years or more and for what reason? There was no escaping the touch of bodies brushing the sides of the tunnel, hands reaching and feeling the same ground as mine now did.

Thirty, maybe forty feet of tunnel angled down, then back up toward the light. I crawled the length of the passage, then squinted in the bright sun as I came out the other side. In front of me was the outer wall of the enclosure. It didn't make any sense. It couldn't have been an escape route from the Viking raids of the ninth and tenth centuries because it didn't go anywhere. Maybe the inner wall was pre-Christian and the monastery was built on the site of one of the many ring forts that dot the west coast? What else could explain the tunnel?

I took another walk around the beehive huts, then back out through the opening of the wall, and stood in the field with the cows watching me curiously. I wondered why the monastery had been built on this point of land. Was it because of the beach, the only possible landing on the island? And if back through all of those centuries the beach was still the only landing, then the Vikings would have driven their high-prowed boats through the surf and onto the sands that were less than a stone's throw from the outer wall. The sails of the raiders would have been sighted coming across the bay from Kerry Head, but what recourse would the monks have had? On an island so small there was no place to hide; the walls must surely have been scaled. Into their lives of prayer and learning must have come terror and death.

What would a place like this have had that the raiders wanted? Chalices and crosses, probably. Perhaps the jeweled cover of an illuminated manuscript. The intricate lettering, which the monks treasured more than the glint of silver and gold, would have meant nothing to the raiders. The pages would have been trampled underfoot or thrown on the flames that consumed thatch and field. These island monasteries offered easy pickings for the square-sailed boatmen of the north.

On the way back to my boat, I met a German lady whose family was renting the cottage on the island. She had been walking the shoreline, collecting bits of shells and rocks, and had seen my boat resting in the sands. We talked about the ruins, how they evoked more questions than they answered and how we had been moved by the silence of the stones.

She asked where I had paddled from. I told her I had crossed Brandon Bay that morning and that I was paddling around Ireland. She looked shocked, pointed, and asked, "In the little boat on the sand?"

"Yes," I said. Then to break the awkward silence I told her when I started and that I was headed for the mouth of the Shannon River in the morning. She still had a puzzled look on her face.

"And you are alone?"

I could see where the conversation was going and tried to answer her questions, the same ones I heard many times in the last weeks, patiently.

She invited me over to the cottage to meet her family and another couple that were staying with them. I thanked her, explained that I wanted to do some writing in my journal but that I would like to visit later in the evening.

I finally gave up on the writing when it was too dark to see the lines on the paper. I double-wrapped the journal in plastic bags and pushed it safely behind some clothes in the forward compartment. The day's feelings and events were now recorded on a page that began: July 19.

By the time I knocked on the cottage door, the island was losing the day's heat to the clear twilit sky. I was welcomed by everyone sitting in front of a huge fireplace that had been stoked with peat for the evening. Half empty glasses of wine rested easy on the arms of chairs that showed heavy wear. I was offered a seat close to the fire and a glass was filled for me.

After years of being used to store hay for the cows, the cottage had been recently fixed up. A new roof, windows, and doors, but the old cupboards and worn flooring spoke of the years when the cottage was home to the owner who had grown up on the island. An iron arm with notches cut at various spacings swung from the side of the five-foot hearth opening. Blackened pots and a kettle sat on the stones within the fireplace, out of the way of the cook but warmed by the sputtering turf.

As the visitor, the receiver of the hospitality of warm fire and drink, I answered the questions that travelers are asked. My hosts, two families from Bonn, could not believe that I would set out on such a journey. The question of why kept coming up in a variety of forms.

"Do you not have work in America?"

"What is the purpose for this trip?"

The questions were asked in the kindest of ways. Two middle-aged couples with teenage children who were fascinated with my stories of the sea but confused by my desire to live what appeared to them a reckless life.

One of the two men asked, "How is it you know where to camp? With so much rock, maybe you will not find a beach one night?"

I tried to explain. "When you travel slow, you see the land as it was formed, ravines that might offer a little cove of protection or a hook of land that breaks the swells enough to get ashore. It might not always be where you need it, but there is always a place to land. I don't always want to know where I'm going. If I do, then I have a plan and expectations of time and what I'll see when I get there. I'd rather not know and rely on what my eyes and sense of the sea tell me."

"But still it is dangerous, no?"

"It isn't the danger of the sea that I worry about. It's the fear of growing old and someday saying, I wish I had done this thing or that."

For the first time in the trip thoughts and feelings of the paddling surfaced in spoken words. I heard in my voice the passion I felt for the journey and let it flow unchecked.

The peat burned with slow flames of yellow and orange, an occasional flicker of green that colored the fire, then faded. As many fires do, this one pulled us into its warmth, its flames reflected in our eyes. Each time the peat burned low, someone stood and coaxed it back to life. It was long past midnight; the conversation quieted, but no one was anxious for the evening to end.

Maybe it was the cottage, thick whitewashed stone walls with sills of windows wide enough to sit in; low-beamed painted ceiling holding the heat and the melody of accented conversation; the soft light of a few candles flickering, casting shadows on walls lit by the silent burning turf. Maybe it was the history of the stone and the warmth of the fire that made the evening an experience from another age. An age when people valued the art of the spoken word and must have sat by that hearth and told stories as old as time itself.

In the early morning hours I found my way back to the beach, pulled the sleeping bag from the front hatch, and with the company of the stars walked into the stone enclosure. Beside one of the beehive huts I spread the bag and lay down with the smell of cut hay, and a thousand lights overhead.

I awoke to the warmth of the sun on my face and the sounds of song-birds, terns, and the cry of kittiwakes. Beyond the wall, the rumbling surf broke on the sands, then fell hushed until the next swell rolled in and collapsed. Around me the ruins were lit with the soft touch of morning. The sun was already drying the stones from last night's dew.

I made breakfast while my sleeping bag dried out on the rocks near the boat, then finished packing for the crossing to Kerry Head. I slid into the cockpit, snapped the spray deck on, and waited for the next swell to wash me free of the sands. Once on the water, I fastened the belt around my waist, the wrist strap on the paddle, and took the first strokes of the day.

A hundred yards out, I twisted in the seat for a last look at the island: the ruins, the blue-green waves breaking into a band of white on the beach, the gentle roll of land, and the cottage tucked into a little depression. I wanted to take this image with me.

It was a ritual that I practiced each time I set off from a special place on the journey, this act of stopping the boat and saying good-bye. How many times had I done this? More than I could remember; the headlands, lighthouses, and islands began to blur with the miles and weeks of paddling.

Movement near the cottage caught my eye and what I saw brought a tightness to my throat. On the highest ground near the cottage stood four people waving in the morning light, waving good-bye to a stranger who had shared their fire and evening. Their tiny silhouettes raised emotions that almost made me paddle back. But what then? The journey beckoned, with seas as smooth as glass, and a ten-mile crossing before the next land-fall. I lifted the paddle, white blade toward my friends in farewell, then set the bow on a point of land that barely rose above the horizon.

The two-hour paddle to Kerry Head was the smoothest water of the trip. Across the ten-mile bay the only disturbance on the mirror of sea and sky was the boat's wake spreading in a "Y" behind me. Fulmars and shearwaters glided inches above their own images, then lifted as if by magic a few yards from my bow, silently gliding past. Pairs of guillemots, mothers with single chicks, ignored the speed of my approach until the last second, then dis-appeared in a flurry of upturned tail feathers for the safety of the depths. Ahead of me, a bank of fog sat off Kerry Head, the mouth of the Shannon River.

The Shannon was another ten-mile crossing, one that I had been warned of along my route. I couldn't remember who or where, but it was the ebb tide pouring out of the estuary that was the problem. A wind or good-sized swell running against that tide gave the rivermouth its reputation. The winds and sea conditions were good, but the thickening fog and the ship-ping that ran upriver to Limerick ruled out a crossing. I'd have to go upriver where it narrowed to within a few miles and cross there.

I came around Kerry Head and turned with the swells running into the river. I hadn't noticed their long easy lift on the open water, but now, running against an ebbing tide, they surfed the boat past jagged fingers of rock that guarded the shoreline. As far as I could see, hills of green capped this wall of low cliff. There was no place to land and I was feeling the lack of last night's sleep.

A quarter mile ahead, in close to the rocks, a boat was moving along a line of buoys. It was a lobster or crab fishermen working the ledges near the cliffs. The shear of the boat and the way it seemed to almost leap out of the water at the first sound of the engine was peculiar. I had heard that some fishermen still used currachs, the tarred canvas boats of another era. Could it be?

I needed to find a place to land. If I could close the gap before the fishermen ran the length of their pots, I could find out where they put in on this coast of solid rock. Each time I got close, the fellow in the back would finish cleaning the trap, rebait it, and drop it over the side. No need to look back. They zipped over to the next buoy, the man at the outboard holding the bow into the current while the other reached for the floating line and the next buoy. Hand over hand another trap was pulled. Small crabs tossed back. Fresh bait placed in the bottom and the trap would hit the water a fraction of a second before the *slap-splash* reached my ears.

Now I was close enough to see that it was a boy up front, wearing the same black cap as the man at the throttle. Both stood wide-legged, loose sweaters of dark blue almost as dark as their boat, the boy a mirror image of the square-shouldered man at the stern. As the engine kicked out a boil of water, they leaned into the thrust, their legs slightly bent to absorb the pounding of the hull. This time they swung wide of the next buoy, and the boy caught sight of me. He didn't point but nodded with his cap in my direction. As the man saw me, he throttled back, and I could see the surprise on his face. It must have appeared as if I had dropped out of the sky.

As I paddled closer I could see the boat was indeed a currach, the tarred fabric stretched taut over stringers and ribs, a small outboard housed in a well at the stern. Two oars, long and almost bladeless, rested in the bow. A pair of wooden thole pins on either gunwale would hold the shaft of the oars. Even with the catch of the day, engine, fuel, man and boy, the boat floated with the grace of a feather.

"Hello," I called out.

The man nodded and cautiously replied, "Hello."

"Can you tell me where there's a place to land?"

There was a pause while he looked over the length of my boat. Then, "Where is it yev' come from?"

I thought, "Oh boy, here we go again. I'll tell him I've come from the Magharees. He'll repeat what I just said, ask me where I'm going, then somewhere in the next ten minutes tell me I'm mad."

"I left the Seven Hogs this morning," I answered.

"The Magharees?" he asked.

"Yeah."

The look of surprise on the fellow's face turned to shock. "Yev' come from the Magharees in that?"

"Yes," I said.

"This mornin'?"

"Yeah. About four hours ago."

"Yev' come from the Magharees in four hours in that boat?"

I couldn't hide the smile. "Yes," I said. And waited for the next question. I knew what it would be.

"And where is it you're going?"

Okay, I thought, I may as well just tell the whole story. My legs and back need a stretch and we could sit out here and trade startled questions and answers for the next hour. My reply had long ago started to sound like a taped recording, but . . . "Well, I'm paddling around Ireland," I said. "I started in Dublin the first of June, went south, came around the Mizen, and now I'm heading north. Should be back in Dublin sometime in September."

All of that was a bit too much for the boy, who stood in the bows and looked first at me, then back to the man, as if he didn't believe what he was hearing.

"Yer goin' all round Ireland in that little boat?" Then, as an afterthought, "By yerself?"

And so the conversation went, as it had so many times before. The tide drifted us back downriver as I answered more questions and asked a few myself. Daniel and his son Donall worked the pots every other day, pulling, resetting them, and taking the catch ashore. Daniel had built his boat, the other one as well that he pointed to working further upriver.

"I build one a winter. Sometimes as big as this one and others bigger or smaller, depends what she's to be used fer."

The boat looked fragile, the ribs easily showing through the canvas stretched skintight and shining as the waves slapped against the hull.

"How long will they last?" I asked.

"Aoch, well, if ye take care of 'em, they'll last ye fifteen, maybe twenty years. But I built one for a farmer a few years back, he used it to bring his sheep out to the islands. Now they'll do the job just fine, but inside of three seasons she was a wreck, wasn't good for anything but the fire." He shook his head with disgust. "Farmers, they don't know how to care for a boat."

The sound of an outboard grew louder. The other currach, finished with its line of pots, was heading in toward a shoreline of solid cliff. One second it looked like it would plow into the rocks, the next it simply disappeared, taking the high pitch of its engine with it.

"If yer lookin' for a place to pull out, ye can follow us. We've got a few pots to pull yet but ye'll catch up. Keep an eye on the rocks and follow us in."

I watched father and son lean again into the thrust of the engine: Daniel, one hand on the throttle, the other held palm out in the small of his back. Donnal, in the bow, standing like his father, his hands folded in the same manner and leaning into the turn toward a buoy.

A half hour later I watched the currach snake through a cleft in the rock that I would have paddled right past. Deep in this fissure was the other currach, its engine out and sitting on a pile of raingear and line. Two men pulled a floating crate in position to unload the second boat's catch. Daniel pointed to a ledge where I could land, slipped the engine out of gear, and set the oars into the pegs. In ten minutes both boats were hauled out on the rocks and turned upside down.

There wasn't a lot of talking; this was work that the three men and one boy knew well. Before I knew what was happening, the stern of the first boat was lifted, the men ducked under, and suddenly the black-curved hull was a giant beetle walking on six legs toward a rack where the boat was gently lowered. The second boat was lifted the same way, the remainder of the gear stowed under the hulls.

What I witnessed was a way of life that, except for the outboards, hadn't changed for generations. Father and son in one boat, brother or cousin in the other, they worked this stretch of coast and used the tiny protected harbor where no other boat could.

When the work was done, the four fishermen gathered around my boat. Daniel must have told the others about me. They tapped on the deck, lifted the stern to feel the weight, and looked into the tight cockpit. They each tested the boat, then stepped back with a shake of their head, arms crossed as if a judgment were to be passed. Comments were traded back and forth,

" 'Tis a fair paddle right round."

" 'Tis so."

"I wouldn't be takin' it outta the harbor."

They smiled, shook their heads lightly, and didn't say very much. They were all looking at my boat. Occasionally, one of them would glance at me with a slightly troubled expression, then look again at the boat. I knew what they were thinking. There were a few words of caution about Loop Head, the headland on the far side of the river, but other than that they just kept looking at the boat. One of them reached into a stained nylon bag, the kind that farmers buy feed in. He pulled out two handfuls of crab legs and a single lobster claw and held them out to me.

" 'Tis a good way from the Magharees and you'll be wantin to have yer dinner soon."

Crab and lobster? Wow. I was almost drooling as I found a place in the back hatch for that night's dinner. I turned to thank them again for the advice on the crossing, and their gifts, but already they were making their way up over the rocks. Two of them were out of sight. The third with the bag over his shoulder and the boy at his heels clambered over the last rock and through the thick grass at the top of the ledge.

I stood alone. Alone too quickly. Did all of that really happen? The two currachs rested high and dry on their racks; a trail of wet bootprints led over the dry rocks and faded into the cobbles leading up to the boats. It was almost too much to believe. One minute I was part of another era and the next I was standing alone on the edge of the Shannon, the far shore lost in a haze. It could only happen in Ireland.

I slid the boat back into the water, took one last look at the currachs, and eased out of the narrow rock channel.

Four days later I was camped on the north side of the river, my first attempt at Loop Head fresh in my mind. The tent was pitched fifty feet above the boulders I had landed through after getting turned back from the headland. I was waiting for a break in the weather. The tent opening unzipped, I could sit out of the rain and wind and watch the rollers come in from the north. Gray-black, like the sky and the cliffs leading out to the headland, they rolled on hour after hour, through the night and into the next day. Two more days of heavy fog and I began to think of how far I still had to go.

I was less than halfway into the trip, almost seven hundred miles remaining, and already it was late July. The weather up north was supposedly colder, with bigger seas, at least that's what I heard from the locals. Could I make it back to Dublin by September? And if not, what then?

During the hours of sitting and waiting I studied the map, unfolding it so the whole country lay before me. The west coast looked as if it went on forever. So many islands and crossings. I stepped off the distance from Loop Head to Malin Head, my fingers spread in a crude compass that covered the distance in twenty-mile increments. Four hundred miles. What would I see? Who would I meet and what stories would I hear? The wind carried a sheet of driving mist into the tent, speckling the face of my map and interrupting my thoughts. I took another look at the headland, its outline fading in the rain moving in from the sea, engulfing field and cliff. Would the sun ever return, the winds die down and let me pass?

I reached for the tent zipper, shut out the view of the sea and approaching rain, and listened to the patter of the first drops.

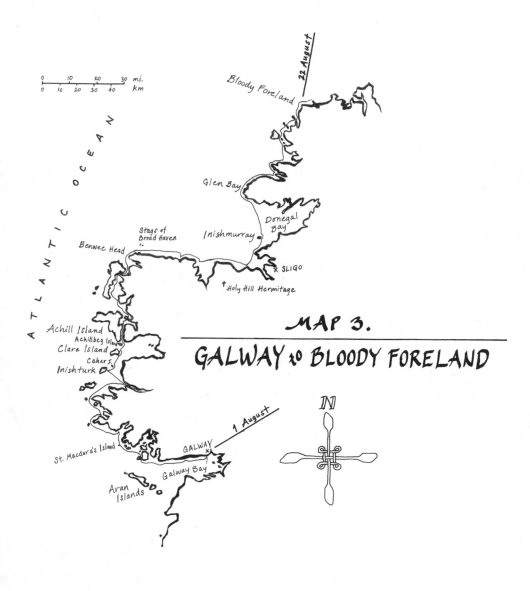

MAP 3.

GALWAY to BLOODY FORELAND

0   10   20   30 mi.
0   10 20 30 40 km

A T L A N T I C   O C E A N

Bloody Foreland

22 August

Glen Bay

Donegal
Bay

Stags of
Broad Haven

Inishmurray

Benwee Head

X SLIGO

† Holy Hill Hermitage

Achill Island
Achillbeg Island
Clare Island
Cahers
Inishturk

1 August

N

St. Macdara's Island

GALWAY
X

Galway Bay

Aran
Islands

Expedition Lows

And a youth said, "Speak to us of Friendship."
And he answered, saying: "Your friend is your needs answered.
And he is your board and your fireside. For you come to him with
your hunger, and you seek him for peace."

—Kahlil Gibran, *The Prophet*

etween Loop Head and Galway Bay, there are a half dozen beaches to land on if the surf isn't bone-crunchingly large. On a calm day, they would have been tempting, but just the thought of trying to surf a fully loaded kayak through ten- or twelve-footers was enough to make me stay offshore. Too many times in past trips I have had to land in big surf, and try as I might, the end result was usually akin to being thrown upside down into the world's largest washing machine set on spin cycle. The boat is pounded and bounced over the surface like a water-logged tree and the paddler has all he (or she) can do to tuck tight, jam thighs against the cockpit, and try to hang on, not only to the boat but also to the paddle that is acting like a giant lever against the tendons and ligaments of the shoulders. Seconds stop ticking. Giant hands seem to shake the body, tearing at it with side-to-side blows. Lungs burn with too little oxygen and the mind screams: "Bail out! Bail out!" A deeper voice of experience counters with, "Hang tight. Let it pass." The voice of reason knows that a swim could be fatal: a rip tide can carry the swimmer offshore or a violent tumbling in the surf can knock the wind out of gasping lungs. In the boat, if the paddler can stay calm and hang on long enough for the first hint of the wave passing, he can roll. The boat will still be in the path of the next breaker, at most eight to ten seconds away, but at least he has the buoyancy and protection of the boat under him.

When I was ordering equipment for the trip, friends and family asked if I was going to take a VHF radio. It could be used for weather reports as well as to call for help in an emergency. I hesitated. How would I keep a radio handy, yet out of the way, and also dry during three months of exposure? They countered with the argument of a rescue. The cost, the limited space, plus the effect of the salt made it a difficult choice. I eventually ordered one thinking it could be returned last minute if it didn't feel right.

The radio arrived double-boxed and shrink-wrapped in plastic. Within the inner box were two halves of Styrofoam perfectly carved to hold the plastic-bagged black radio. A short screw-on antenna and a separate battery pack lay similarly protected. It had the dense weight of compact technology straight from Silicone Valley. In a bizarre way, it appealed to me. I didn't own a TV, VCR, or fancy stereo. Maybe because of that, with this single piece of gear, the trip suddenly felt like an expedition. Mountaineers, sailors, skiers to the North and South Poles all have base camps, support personnel, and elaborate forms of communications. The VHF was a step toward that technology. It felt important and added some technological weight to the trip. Yeah, maybe I would take it.

Two days later I looked at it again, its novelty fading as it sat amid the other low-tech gear. Did I really need it? I had an AM/FM radio for weather and news, which in itself was a deviation from my ascetic approach to paddling. That left the safety issue.

Big offshore swells and waves, even if they are breaking, are not necessarily dangerous. They have the potential of throwing the paddler over, but with a "bombproof" Eskimo roll you are back around in four or five seconds. The test of my ability to survive a large offshore rogue wave had occurred three years earlier.

With my friend Erran, we were halfway through a two-week trip along the west coast of Vancouver Island. The swells were smooth but running ten to twelve feet, large enough that although we were no more than twenty yards apart, we were often out of sight of each other. We were several hundred yards offshore, Erran further out to sea but parallel to my course. All morning the waves had been a steady roller-coaster ride of giant but safe proportions. Five miles away was our destination, a point of land that promised a sheltered landing from the westerly swells. Out of the corner of my eye I caught a glimpse of a huge wave, its face a slick wall rising high over Erran's head, the top seven or eight feet beginning to curl and racing with deadly speed toward us. I yelled a warning. Erran braced, and cut over the top of it a second before it broke with the noise and power of a fifteen-foot breaking sea. Where there had been gentle big rollers one minute, now, because of some quirk of wave dynamics, I was in the path of a wave that champion board surfers dream of and sea kayakers have nightmares about.

With this rogue wave, a rumbling freight train of white terror, thundering down on me, my instincts went into overdrive. I had three choices: (1) Try to turn the boat into the wave and hope to cut through it without getting thrown over end-for-end; (2) side-surf it by leaning into it, pray that it wouldn't rip my shoulder out of its socket, and hopefully it would let me go before crashing me onto the shore rocks; or (3) take a deep breath, roll a second before it hit me, and hang on—maybe the drag of my body through the water would slow the boat and let the wave crash and break over me. Eventually it should spit me out the back of the wave and I could roll back up.

There wasn't time for the first option. Sea kayaks are not designed to turn that quickly. The second choice was too dangerous and time had almost run out for decision making. The only choice had been to roll. I went over and the wave hit. It lifted the boat and slammed it back down, shaking me like a wet rat, tearing at the paddle with the fury of a watery tornado, and filling my ears and sinuses with stinging cold seawater. I waited for the roar of breaking water to subside, forced the paddle into the setup position, and executed an Eskimo roll. Aside from feeling like I had just had an hour of Turkish massage, I came out the back of the rogue wave intact and headed for deeper water, away from the submerged ledge that had caused the huge roller to break.

After the Vancouver Island experience, I knew that I could handle just about any offshore waves. Deep water was not where I would need the help that a radio could provide. The surf, though, was a different story.

A cubic yard of seawater weighs almost a ton. At ten knots, the wall of a breaking wave has enough power to break a boat in half, snap a paddle like a matchstick, or rip a shoulder out of its socket. It is in the surf zone, not the open water, that help may be needed. It is also where help is least likely to be available.

A VHF radio has line of sight capabilities only. If I needed help in the surf, I would most likely be out of the boat in large breaking waves. Transmissions would be near impossible, nor is it likely that anyone but another kayaker, or perhaps a helicopter, could come to my assistance. The fact is that in big surf paddlers have to accept that they are on their own. The best thing to do is to avoid any surf landings.

I kept the radio for a week and realized it didn't have a place on the trip. I reboxed it, taped the corners shut, and mailed it back.

Those thoughts were on my mind for the forty-mile paddle from Loop Head to the Aran Islands. From a mile out, the beaches looked inviting, at least until the crunch of tons of dumping surf echoed off the low cliffs. I wanted to land, but not badly enough to take that kind of risk. Somewhere ahead I would find a better place.

I crossed Liscannon Bay under a sky that promised rain. It was cold and damp, the kind of cold that didn't make sense for July. The water dripping off the shaft of the paddle was warm compared to the chill of the air. Ahead of me, massive waves rolled over a reef, lifting black and shiny, curling higher and steeper until whatever held the wave intact finally let loose and it collapsed in a deafening rumble of white. It was a crushing, terrifying power that re-formed, reaching around the ends of the reef and racing onto the cliff face I was paddling parallel to. I had landed for a quick break on a ledge beneath the cliffs, protected from the outer swell by this very reef. Now I was heading back out and thinking I should have stayed ashore. If it hadn't been for the rising tide, the ledge disappearing by the minute, I would have. Another swell rolled in, lifted as it raced over the shallows, and folded. Again and again the cycle repeated. Each time I was twenty yards closer to the reef and the headland above it. I changed course, angling away to deeper water.

I was watching for the rogue wave, the one in a thousand that was deeper, more deadly because it would break where no other wave would.

Veils of mist drifted below the cliffs, vapor from the thunder of the reef and the waves climbing twenty feet onto the cliff face. Beyond the rocks, the sea settled into the hypnotic rise and fall of deep water. The seaward side of the waves looked benign. That's what made it dangerous, to get lulled into the rhythm of the swells and wander too close. I paddled wide of the point, clear of any possible breaker, then turned and saw beyond the headland.

Hags Head was the beginning of a line of cliff broken by huge pieces of rock torn from the face, leaving caverns and sea stacks to stand alone against the ocean. In a jagged line, black against gray sky, the towers climbed, plummeted, and climbed again. Magnificent and dramatic in the weighted gray of the day, yet dwarfed by a mountainous wall of cliff that rose beyond and above them.

I had been anticipating this moment for days—my first glimpse of the Cliffs of Moher. The noise of the reef faded as I paddled around Hags Head and slowly drew closer to the cliffs. Over six hundred feet high, the single mass ran unbroken for three miles, bold and impenetrable as any fortress. Bands of white sedimentary rock separated fifty or sixty feet of darker layers, giving measure to the heights capped in green. Towers of rock, two hundred feet tall and bearing the same striations, stood cut off by the water, a geological indicator of where the cliffs had once reached further out to sea.

In the light rain, darkened skies, and heavy swells, the visage of the cliffs was intimidating. I stayed a half mile offshore, wanting to be in closer, to look straight up the face of the cliff, but afraid of the confusion of rebounding waves at the base.

A swell lifted then lowered me into a trough that stole the bottom three hundred feet of the cliff from view. It rolled away toward the land and another cycle began, another onslaught of rolling energy gathering speed in the shallower waters around the towers, crashing in rings of white, then hitting the outermost points of the cliff. A split second apart, three faces of wall silently exploded. For a mile on either side, a line of white powered into the cliffs, hung for a second, then disappeared. Seconds later I heard a muffled rumble, another bank of wave approached the stacks, and the cycle of impact and sound confused my eye and ear.

I was chilled, the rain soaking through my hat and sending a shiver between my shoulders. I wanted to stay, watch one more cycle, but knew I had to get moving. The weather was changing fast and there was no place to land for the next five miles. Already the two outer Aran Islands were lost in cloud and rain. The third and closest was more shadow than land.

With the front moving so rapidly, there would be wind—wind I didn't want to deal with. Suddenly there was a sense of urgency, fueled by the energy of the cliffs and the approaching storm. Black on black: the water, cliffs, and sky were one.

The paddle sliced into the swells, churned the water, and slowly the boat began to move. Four strokes, six, then eight. The bow wake surged with each pull. Running parallel with the swells the boat lifted with each wave, two strokes on the crest, then dropping sideways into the trough for another two. Back up on the shoulder, over the top for a quick look around, then rolling into the trough again. The slight burning in my shoulders faded as I warmed to the pace and the automatic movements of my body took over. Toes, knees, and hips were the contact points, relaxed yet firmly planted while the rotation of upper body, stomach, back, and shoulders did most of the work.

The paddle shaft flexed, pulled against fingers, and released as one blade leaped out of the water and the opposite one dove in. Moments would pass and I was lost in the magic of reaching and pulling, feeling the blending of storm, swell, mind, and body becoming one. The threat of being caught out on the open water by the storm had been the impetus for the charge of energy running through me. On the crests was the point of land I was heading for. Reach and pull, storm darkness overhead. Wind waves started to cover the swells and grabbed the paddle in warning. I was barely ahead of the storm, engrossed in the moment, trying to win the race and at the same time almost hoping it would catch me.

As the first rain drilled into the deck, I paddled into Doolin Harbor and dragged the boat up between some boulders. Sea to land, the transition was always so sudden. The sky opened up with fat cold drops. Thoughts of the last hours of paddling were pushed aside and the immediate concern of finding a place to camp took over. The only level, dry ground was a tourist campground three hundred yards from the high water mark.

On the first trip I set up the tent, the priority, to keep the gear as dry as possible during the unloading. Three more trips around boulders and great slabs of rock that teetered with each misplaced step and I was exhausted. The air was filled with the sound of heavy rain drops, sheets of it that splattered on rock and harbor. I tasted the salt washed from my face and felt the rivulets running over my hands and dripping from each finger. Empty of energy from the race with the storm and the trips up and down the beach, I stood and looked at the boat. I dreaded this part, lifting the seventy pounds of boat and gear and carrying it over the rocks. One wrong step and the weight of the boat balanced on my shoulder would drive us hard into the rocks. Broken fiberglass, broken bones. I pushed the thought away.

There was no use standing in the downpour and thinking about it. I turned and reached for the cockpit combing, and paused. Two guys were heading my way through the rain-slicked rocks. They had seen me coming over the rocks with bags of food and gear, then disappearing for another load. Fortunately for me, they were kayakers and knew the hassle of trying to carry a boat solo. After a quick introduction we split the last of the gear and carried the boat through the rock maze.

Marty and Garth were on a weekend break from jobs in the North. They had gotten rained out on a rock climb and were camped, waiting for a break in the weather. They wanted to hear about the trip and offered a ride to the pub a mile into town. I threw the last of the gear into the tent, tied the boat to the windward side, and piled into their car beside packs, ropes, and climbing hardware.

The pub was crammed with people escaping the rain—Germans, Americans, Japanese, and Irish. People milling in a blur of colored raingear and wet heads. Everyone smiling, ordering rounds of Guinness, and crowding tighter around the tables when another friend came in dripping wet.

We found a table against the back wall, ordered fish and chips and a beer each, then settled into talk of sea kayaking, river paddling, and climbing. We talked about stretches of the coast we had all paddled, how the rock formations and caves had looked, and where we had camped. I asked if they knew Jim Kennedy, a paddler I had met on a dock in Schull, County Cork. Sure enough, they knew him; in a country as small as Ireland and a sport as tightly knit as sea paddling, everyone seemed to know everyone else.

The food was gone and the glasses nearly empty for the second time when the conversation suddenly shifted. Garth asked, "Did you hear of the bombing in Atlanta?"

I froze. "The bombing? What bombing?"

He told me what he knew. The previous day, a bomb had exploded on a street near the Olympics Stadium. One person was killed, others injured. No one was claiming responsibility.

My isolated world of headlands and ocean suddenly vanished. Something closed around my chest, fingers reaching in and squeezing the life out of the day. Stealing the magic. Ripping it out of me like it was my heart and filling the space with anger and confusion. The sounds of the rain, smells of wet clothing, the noise and confines of the pub suddenly felt claustrophobic. I pushed the glass of beer away and wished I could do the same with what I had just heard.

Not again. Please, not again. First it was the Troubles in Northern Ireland, then a week ago the crash of the jet liner off Long Island, and now this. In the corner of that Irish pub I felt like crying or screaming, I didn't know which. I just wanted the madness to stop. No more. Please, no more.

Later that evening I sat in the tent, the journal resting on my lap, sheets of rain drumming against the nylon. My clothes, the sleeping bag, everything in the tent felt damp and added to the heaviness of my heart. Where had the joy of the trip gone? I could no longer feel the beauty and power of that morning's paddle. I was fragile, empty and alone. I wrote in the journal:

> Why, why, why?! Who is the bastard that would do such a cowardly thing—I am both depressed and angry at all this bombing and killing. My soul cries out, Dear God, Dear God—it is a prayer . . . of what? A desperate plea for peace, for harmony, for the things that Christ taught and lived. How can there be any hope for a bright future when a madman can so easily kill innocent people?

I looked at my own handwriting; the word "bastard" was something I had never written before. It felt ugly, full of hate. I closed the book, tired and confused by my emotions. The leather cover felt soft, natural in my hands. It was the one thing that I valued more than any other possession in the boat. There was nothing sacred or holy about it, yet I handled it reverently, wrapping it carefully, as I did every night, and placing it under a pile of protective gear. On the pages of that journal were all the highs and challenges of the trip. The people, the sea, and the mystery of this ancient island country. Now there was a blemish. A dark entry that was as real as all of the others and frighteningly honest.

I was shocked at how vulnerable the news of the bombing had left me. Maybe it was the nature of the trip, the willingness to be open and unguarded when suddenly something evil slips through and temporarily lays waste to the richness of the journey. Maybe it was the fatigue of two months of camping: the seas, the winds, and the headlands that I loved but that also scared the hell out of me sometimes. It wasn't any one thing but a combination of many that had lowered my emotional and physical reserves. The news of the bombing brought it all to the surface where I couldn't deny that the trip was taking its toll. I needed a break.

The next morning I crossed to Inisheer Island, hoping to escape from the demands of the expedition for a few days. What I needed was a place to rest, eat well, sleep as long as I wanted, forget about the tides and wind, or the worry of the summer rapidly slipping by.

What I found was an island that must have been beautiful twenty years earlier but now was being overrun. Farm tractors pulled carts filled with tourists from the ferry to the pubs, and the bed and breakfasts. I walked through one of the pubs, looking at photos of a time when the Aran Islands were an isolated community of fishermen and small farms. The black and white photos showed the classic toughness of hardworking men and women, poor in material possessions but rich in their simplicity. An earthy, no-frills life of farming and fishing.

Above the photos, a thirty-six-inch TV flickered its colored message to no one. Everyone was watching an Irishman in a black shirt and white collar, made from a paper plate, imitating an overly pious priest. He was heavy for a man of my own age, loud and a little drunk. The crowd loved the thick accent and the way he used the cane, daggerlike with pointed accusation, to chastise the evils of drink and nonchurchgoers. I stepped around him on the way out, uncomfortable with the mockery and thinking this wasn't the Ireland I knew or wanted to see. The cart paths and cottages were still part of the island character, but everything else on the island seemed to be for the tourists. It was no longer the land or the sea that paid the taxes and fed the people. Now it was tourism that brought in the money.

That night as I lay beside the boat, a floodlight glared over the ferry dock and a backhoe moved into position. With the pointed steel finger reaching over the edge of the dock, the evening peace was shattered by the concussion of expansion jack hammering into concrete.

I thought of the five miles of open water and the slim chance of finding a safe landing on the mainland. It was the fear of the swells and the rocky coast that kept me from foolishly paddling away. I stared at the stars, watched their blinking, and thought of other camps and islands. Other times.

It was ironic that it wasn't on an island that I should find the rest that I needed but rather in a city. A month before leaving home, I told family and friends that one of my mail stops would be the general post office in Galway. The words "poste restante" after my name would hold the letters for up to three weeks. As low as I was feeling, I didn't like the idea of dealing with a city, but the promise of mail was a different story. As it was, it took two days of sitting out high winds and seas too big to chance before making the final crossing of Galway Bay.

I didn't know anything about the city, much less where the post office was. The map on the foredeck showed the city center at the end of Lough Corrib, where a river flowed into the bay. From three miles away, I could see a cut in the land, figured it must be the lough, and angled toward it.

Twenty-mile-an-hour winds and four-foot waves made the paddle across the bay more like a wild surf ride. I could feel the stern lift, the bow bury into the back of the wave in front of me and off I would go, cradled between the two waves and racing along at twice the speed of paddling. It didn't matter that I was miles from land, the water as black as the sky, and the winds pushing the waves until they broke with tumbling white froth. What mattered was the wave I was riding and the energy pouring in with the winds from the southwest. The ocean funneling into the bay and driving me wildly across the darkened waters lifted me out of the doldrums I had been wallowing in. The bow split the wave, clear ocean water ran over the fore deck, and I leaned back on a stern rudder that kept me dead-on to the following seas. I could have counted on one hand the number of days where both sea and wind had been at my back. Now when I needed it the most, their combined energy surfed me through a stormy morning and on to the promise of mail.

A hundred pounds of gear, food, and water have to fit in my
eighteen-foot-by-twenty-one-inch kayak.

A corner of the gannet colony on Great Saltee Island.

In the calm of the South Coast, I could paddle through arches and sea caves.

Cottage ruins on the Rabbit Islands in Country Cork.

The serrated teeth of Clear Island, the last of the calm waters before starting up the West Coast.

Mizen Head—the
beginning of the
West Coast.

Morning light
bathes the
Martello
Tower on Black
Ball Head.

Skellig Michael—
a ten-mile
paddle out to
the mystical
sixth-century
monastic ruins.

A section of the 600 steps
built by sixth-century monks
on Skellig Michael.

The beehive huts on Skellig Michael, long abandoned but filled with the spirits of the
sixth-century monks.

The spirits of ancestors seem to ride on the wings of visiting sea birds.

The cart path and stone-lined fields of Great Blasket Island.

The father and son
fishing team off the
mouth of the Shannon
River.

A gift from the
Shannon lobster-
men.

The lobster fisherman Gerry O'Shea, pulling pots off Loop Head.

The calmest waters of the entire 1200-mile journey—seven miles from land and a fulmar sweeps by for a visit.

The results of the potato famine. This wind-blown abandoned village sits on Mason Island, off the coast of County Galway.

A seventh-century chapel on St. MacDara's Island.

The Standing Stone on
Caher Island keeps
watch over the tiny
cobbled beach.

Atlantic swells hammering
Achillbeg Island in County
Mayo. A safe refuge is still an
hour away.

My tent sits in the shelter of the Headlands—but what lies beyond that rock?

Breaking waves have chiseled away at Downpatrick Head, creating a beautiful monument to the power of the sea.

The seventh-century
monastic site on
Inishmurray Island.

To be washed by the spray of the sea—one of the many gifts of the journey.

County Donegal's rugged coast: fifteen miles of cliff, sunshine, and soaring spirits.

Two retired fishermen making
the run from Inishbofin to the
mainland—County Donegal.

The surprising calm of Fanad Head, one of the northern headlands of Ireland.

The abbey ruins on Inishdooey Island in County Donegal.

The poetry of heavy seas, miles offshore.

Further into the bay and around a couple of small islands, the waves lost their power. They were choppy, confused and trapped by the lands closing in on all sides. I felt the same way. It was as though we had both been pushed into this corner, fooled by the winds that drove us to a high, then veered off to leave us looking over our shoulders at the open sea. Transitions again, physical as well as emotional. I could feel the high draining away.

It took me awhile to find the rivermouth, and when I did, I was sorry. Raw sewage floated on water that stank like none I had smelled before. No place to land, even if I wanted, beneath the concrete walls and sludge of low tide. I retreated to a cobble beach, timed the waves, and landed below a park full of wind- and rain-damaged tents. There were lots of young people, eighteen to twenty years old, camping amid the debris of a concert two days earlier.

Between the blast of winds that were increasing and the flapping of torn rain tarps, I heard the warble of a didjeridoo and the beating of a drum from one of the tents. Three wet and rumpled-looking guys walked over to check me out. They were friendly and asked where I had come from. I wasn't in the mood to explain, but told them I had crossed the bay that morning and left it at that. I asked if they thought it was safe to leave the boat for a couple of hours. They said they would keep an eye on it, but that it wouldn't be safe after dark. I assured them I would be back long before that, thanked them, weighed the risks, and carefully placed the compass, camera, weather radio, journal, wallet, and passport in my backpack. This was the other disadvantage of traveling solo: leaving the boat unguarded. I slipped the two-piece graphite paddle apart, stuffed the blades into the pack, and turned the boat over against the seawall. Luck, maybe karma, would have to guard the boat.

After a few stops for directions I found the post office, showed my passport for ID, then waited as the lady turned and sorted through a stack of letters for other travelers. As I looked over her shoulder, one, then two letters were pulled from the pile. A pack of five or six held with a rubber band were added to the first two, then two more. This was too good to believe. Were they all for me?

When she turned and handed me the stack, I felt the rush that world travelers are familiar with as a stranger slips their mail through the clerk's grid. The sight of my name—such a wonderful feeling of identity—"Yes,

yes, that's me. Thank you very much." It was a mix of giddiness, of holding a treasure I wanted to tear open the moment I felt its weight, and yet wanting to savor the unopened gifts. A smile spread across my face and I felt like a child on Christmas morning. Which one to open first? I stepped back from the counter and flipped through the return addresses. I would find a quiet place to read them later. For now, I just wanted to see who had written. There were letters from my parents and sisters, three or four from friends in Port Angeles, and one from my uncle, hopefully a reply to my letter about the family history. I counted them again, checked the addresses to make sure I hadn't missed any, then zipped them safely into the top compartment of the pack.

As I walked back to the boat, the wind rushed through the streets, scattering trash and slowing my steps. The narrow streets were busy with shoppers and the kind of cars you see in European cities, small, with short wheel bases. Everything seemed small: the grocery shops, the separate meat and fish shops that displayed their goods through scrubbed glass windows. It was still early morning; delivery trucks blocked half the width of the sidewalks and many of the stores were closed. I passed a camping shop, its windows filled with boots, stoves, and clothing. I tried the door but it was locked. Too bad; it would have been a nice place to get out of the wind and rain.

By the time I got back to the boat, the winds were blowing the predicted Force 8, almost forty mph. The last of the concertgoers were packing up and it looked like the grassy point would be abandoned to the sheets of wind-driven rains. Good. No one would bother coming out to the point in this kind of weather. The boat was safe for awhile and I would have some time to figure out a plan. I walked back to the city center, toward the camping store.

When at last I walked in, soaked and miserable, any pride or embarrassment at pleading to a stranger for a place to dry out was gone. It was a long shot, but in a jumbled introduction I told the woman at the counter who I was, that I was trying to paddle around Ireland, and that I desperately needed a place to stay. While the water dripped off my raincoat and turned the carpet in front of the register dark brown, she listened, asked a few of the questions that everyone always asked, then casually said she knew a paddler who had attempted to do the same trip earlier in the spring. His name was Jimmy O'Toole. Maybe he could help. As she dialed his number,

I couldn't believe it was purely coincidence she knew someone that I had been hearing about for the past month and a half.

Somewhere along the coast of County Cork I had heard of a trio of paddlers that were two weeks ahead of me. It must have been a fisherman or a shopowner who originally told me of them. As my journey progressed, I kept meeting people who had met them. The nature of Ireland is that everyone seems to know everyone else or at least takes an interest in strangers traveling through. The villages are small and word travels quickly, especially when the travelers come in from the sea. Given the few towns and the rugged coastline, it wasn't surprising that I should seek food and shelter in the same villages these other paddlers had. What was surprising was that here in a city, big by Irish standards, I should once again hear of them. And by the sounds of the phone conversation, I was going to be meeting one of them.

As soon as Jimmy walked into the shop, I knew my problems were solved. He had an energy and openness that were immediately welcoming. I could stay with him for as long as I needed and the boat could be stored in the back shed. Without wasting any words, he asked where my boat was. I told him, then barely had time to thank the woman at the counter before we were out the door and heading back to the park. He didn't like the idea of leaving it unguarded.

On the way to the boat, Jimmy asked about my trip. Where had I started and where had I been on particular dates? He remembered the villages where they had stopped, the headlands that had given them problems, mostly because of the winds, and the magic of traveling along the coast. The disappointment was thick in his voice when he told me how they had to quit when they were within two hundred miles of finishing their trip. Time and bad weather had beaten them, but his enthusiasm and love for the adventure were still there.

As I tried to keep up with him through the crowded streets, he would wave, call out a greeting to friends in shop doorways, and dodge in front of cars, often leaving me on the far side of the street. When I finally made it across, he would slap me on the back, laugh, and say, "I forget how busy the city is. 'Tisn't like this on the sea, is it?" Then it was back to talking about the coast and the love we both shared for the sea.

No, the city was nothing like the sea, and if it wasn't for Jimmy's warmth and unselfish energy, I don't know what I would have done. We retrieved the boat and carried it on our shoulders along the sidewalks and across the busy streets of Galway, the motorists bewildered by the sight of the bright yellow boat and Jimmy's disarming wave as we threaded our way through the cars. There aren't a lot of people who will carry a hundred and fifty pounds of boat through a city, not uttering a single complaint about the keel digging unmercifully into their shoulder, and do it all with such grace.

When we got to the house, Jimmy knew what I needed before I asked. The hot water was switched on for a bath, floor space was cleared in a back room for my gear and a place to sleep. More important, he gave me space and time to unwind. I didn't have to explain that I needed to just sit and let the weight of the trip fall from my shoulders. He knew. As I sat reading my mail in the comfort of an old worn chair, Jimmy would come in with another load of peat, carefully place a few bricks on the fire, and then disappear again.

Many times on this trip, and others, I had difficulty making that transition from the world of solo paddling to the sudden barrage of questions that the trip initiated. People wanted to know everything about me: where I lived, why I was doing it alone. Everything from how I could afford three or four months off to how I peed when I was out at sea. I felt their curiosity and wanted to answer their questions, but there were some answers that took more time than a brief encounter would allow. At times I was happy to try and offer insight; other times I was just too tired to explain. I wanted them to see more than just the sleek boat, the romance and adventure of traveling solo, and the physical nature of who I was. Sometimes I wanted them to know the questions in my own mind, the quest, the soul journey that kept me going. I wanted them to feel the fatigue, and know the doubts when I questioned what it was that I was doing. Jimmy knew the emotional highs and lows of traveling solo. He had hitched across the Sahara Desert and worked in Africa for two years (doing what I wasn't sure), but it was this traveling that gave him the insight into what it was I needed. For the first time on the trip, thanks to him, I had the luxury of sleeping under a roof, not worrying about the tides or weather, and just letting go for awhile.

For three days I ate well, napped, read my mail, and wrote letters. There was nothing to do but stay warm, and listen to the winds and rain rattling against the windows. Listen, and be thankful for the fire in the living room and the walls around me.

The day before the weather broke, I was wandering through the streets of Galway, stocking up on food for the boat stores, and treating myself to sweets displayed in the bakery windows. I was on a back street, narrow and crowded with old buildings that seemed to lean out into the street. The crowds of the city center were several blocks away and the area had the feel of a neighborhood.

Up one street and down the next, people I passed along the way looked me in the eye and said good morning. It was still cold enough for a coat or heavy sweater but the sky was brighter and folks were moving about. I came to a junction where two roads met, not in a way that carefully laid out streets do, but in a haphazard way of one meeting the other at an odd angle. I took the left fork, stayed in the middle of the street for a hundred yards, then moved to the sidewalk when I saw a crowd appear around a bend. There were forty or fifty people in the road and they crowded past the cars parked on the curb. People were occasionally looking over their shoulders or toward the throbbing of a helicopter I became suddenly aware of. No one was moving fast, just steadily away from whatever was happening behind them.

I let the first few couples pass, then stopped and asked three girls walking together what was going on. They wore identical light blue dresses with their names printed on pins that had a store emblem on one corner. They were young and nervous, glancing back and walking with arms interlocked as if for reassurance, their shoes not made for the steep, uneven road surface.

"It's some kind of a bomb scare." It was more a question than a statement that the middle girl offered.

"The police are closin' the shops and makin' everyone leave the center."

A bomb scare? In Galway? I knew the Troubles were heating up and there was new violence in the North, but I hadn't expected to literally walk into it here in the South. The high-pitched whine and throb of the helicopter banking into a turn drowned out all thought and sound of the crowd moving past.

I immediately wanted to know where the bomb was, how to move away not only from the spot where the image of blown-out windows filled my mind but also from the crowds filling the street in front of me. I didn't want to be in the path of that panic if a bomb went off. I knew roughly what direction Jimmy's house was, but it was straight across the city, against the flow of people emptying the center through the alleys that led into this normally quiet section of town. What I didn't know was how to get around the center and back across the river to where my boat was. Funny how that was the first thing that came to mind. My boat.

It must have been the nature of the trip, thinking defensively, and avoiding trouble. I took the first side street that wasn't blocked by the police or filled with the moving crowds. In a tiny café I found a table near the window, then thought better of it and moved toward the back. I ordered tea and scones, extra butter, and watched the people.

No one seemed upset or even aware of what was happening a few blocks away. Maybe they didn't know or maybe it was something they were accustomed to. Couples, small groups of young people in bright clothes, with multiple-pierced ears, sat around drinking coffee and smoking. I thought how strange this city life was, how out of place I felt one moment and how capable of surviving the next. Ten, maybe fifteen miles away was another world, one of clear ocean swells, gulls, and diving seabirds. Two worlds so disconnected—one that I loved and that fed me with its energy and wildness and one that threatened me with unpredictable currents I couldn't read.

I sat, drank my tea, and knew that whatever the weather did the next day, I was going to leave. I was calm, alert to the danger, whether it was a real bomb or just a hoax, but certain in that moment I would rather deal with the hazards of the sea than blindly stumble into something in a city where I was just one of tens of thousands.

On August 1, two months from the start of the trip, Jimmy helped carry the boat across the draining sandflats below the park. It was raining hard, but the winds had dropped considerably since the day before. The bomb scare had been just that, a scare that shocked Jimmy as much as it did me. He understood why I was anxious to relaunch, to get out of the city and back to the freedom of the sea. Like everyone else, he was puzzled by the madness of the violence bleeding across the border. The news was filled with images of people in conflict, two sides separated by a line of helmeted police with interlocked Plexiglas shields. Religion? Politics? Or was it something that happened three hundred years ago under the guise of righteousness? People no longer knew what it was they were fighting about, just that one side was pitted against the other as their parents, grandparents, and past generations had been. The majority of the people, like Jimmy, didn't understand it. I knew I never would.

In a pair of shoes that he had bought the day before, the first new ones he had in years, Jimmy sloshed through the sand and strips of algae to the tideline. I wanted just to drag the boat across the flats, but he wouldn't hear of it. The first hundred yards with the fully loaded boat weren't bad. The second stretch had us breathing hard and staggering out of step with each other the closer we got to the water. We gently set the boat down at the water's edge, turned our backs to the rain and wind, and stood looking at the puddles gathering in the seat. It was a miserable day to be setting off, no reason to it except the feeling that it was the right thing to do.

Jimmy hadn't questioned my decision to go; he simple rearranged his morning plans to help me get the boat back to the water. Now he stood with the tide staining the leather of his shoes, his hand clasped in mine. I thanked him again for all of his help. He passed it off with a statement I had heard him say many times, "It's just part an' parcel of the whole." Then, "Ye take care on the sea and drop me a line when ye get back to Dublin." And with that, our farewell was done. He turned and walked across the flats. I eased the boat through the shallows, then turned into the wind and started out of Galway Bay.

I didn't get far in the wind—three and a half hours of digging into the short chop and getting soaked with the spray—but it was far enough to clear my head and feel that I was on the move again. The shoreline was low, guarded by rocks as usual, but with plenty of places where I could pull out of the wind and rest.

Ten or twelve miles up the coast I spotted a fisherman anchored in a natural harbor between fingers of rock. A couple of currachs floated lightly on the sheltered water nearby. Beyond the boats gently tugging at their moorings was a cobble beach and a grassy ledge that looked perfect for the night's camp. As I paddled closer, I watched the fisherman sort through a bin. Along with bits of seaweed he would occasionally toss a crab or lobster over the side of the boat; maybe they were too small or the shells were soft. Methodically sorting and cleaning, he was lost in his work and didn't see or hear me until I was almost alongside. I kept my voice soft when I called out a greeting but he was still startled as he straightened and looked around in surprise. He shook his head and said, "Ye gave me a fright, lad. I didn't think there was anyone out here but me."

I apologized and he laughed as he leaned on the gunwale, grateful for an excuse to chat and rest his back. He looked to be in his mid-forties, short, with the agile build of an athlete. I watched his eyes and the tilt of his head as he studied the lines of my boat, then asked if it was an Eskimo kayak. I told him it was a design taken from the original Greenland style of kayaks but that it was built in England. With a nod he said, "She's a fine-looking boat, she is, and good in the likes of a day like this, I suppose."

He talked about the winds of the last few days and how he hadn't gone out to check the pots until this morning—"Too rough to be pulling pots over the side." He asked me where I had come from, and I told him Dublin. That got the usual response of disbelief and then the battery of questions that today I didn't mind answering, especially from a fisherman who could appreciate the sea and the winds. When he asked where I stayed at night, I told him I camped, and that was the reason why I had pulled into the break in the rocks. He assured me it would be fine to camp on the grass, then asked if I wanted a lobster for my dinner. Before I could answer he reached into a bin, tossed a few aside, and chose one that he thought would suit me. He slipped a rubber band over each claw, and tipping the gunwale of his boat, leaned over with the offer.

"You'll have to pull her high above the rocks, the tides are full the next two days. But you'll be fine up on the grass."

After the last week of feeling down and worn out, this fisherman re-minded me of what it was I loved about Ireland. It was the same thing I had seen in Jimmy: a complete interest and openness to strangers that made me feel so humble. I had nothing but the stories of my travels to give, yet the hospitality that I received didn't even ask for that. It was given freely, as if the giving itself was the reason for being alive. It was this gift of meeting these wonderfully warm and hospitable people that kept me going. This was the Ireland that I loved.

That evening as I sat writing in my journal, three fellows drove down the packed earth track that led to the cove. They piled out of the dilapi-dated little car and started loading fishing gear into one of the currachs. They carefully stepped over the gunwale and settled into the nimble boat, the bowman tending the forward lines while the fellow in the center lifted the oars in place. A minute later the fishing gear was stowed, the mooring lines cast off, and they were underway with the sound of the oars knocking against the thole pins: *clunk*; a long, silent sweep; another *clunk* as the oars lifted clear of the water and reached forward for the next stroke. As they left the protection of the rocks, the fellow at the oars leaned harder into each sweep, his legs spread wide and his back straight as he pulled with long, even strokes. The blades of the oars were barely wider than the long shafts and didn't look like they would have any bite on the water, yet with each pull the boat surged forward. The waves smacked the windward side of the tarred boat, sending spray into the wind that swept over the fishermen clad in yellow raingear. On an evening when the water was covered with whitecaps, I wondered what inspired the men to go out.

It was nearly dark when they returned, the sound of the oars and their Gaelic voices drifting through the dampness of the night. I set the journal aside and looked out the tent opening as they tied the currach to a buoy, pulled themselves ashore in a dinghy, and climbed over the rocks. They were wet but happy. The first fellow carried the fishing rods, the second the long oars over his shoulder, and the third a gunny sack bulging with the catch. As the fellow with the sack passed the tent opening, he held out three gutted mackerel, his hand stained in half-dried fish blood. He didn't say a word, just stood there in front of the tent in black, knee-high rubber boots and open raincoat with a fistful of shiny blue-black mackerel. I reached up with both hands and accepted the gift. I thanked him. He nodded and turned to catch up with his friends. A minute later they were gone, the sound of the car's engine fading as it labored up over the hill.

With some leftover rice from the lobster dinner, I made another meal of the mackerel. Cooked in a bit of olive oil with salt and pepper, the fillets browned lightly and curled on the ends. I turned the stove off and sat in the tent doorway, holding the warm pot in my lap. The wind was dying down, the seas quieter than they had been an hour earlier. The sides of the tent were slack. In the silence and fading light I knew how simple and fulfilling the moment was. There was change in the air. The clouds were moving swiftly in the night sky and showed signs of breaking up. The storm of emotional lows that had been brewing inside me was also weakening with the return to open waters. Maybe I needed the low of the last week to realize how rich the simple gifts of the trip were. And maybe the best way of balancing the pain, the brokenness of the world was to be silent and let the acknowledgment of these peaceful moments bring life back into balance. A simple meal, a quiet evening of writing, and the gift of food from total strangers were a perfect start for the next leg of the trip.

Island Tapestries

This is the place. Stand still my steed,
Let me review the scene,
And summon from the shadowy past
the forms that once have been.

—Longfellow, *A Glean of Silence*

My map had been folded and refolded so many times the
creases had begun to tear. Across the center from Dublin to
Galway, there was little that held the two halves together. I
carefully pulled the fibers apart, separating the map in two and folding the
lower half of Ireland into a plastic bag for safekeeping. It was symbolic of
the halfway point in the trip.

In the bottom left of the map, I found Gorumna Island, my present
camp, and traced a route connecting islands, headlands, and long reaches
of exposed coastline where there would be nothing to protect me from the
swells and winds. I took a route that would take me from County Galway
into Counties Mayo, Sligo, and eventually Donegal. From there I would
be over the top of Ireland and into what I thought would be the more
protected waters of the north and east coasts. I followed the coastline back
into the Irish Sea and south to Dublin. It seemed an impossibly long way
to go. Too far. Too much exposure to think about. I folded the map so
only the next hundred miles showed through the plastic and instantly the
trip felt feasible again. It is a tactic I have learned to use in my life: Focus
on what is immediate and let the future unfold in small steps. On the map

was a chain of islands that led out toward Slyne Head, islands that I knew were just out of sight over the crown of land in front of the tent.

The next morning, I struggled to get going early. The night had been unusually cool, and the warmth of the bag was hard to leave. I unzipped the tent to a world of blue sky overhead while all around a blanket of fog lay on the water and contours of the low hills. The clear night skies had let the heat of the land escape, and a heavy dew clung to the grasses and dripping tent. I waited for the sun to burn off the fog and dry things out before breaking camp and paddling through the reflection of a low bridge connecting Lettermullan Island to Gorumna Island.

Behind Lettermullan, the tide pulled me out toward open water and through several small islands, ridges of rock crowned in grass and ringed by aqua-green shallows. The sun floated on the water's surface, sea and sun barely touched by the gentlest of breezes. Not a cloud dared venture into the skies above, while inland the Connemara Mountains were half hidden in swirls of charcoal gray wrapped around sharp peaks. The mountains were getting blasted by one of those summer thunderstorms that bring violent roiling clouds one minute and dazzling sunlight the next. From the comfort of the calm seas, I watched as the storm thickened, then receded. Occasionally the sun would break through and bathe one of the peaks in brilliant light as if it were some enchanted land guarded by the forces of the gods.

Two hours of sunshine and the reach of paddle blades meeting their own knifed reflections brought me to an island of crushed shells and sand dunes broken by tufts of grass. The shallows around the island were marked by the same abrupt change in colors I had seen earlier, the blue of the deep water fading and turning aqua-green over sand and shells extending from the beach. I eased the boat behind a ledge of rock that blocked the low swell, and coasted silently over the shallows until the bow gently nudged the island. The soft crunch of the keel sliding into the shells was the only sound. A dozen oystercatchers stood like decoys on the beach, all facing the same direction and taking to flight in the same wave when I stood up in the ankle-deep water.

Millions of fragmented shells sloped to the water's edge: a falling tide marked by a damp line of weed three feet from the tingle of wavelets. I left the stern barely floating and the bow held by the fingers of the shells.

The falling tide would assure that the boat was safe for as long as I was ashore.

As I walked up the beach, the interior of the island spread out in front of me. In the foreground, sand dunes stood like motionless waves, their faces eroding, while their backs were covered in close-cropped grass. Cows lay in the sun-warmed sand, chewing their cuds, momentarily pausing, then continuing their ruminating as I crested the lip of the beach. Beyond the dunes were two parallel stone walls that seemed to push away the stones of the field to either side of their course. It was an old cart path, dividing the island in half and leading from the beach to a cluster of crumbling cottages, the remains of a long-abandoned village.

In the calm and warmth of the day, I walked down the center of the cart path, accepting the ease of passage rather than the thistle, nettle, and rock ledge beyond the walls. On either side the walls ran shoulder-high, tons of rock that had been lifted from the fields and set one upon the other. In places, the walls had crumbled. The lines of rock were broken, fallen back into the fields where they had been picked. Grass and moss covered the fallen rocks and were gradually reclaiming them. There was no creak of a loaded cart, no slow turning of wooden wheel over stone and grass, and no rich smell of peat or fish being brought to the tiny houses on the hill. There was only the loneliness of the path, and the smell of the grass that hadn't felt the weight of a laden cart since the first carefully laid stone had shifted and tumbled. The walls ran true to each other, broken in places by time, but still solid in purpose.

I walked to the first cottage and let my eyes wander over the ruins. Nettle and thistle crowded the outer walls and grew thick amid the tumbled rock inside. Doorways and windows stared lifelessly, funneling the breeze through their openings, and standing solid with stone lintels bearing the weight of the years. What had once been a tiny home was now just four roofless walls against a blue sky. The cottage stood abandoned, holding the tragedies of poverty, famine, and emigration in its interlocking squares of lichen-covered rock.

The only clue to the people who had lived here was the care with which the walls had been built. Beautifully solid, even in their ruins, they were a testimony to a craftsman's work, the weight of each rock carefully shouldered against its neighbor and straddling the two it rested upon. The interplay of sun and shadow, brilliant orange and feathery gray lichen, massive rock set against perfectly matched neighbor, tied the walls together in a marriage of colors and texture. These walls, like those of the cart path and the other cottages scattered across the stone-covered island, had been built with patience and an understanding of time.

Through doorways framed by carefully selected flat-sided stones, I walked into the homes of people who had lived and worked this island. The low doorways opened into a single room, twelve feet by twenty, with a tiny bedroom behind the fireplace at one end. Unlike Great Blasket Island, here nothing remained of the people's lives, no hint at what simple comforts they may have had or how the large families would have fit into the cramped quarters. In the empty rooms where the grass and nettles grew, I felt as if I were being watched, as if an old man or woman from another era might suddenly appear around the end of a wall, a soul wandering through the ruins searching for something left behind.

The builders of these stout cottages had set their walls against the forces of nature, of winter rains and gales that would carry the ocean's spray in drifting mists over their island. The walls had stood soundly against that threat. What no stonemason could have foreseen, though, was the combination of politics and famine that would slowly bleed dry the life of the island and that of the rural lands of the mainland. The paths, the fields cleared of stone, and the emptiness of the houses spoke of one of the darkest times in Ireland's troubled history.

At the time of the first potato blight in the 1840s, Ireland had a population of almost nine million people, the most densely populated country in Europe. In contrast, today there are three and a half million, and across the length and width of the land are the ruins of those previous times. In the nineteenth century, most of the people lived in the rural areas, pushed off the better lands by the English, who milked Ireland as a feudal state and gave little in return. The people lived in squalor; pigs, chickens, and cows, if the family was that wealthy, shared the same shelter. Others lived in nothing more than sod-covered hovels. The potato was the one crop that would grow in the thin soil, or along the coast, in a mix of seaweed and sand carried in willow baskets to a place where the wind and sea mist wouldn't tear at the plants. There is a saying in the North of Ireland to this day: "The English got the good land and the Irish got the views." Before the blight, Ireland was precariously balanced on the edge of disaster.

Overworked land, disease, and a people weakened by poverty stood little chance when their main staple began to rot in the ground.

The first major potato crop to fail was in 1845. The early harvest had been promising, plenty of "tubers" and no sign of the devastation that would wrack the island for the next five years. Subsequent harvests yielded potatoes either blackened by the blight or apparently healthy ones that later rotted in storage by the ton. The 1846 crop unearthed the same blight that ran like a panic throughout the country. There was starvation in the rural areas and soup lines in the cities. By the third year, the fungus that triggered the devastation had weakened, but the crop was dismally inadequate. In desperation, the seed potatoes for the 1847 crop had been eaten and there was nothing in the ground to harvest.

On a summer day, with hundreds of tiny yellow flowers growing amid the greenery of the island, it was hard to imagine the forces that had scattered the inhabitants. Was it the blight that caused the first person to pack up and leave, or was it the lure of a better life in America that a relative wrote of? Maybe the cycles of fish stocks hit a low at the same time typhus, measles, or whooping cough had taken another member of a family. Maybe, like the Blasket Islanders, these people had exhausted the peat, or perhaps after a time of too many people leaving the island there simply wasn't any reason to hold out longer as the last door was shut against the west winds. Whatever the reason, one by one, like families all over Ireland, the survivors abandoned their homes and left. Between 1846 and 1851, an estimated one million Irish died of starvation and disease while another two million emigrated.

Where had the people of this island gone? Canada, America, Australia? In the misery of cramped ships full of emigrants fleeing the same starvation, poverty, and disease, these island people had headed across the Atlantic. From ports throughout Ireland the ships set sail. The captains were paid by the numbers they could pack into their holds; thousands of people already weakened by years of famine. These were desperate people, who risked everything for a chance at a brighter future. The ships were called "coffin ships" because of the numbers that died during the passage.

In my uncle's letter, which I had picked up in Galway, he sent a copy of a letter my grandfather wrote at age eighty-five to my aunt. In it he tells her what he knew of their Irish roots and mine as well:

You have asked me to fill you in as regards to my ancestry. I have not at hand all the facts but here are the salient ones in my mind. My father's mother and father were born in Ireland and later, due to hard times (Potato famine), decided to leave the strickened country and cross the sea by boat to reach the "Land of Promise," America. During those times one had no choice, either of boats, sailing times or destination. Any landing port on this continent was the goal. It happened that the destination of their boat was St. Johns, New Brunswick, where they finally arrived safely. My father, Bernard Henry O'Kane, his two sisters, Mary and Helen, were born in New Brunswick. These three finally reached the goal of their parents—Portland, Maine; and thence became citizens of the United States.

My grandfather's account says nothing of what the O'Kanes were fleeing, but I have no reason to believe they were any different from the millions who went west with nothing but what they wore. From a small rise in the center of the island, I could see the cart path leading from the ruins to the beach. Two miles away, the fields of the mainland climbed into the distant hills and turned somber beneath the clouds of the Connemaras. I looked around one last time, then reluctantly, not wanting to break the thread that wound back through the generations, walked the path to the beach. In another age, I would have been dressed in wool coat, coarse shirt, and leather shoes. A bag over my shoulder or a box containing all the wealth I had would have been swung into a currach and the journey to the Land of Promise would have begun. Four generations after my ancestors left Ireland, I was back looking for something America could not provide, the shadow of souls that link the generations and welcome a stranger home, if only for a visit.

It was hard to shift gears when one moment my heart and emotions were deep in the lives of people of the past, my own past, and the next I was back in the boat, feeling the sea wrap around me and demand that I live in the moment. Throughout the trip, I struggled with that transition, wanting to stay with the emotions, to explore them and feel their depth, but knowing that once I was in the boat I had to let it go and pay attention to my surroundings. The rhythm of the trip was like that: while my experiences on the land were as intense as those on the sea, it was a life of constant transitions.

Day after day, weeks flowing into months, I had seen and experienced more than I thought was possible. Every time I thought I had reached the peak, that the passion for the journey must certainly begin to wane, I would stumble on another experience that pulled me onward. Stroke by stroke, four miles an hour, Ireland was filling me with its life blood. At times the awakening was one of haunted loneliness, a severed connection to the people of my own beginnings. At other times it was the high of feeling free and running with the abandonment of winds and swells. Still others, it was sitting in complete surrender and awe beneath great walls of cliff that reminded me how very tiny and insignificant I really was. It was ironic, yet at the same time uncannily natural, that I should come back to a land my ancestors had fled. Somewhere in this country were the ruins of my family, the stones and earth that had known my blood relatives. It was no wonder I felt so alive, so open and willing to take the risk of being both physically and emotionally vulnerable.

While I paddled, my mind was free to move through these thoughts, exploring the images and feelings of the trip and letting them go again when the sea demanded my attention. That was the beauty of the journey. I could move freely from one realm to the next, the constant dip and pull of the paddle a mantra that connected both worlds.

I paddled on the inside of Slyne Head, happy to have the reefs and islets that extended out to the lighthouse breaking the power of the bigger waves. A mile offshore, the light tower stood on an island and warned of the shallows. As regular as the swells, huge explosions of white broke against the seaward side of the island and mutely climbed into the air. In closer, smaller waves broke over hidden rocks, lifting and cascading in bands of brilliant white on deep blue. They broke with a regularity that marked them separately from the smaller whitecaps covering the sea surface. Most of the breakers I ignored; they were close but not close enough to be a threat. The others I watched and eased the bow to either right or left as I came up on them.

That night I slept beneath the sand dunes in Mannin Bay twenty sea miles from where I had started the day. Massive dunes stood side by side, crowding the beach and spilling sand into the blasts of wind that buffeted the tent, the same winds that had pushed me around Slyne Head. The forecast was for strong southwesterlies, shifting to northwesterlies by dawn. During the night I awoke several times to the slamming and popping of the tent inches from my head. I drifted in and out of a disturbed sleep and later woke to a sudden calm. Perhaps the winds had blown themselves out? I needed rest desperately and finally settled into the first deep sleep of the night. I should have remembered the forecast.

It seemed like moments later when the next blasts hit the tent from the other direction and suddenly the rain-soaked nylon collapsed over me. I was instantly awake, groping for the headlamp and crawling out from under the gritty mess of sand-covered nylon. In the driving wind and rain, I searched for rocks to pile on the tent corners and shifted the boat to the windward side. Anchored again, I reset the tent and laughed at the image of myself working in the wind and rain with nothing but a headlamp on. I crawled back into the tent, did my best to shake the sand off everything, and shivered in the sleeping bag until dawn. I was gritty, cold, but for some reason, perhaps madness, I was happy.

Two days later, I paddled out of fjordlike Killary Bay. The northwest winds had forced me off the water, and I had turned and run with them into the calmer waters of the bay. Now the winds had shifted back to the southwest and I was on my way again. Two thousand–foot peaks half hidden in mist framed the open ocean I was paddling toward. Gusts of wind raced over the surface and covered the water with whitecaps.

As I left the shelter of the bay and paddled past a few rocky islets, I could see a low, gray shadow on the horizon. It was drizzling and there were three-footers coming out of the southwest. The waves rolled in broadside to the boat, balanced it briefly on the crest, then rolled away and dropped me into the next trough. By some stroke of fortune the angle of the waves set me on a perfect course for the shadow I had seen. Inishturk Island lay ten miles offshore.

I had a choice of staying in close and paddling the long sandy beaches of the mainland or gambling on the weather, primarily the winds, and trying for the islands that lined up in a northerly direction. If I could make it to Inishturk before the winds changed, I would have the seas broadside, then at my back for the crossing to Caher Island. If the winds were still southwesterly, I could get a free ride to Clare and on to Achillbeg. Everything depended on the winds; but I liked the idea of island-hopping better than the exposure of paddling along a crashing surfline and sandy beach. The winds were holding steady at Force 3, fifteen miles per hour. The sky was a single sheet of flat gray that dropped into the sea. With the unstable winds of the past few days it was risky, but I decided to try for the islands.

With nothing to focus on, no colors or light playing on waves, no land but the vague outline of Inishturk that never seemed to get any closer, I slipped into the mechanics of timing the paddle strokes with the waves rising on my left side. They were short and steep, shoulder-high, presenting a smooth blackness that I slid the blade into. A full stroke through the crest, the paddle exiting just as the wave passed under me, and I would slide sideways into the next trough. A right stroke through the back of the wave. Left stroke at the bottom of the trough, one more on the right, and I would feel the lift of the next wave. Hour after hour the cycle of crest and trough continued.

Four hours after leaving Killary Bay, I paddled into the lee of Inishturk. Two currachs were tied to a line that ran from a buoy to a weathered gray post jammed into a crack of rock. I stopped paddling twenty yards from a cleft that formed the sheltered anchorage and let the boat slide out of the swells into the calm beside the tarred boats. Suddenly there was quiet. It was like stepping through a doorway and leaving the noise and rolling of the sea outside.

I climbed out of my boat, left it resting above pools of seawater cupped in the fissures of the ledge, and walked over a crest of grass and rock. In front of me was the island harbor, big enough to hold several mid-sized fishing boats tied to the pier that left only a narrow opening to the sea. A fisherman was pulling crabs and starfish from a tangle of netting on the back of his boat. The crabs were dropped into a bucket, the starfish thrown over the side to settle on the bottom of the clear water. Aside from two women staring at me from the doorway of one of the houses above the harbor, there was no one else around. Island life was as quiet as the currach anchorage.

I had read in a guide for the west coast that there was a standing stone on the summit of Inishturk. That was one of the reasons I had paddled out, but not the only one. I also wanted to meet the people and see how they lived. I walked over for a chat with the fisherman.

When I said hello, he looked up from under a leather hat, the kind that Australian cowboys wear in the outback, and nodded as if he had been interrupted a hundred times that morning. He then went back to picking through the netting with yellow-gloved hands. Another couple of starfish were ripped out of the monofilament and hit the water with a splash. I asked him about the fishing. He said it was fair and broke off the legs of a crab tangled in the net. As the crab was tossed into the bucket and another handful of netting was shaken free of weed, he patiently answered my questions about the island. He didn't know anything about the standing stone but told me that ninety people lived on the island and that power from the mainland had come out nine or ten years ago. A boat from the mainland came out twice a week, if the weather was good, and brought mail and groceries. He spoke fast, and with a brogue so thick I caught only the gist of each sentence. When he asked how I had gotten out to the island, I told him. He stopped the net cleaning as if his hands had to be still to hear what I had said. "You've come out in a canoe?"

"Yeah, from Killary Bay."

With disbelief in his voice, he asked, "And where's yer boat now?"

"Well, I thought the harbor was where the currachs are tied. I came in there and left it pulled up on the rocks."

He looked at me with that familiar shake of his head that I had seen all along the coast. "Yer a hard man if you've come from Killary in a canoe."

I wasn't sure if it was a compliment or a question as to whether I had really paddled from the mainland.

When I told him I was headed for Caher, then Clare if the weather held, he said there was a road to the summit that would give me a good view of both islands. Maybe I would find the stone I was looking for. I thanked him and set off on the narrow lane that curved around the harbor and disappeared over a rise between two fields.

The road ended at an iron gate set in an opening of stone wall. I let myself through and carefully replaced the chain looped around a corner of stone. A grass track followed the folds of hills and slowly climbed to the interior. In places, the land leveled out and the track was wet with the same boggy waters that filled the depressions between the slopes. A few sheep grazing the hills jerked their heads up and bolted when I appeared around a bend or hump in the track. Eventually I left the track and headed straight up to the summit. Even on the steepest slope the ground held water like a sponge until my weight sank into the softness, and brown water ran over my toes. It was no wonder that the hills were so lush.

From the summit I could see the tiny wedged-shaped island of Caher three miles away, and further to the north the much larger island of Clare, looking inhospitable in the gray light. On the mainland, set aside from neighboring peaks by its near-perfect symmetrical form, was Croagh Patrick, the pilgrimage mountain. Each year hundreds of devout Catholics would climb the mountain, some barefoot, and pay homage to St. Patrick.

Five hundred feet below, the sea was a single plane of ripples that spread from horizon to mainland, empty except for the islands that bent the lines in breaking rings. If I watched a spot long enough, a white speck would appear, hang for an instant, then melt into the rows of waves that looked motionless across the expanse. I didn't realize ten miles of open water could look so empty. If it had been a sunny day, the summit would have been a perfect place for a nap. But the chill wind cut through the fleece clothing I was wearing and it wasn't long before I started down.

I half ran, hopped, and splashed my way off the summit, chuckling when my feet flew out from under me and I caught myself on the next clump of matted grass. Life was as good as it could get, simple and free as the sea and the hearty climb through the hills. What a marvelous moment, walking down a grass track in the middle of an Irish island without a care in the world and the blessing of a mind and body that were healthy and strong.

On the way back to the village, I saw a boy herding a dozen sheep through the gullies between the hills. He came up over the edge of a steep drop with a stick in his hand and two sheep bounding in front of him. I wanted to stop and talk with him but he was out of breath and the two troublesome sheep weren't following the main flock down the easy track. They doubled back on the lad and headed for higher ground, away from the dirty gray rumps of the other sheep grazing along the edge of the track. Frustration was written all over the boy's face.

I eased around the sheep, which ignored me, and eventually came to the gate and the road that led back to the harbor. I had been thinking about a hand-painted sign for tea and scones I remembered seeing in one of the cottage windows. It would be a nice way to cap off my visit to the island.

I knocked on the open door. There were muddy boots kicked off to one side and a sweater or coat tossed easily on the back of a wooden chair. It had the feeling of a working home, a comfortable welcoming feeling. A stout lady with an apron and rolled-up sleeves came down the short hall and welcomed me in. She led the way past the kitchen and into a room with a long wooden table and windows that looked out over the harbor. I could see a fellow working on one of two currachs turned over on the cobbles above high tide. He was painting or tarring a patch in the canvas. The crab boat with the fisherman I had talked to earlier was gone, maybe setting the nets again or checking his pots.

I asked for a pot of tea and scones, and while a teenage girl heated the water, the woman sat down at the table with me and chatted. Her name was Mary, an independent woman, strong and obviously someone who knew a hard day's work and how to get by when things weren't easy. She had that tough-love, no-nonsense way about her. The tea and scones came to the table steaming, and we talked.

Unlike some of the other islands, there isn't a ferry that comes out to Inishturk. Anyone who visits comes out on the mail boat or catches a ride with one of the fishermen. Visitors were not that common, and I obviously wasn't one that came off the boats or she would have known about me already. Mary's daughter came in and sat at the table while I told them about my paddling, where I had started, and what my impressions of Ireland were. It was an even exchange. I told them about the trip and Mary told me about island life.

"I grew up on the island, I did, but went to Dublin for work. Everyone does that, leave the island for money, and see 'tis the island way that we all miss. The young always go off. Ah, the city is fine for the young. I did it, but I wouldn't be leavin' the island now except for a visit."

Mary had her hands folded on the table, fingers intertwined. She sat facing the window looking out on the curve of the seawall, an endless horizon of sea and sky to one side and the distant green of the mainland to the other. As I dipped the shortbread in the tea and let the buttery treat melt in my mouth, she said, "When I came back from the mainland, I opened an unlicensed pub." Her eyes twinkled with mischief as she explained what an unlicensed pub was. "Well, ye see, on the mainland now, yer supposed to have a license if ye open a pub. Here on the island there was one pub but no one wanted to go to it, so I opened another. And it ran well for the better part of two years. The fishermen would bring out beer and whatever for me until . . . well, the island can be funny sometimes. There was a bit of a quarrel. Someone reported me to the Garda and they came out and shut me down. *The New York Times* did a story about me and the best part of what I'm tellin' ye is that a fellow from New York read that story and sent a letter addressed to the pub owner on Inishturk, saying how he was on my side and the mainlanders should mind their own business and let the islanders be. I have that letter to this day. To think a man from New York who I never laid eyes on would write and tell me he was on my side. He had never even been to Ireland."

I asked her if she knew anything of the standing stone I had read about.

"I wouldn't know about any stone but John Joe might. He's lived on the island all his life. A smart man, he is. He was the boat builder and carpenter. He's eighty-four now, never married. Same with his brother, God bless him. John Joe built this table. And that cupboard behind you. After ye finish yer tea, we'll go see if he's home."

Mary had her daughter pour another cup for the two of us and added a few more cookies to the empty dish.

Later, we walked around the front yard, following a curving path through high grass to the open door of another cottage. I followed Mary as she went into the dim house and called out for John Joe. Through a doorway with a picture of Jesus on the wall, an old man dressed in a dark jacket buttoned over a white shirt appeared. He was tall for a man of eighty-four, square-shouldered and handsome. Curled shavings of wood clung to his pant legs and he squinted as if the light from the open door was too harsh. His movements were slow but solid.

Mary introduced me. "This gentleman is paddling a canoe around Ireland and came out looking for a standing stone. Would you know anything about that, John Joe?"

He looked at me with an unhurried ease, then extended his hand with a firmness that surprised me not only for its strength but for the time he held mine in his. It wasn't just a cast-off greeting. It was a sincere welcome.

"Yer a hard man, ye are, to be paddling a canoe out to the island. And right round Ireland, yer going? Brave lad ye are." Then, remembering the stone, he said, "Another gentleman came to the island years ago and was asking for the same stone. There was one up on the hill I remember but 'tis gone now, I suppose, maybe fallen down an' covered in the bracken. Aoch, I haven't thought of it in years."

It didn't sound like I would find this elusive stone but it really didn't matter. I was more interested in learning about Mr. O'Toole. He invited us into the back room where wood chips lay where they had fallen beneath a chair pushed back from a table. On the table was a folding knife and a half-finished model of a currach, the hollow of the hull roughed out and the shape of the keel taking form. "I was doin' a wee bit of carvin'." He picked up a finished currach, two feet long, with all the details of the full-sized boats he used to build. He held the model gently in his hands and tilted it so I could see the ribs made of pine, the thwarts and seats of balsa. There was a pair of brightly colored oars. A coil of twine lay beside a miniature lobster pot.

I looked at his hands, large and weathered with sun spots, fingers that knew the feel of wood. Broad fingernails. In decades past he would have worked on the beach or in a stone shed bending the boards of oak or pine to a plan that existed only in his mind. Each boat different, built to what-ever needs the owner had: moving sheep to other islands, fishing for mack-erel, or pulling willow lobster traps.

In the dim light of the room, I knew I was looking at a man of the past: the island boat builder. I envied him not only the skill with which he had built those beautiful light craft but also his place in the community. Car-penter and boat builder, there was honor in both titles. I was certain that within Mr. O'Toole's memory were stories of island life in the twenties and thirties, stories that he must have heard his parents and neighbors tell around winter fires, memories of storms that must have pounded the sea-wall and thrown spray onto the panes of the houses above the harbor. Memories of music and laughter, times of plenty and times of need. In eighty-four years this quiet, humble man who whittled away at models of currachs must have seen it all. To live for a day in his mind would open a window into the island's past.

After we left Mr. O'Toole to his carving, Mary told me John Joe and his brother had been self-taught men, great readers, who knew the world's geography and history through books that found their way out to the island. As we walked the path to Mary's house, I wondered if he would still be alive if I came back to Ireland on a bicycle trip. Would the path be worn from the coming and going of neighbors checking on him or would it be overgrown and the door closed?

The winds were buffeting the wildflowers in the yard when I said good-bye to Mary and her daughter. I thanked them for the tea and scones, which they refused to take any money for. I promised to write as they bid me blessings and farewell. I never found the standing stone, but as I followed the road back to the harbor, then up and over the rocks to where the boat sat brilliant yellow on gray rock, I knew I had found more. The last image of the island was that of a small boy whose face appeared framed in a window of lace, the curtain pushed aside as he gazed out from the protection of his island home. I waved and the face vanished. As I slid into the boat and gently backed out of the sheltered cove, I could feel him watching me again, an island lad gazing with wonder as I leaned the boat over and slowly turned so the bow pointed across the breaking waves toward Caher.

The winds had picked up during the four hours I was on Inishturk, and now the sea was covered in whitecaps and steep waves breaking on top of a larger swell. The morning weather report had called for moderate south-westerlies increasing to Force 5 and 6 by late afternoon. Once again the Irish Meteorological Office, or Met, forecast had been right on. The seas were noisy and boisterous as they grew with the winds that surfed me three miles to Caher.

The fisherman on Inishturk had said there was only one landing on the island, around the back side, that would be sheltered in the southwesterly winds. As I drew closer to the west end of the island, the heavier crash of swells meeting cliff mixed with the rasp of breaking waves and the wind tearing past my ears. The island looked as if it had been upended from the ocean bottom, the west tip a two hundred–foot vertical wall that tapered smoothly to the east, where fingers of rock tripped the waves into a confused rumble of white water. If the winds had been stronger, I could have let them push me around the western tip and would have approached the landing on the leeward side. But I didn't want that shelter. I wanted to feel the exposure of the windward side, to see the gusts of wind race over the contours of land and flatten the grass in waves of lighter green. I wanted to see the island meeting the oncoming winds and seas. I paddled a hundred yards off the windward side, alert to any wave that broke in the same spot more than once and altering course if it did. It was a wild introduction to the tiny island.

I swung wide around the breakers on the east end, then followed the shoreline into the gradually calmer waters of the north side. At a place where the island dipped, I found the landing that the fisherman had told me about. It wasn't much, just a break in the jumble of boulders below the low cliffs. In a north wind, a landing would be impossible.

I rested the paddle across the cockpit and sat looking not at the landing twenty feet in front of the bow but above it, at a slab cross standing against a darkening storm sky. Gusts of wind found their way through the cut in the land and pushed the boat back toward open water. With a few strokes I eased in closer, waited for a surge to lift me clear of a rock, then rode the back of the wave onto a pile of kelp that cushioned my landing.

It was hard work getting the boat above the reach of the waves. I used the padding of kelp to cradle the keel as I jammed my feet between rounded rocks and slowly pulled it to higher ground. I pulled until the stern was almost off the kelp, set the bow carefully down, and went back for an armful of the slippery weed. With a cushion beneath the bow, I would lift the stern and push until the boat teetered on the padding beneath the cockpit. Then back to the bow, lift and pull until the stern was again ready to fall off the green-brown kelp. Three or four cycles of this pushing and pulling, a broken toenail from jamming it under a rock, and I was finally above the reach of the tide. I stood breathing heavily beside the boat and looked up at the ravine and silhouetted stone.

Maybe it was the sky, the clouds heavy and black, that gave the island a feeling of mystery and energy. Sheltered from the winds, I knew that once I left the boulders and walked up the ravine, I would be blasted by the approaching storm. I wanted to be ready for it. With my back to the winds I pulled on fleece and raingear, then sat hunched beside the boat eating a quick sandwich, staring at a wild sea, grateful to be in the relative shelter of the island.

I turned from the cobbles and boulders of the beach and walked up into the wind, which tore at my clothes and watered my eyes. The cross stood on a knoll surrounded by rocks that held it upright. It was four feet high, five inches thick, and chiseled in a strange form of a crude cross. When I was beside it and looked through the confusing patterns of lichens, I could see that it was far more than a cross. On the flat of the stone were shapes cut in relief, raised squares with simple designs that I couldn't make sense of. I stepped closer, lost the image, then backed away again. Out of the patterns of lichen they reappeared, mysterious as before. A third of the way down was a face that stared out on the landing with hollow eyes and mouth agape. A warning? A blessing? The threshold of sacred ground?

Behind the stone in a sheltered hollow was a small chapel, its end gables and walls standing within the remains of an enclosure that was fallen and overgrown. Beyond the outer wall were plots of parallel tillage lines that the thick tangle of green could not hide. I had read that some of these plots may have been laid in Celtic times, hundreds of years earlier than the seventh-century monastic ruins that I was looking at. In an arc extending two or three hundred yards out from the chapel and silhouetted against the black sky were other standing stones and crosses. Stones that knew a thousand nights like this. I could almost see the hooded monks moving from station to station in meditation.

Before I entered the chapel, I wanted to feel the land the monks of thirteen hundred years ago had felt beneath their feet. I took a long, slow walk into the wind, the sky layered in clouds heavy with rain, and the gusts strong enough to throw me off balance. In places my feet sank into tannic brown waters that the matting of grass floated on. In other areas, I walked on gray ledges with fragile sea pinks growing out of the cracked rock and bending double in the wind.

On the western end of the island, just back from the abrupt cliffs was a shallow pond, the source of fresh water for the eremitical monks. I stood at the boggy edge, felt the wavelets wash over my toes, and squatted down to taste the waters. Who were the holy men who had walked this island and drunk from this pond? Did I dare go into that part of my mind and soul to feel their presence, their spirit? Was I worthy? Like the chapel itself, it was a sacred place to go.

Surrounded by the unchanged landscape, the winds, and the distant rumble of surf, I took a deep breath and let it out, heard it leave my body, felt my chest relax, and listened as the void filled with inner peace. In the pause between breaths, that silence of the body and mind when all is quieted, I heard nothing, thought nothing. They were seconds of purity, hallowed emptiness beside a pond on a windswept holy island. A gift of the saints.

When I was ready, I turned with the wind, felt it fill the hollow of my back, and let it push me in the direction I had come. It had been a lonely walk, an hour of feeling the immediacy of the land at my feet, the wildness of nature, and the certainty that others had been quieted by the same rich loneliness. From the crest of a small hillock I could see the tiny chapel a half mile away. Barely sheltered in a depression that was greener than the surrounding hills, it sat in ruins, yet still spoke of refuge. I left the height of the island and slowly moved with the winds into the great circle formed by the standing stones. I walked a few yards, stopped, let the winds blow through my mind, then continued.

The walk had calmed, emptied, and prepared me for the austerity of the chapel. I stood in front of the narrow, low doorway with the graceful arch of stones set on edge. It seemed to be waiting patiently for me to enter. I stooped low and stood quietly, with my back against one wall, my face relaxed, and my eyes gently moving from lichen-covered rock to vertical slit window and finally to a stone bowl resting on a slab of altar beneath the open roof.

The bowl was thick-walled, three inches high and maybe ten inches across. Surrounded by the walls of the chapel whose ledges and cracks held the roots of grasses, it was perfect not in its crude balance of shape or form but rather in its focus. While the winds tore at the stones and filled the air with noise, the bowl sat in crude perfection as it had for a thousand years or more, testimony to the hands that had carved it out of solid stone.

Minutes slipped by as I stood and listened to the walls and the stillness of my soul. Nothing could have been more real than the absolute truth of those moments, the almost frightening feeling of smallness in time and space. The smallness came from knowing that I offered nothing of myself to the moment, nothing but silence. How could I offer anything more? Surrounded by winds, the approaching storm, and the solitude of a tiny island battered by waves heard above the noise of the wind, I knew complete and pure emptiness. I felt it on my skin; heard it in my breathing. Within the walls of that tiny chapel, I knew I stood with other sandaled feet and robed figures.

I crossed the chapel floor to the narrow window above the bowl. Through the thickness of stone I could see an outside altar and several sculptured slab crosses amid the fallen rocks of the outer wall. Weeds bending in the wind revealed the coarse grain of weathered stone, scales of lichen, and the graceful curve of a Celtic cross. Later, I would crouch beside the leaning stone and trace the lines of the carved cross with the tips of my fingers.

The window in front of me was a picture of detailed stone on stone, of gray light and soft shadow. In past centuries, when the chapel was roofed with either thatch or sod, the window would have been the only light in the little room.

Below the window sat the bowl, its roundness resting on a near-perfect slab of stone. A raised bead of carved stone followed the rim of the bowl and showed the patience and skill of the carver. I gently lifted it, felt its weight resting in the curve of my palms and fingers, felt also the age that I held. I turned it slowly, one side thicker than the other, then set it down so it touched the slab with a whisper of contact.

I stepped back, let my eyes wander over the walls, the floor, and the altar, then turned and left as quietly as I had entered.

Later, as the winds bellied the tent fabric and threatened to rip the stakes piled with stones out of the shallow soil, I sat listening to the rain and writing in my journal. I was living in two worlds: deep in the folds of my thoughts and feelings one moment, then suddenly pulled back to the surface by the blast of another powerful gust. I would unzip the tent a few inches, look out at the sea that was ripping past the island in a chaos of black waves and stark white froth, then glance down to the boat turned over on the rocks below. Satisfied, I zipped the flapping tent shut and retreated into thoughts that pulled me deeper.

I thought about why I was attracted to lonely and ancient places such as the Skelligs, Blasket Island, the many ruins I had walked through, and now the silence of the standing crosses and simple bowl of Caher Island. Much of the attraction was to the people who had walked on lands that now were empty. It was their humanness that I wanted to feel, the realness of hands that lifted stone and built walls or carved ancient slabs and stone bowls. The stones—all that is left in these desolate places—provided the link, the spiritual, almost flesh-and-blood connection to that past.

By moving slowly along a land that was empty and ancient, I would have had to have been spiritually blind not to see the contrast and fragility of our own time measured against past ages. Perhaps it was that contrast, that need for something more permanent, which silenced me and pulled me into the quiet of my soul.

On Caher Island, as on the Skelligs, it was the sacredness of the early Christian ruins that pulled me inward. Within the walls of these monasteries, I could walk with the spirits of monks and know that my soul—

that part of me which is the essence of my life—was listening to the same silence that they had in the sixth or seventh century. It was not the rituals of their religion that moved me. It was their brotherhood, the shared awe of reaching across the barrier of humanity and approaching the divine in silence. I didn't know the ceremonies and prayers that the stones of the chapel had heard for hundreds of years. I didn't know the individuals, their strengths or weaknesses. I only knew the same desire, to be still enough to feel the stirring of the soul. Perhaps it was the monk within me that was responding to the same silence the ancient ones sought on these islands.

In the last light of the day, I wrote these thoughts. My eyes were heavy and I wanted the comfort of the bag and the sleep that would quickly close over me as soon as I closed the journal. I wanted to set the pen down; but there was more I had to write.

I thought of the monks again and what they would think of the trash washed up on the only landing on the island. I also thought of the rocks themselves, the boulders that sat exposed at low water, and the smaller rounded rocks that knew the weight of every man, woman, or child who had ever stepped from a boat onto the island. In a world of stone and ancient tillage plots that had felt the passage of centuries and saints, of invasions both peaceful and murderous, the landing now held the glaring color of plastic bottles trapped beneath the rocks.

I didn't want to see the plastic, the waste of our throwaway culture washed onto the rocks of this holy island. Was this our contribution to the island's history? I knew I saw these and the other ruins in a somewhat purified state, the crumbled walls and collapsed roofs burying in time and turf the waste and imperfection of the people from past centuries. I had the benefit of seeing the skeleton upon which I could clothe the past, but I also had the frightening knowledge of a world that had absorbed too much abuse. Instead of bringing to the island prayers and humility, we let our trash find its way on the tides to the rocks below the slab cross.

I finally closed the journal, unzipped the tent to check the boat again, and gazed up at the dark shape of the standing stone looking down on the landing. In the darkness, I could not see the face, the hollow eyes carved into the stone and staring into the blackness. I didn't have to see it to know it was there. For over a thousand years that face had watched over many a stormy night. Tonight would be just one more.

Tales from an Irish Lad

Come away, O human child!
To the waters and the wild
With a fairy, hand in hand,
For the world's more full of weeping
Than you can understand.

—W. B. Yeats, "The Stolen Child"

On the morning I left Culler Island, I woke to winds out of
the southwest at Force 5 to 6, twenty to twenty-five mph. I
hadn't slept much the previous night because of the slapping and
popping of the tent and I wasn't looking forward to the six-mile crossing
to Clare Island.

The storm had passed during the night and now there was more blue in
the sky than tumbling balls of white cotton. Cool shadows of cloud floated
over the island, covering its narrow width in seconds, then raced out to
sea and let the heat of the sun soak into the morning.

In the warmth of the tent with the flaps tied back and the view of Clare
Island framed in the opening, I catnapped and waited to see what the winds
would do. I didn't expect them to drop, not with the clouds racing as they
were, but it was an excuse to catch up on some needed sleep. I awoke
several times, looked at the mainland, at Croagh Patrick mottled in shadow
and light, listened to the wind, and drifted back into sleep.

When my body had enough rest I was instantly awake, methodically
reaching for stuff sacks and organizing gear for the repacking of the boat.
As I set each bag outside the tent, I subconsciously felt the winds; they

were still out of the southwest and holding steady. The seas would be at my back, coming over my left shoulder. The crossing would be fast, and a little wild, but now I was eager to launch. Within a half hour, all the gear was packed away and I was dressed in my paddling clothes: a pair of nylon shorts, lightweight quick-drying shirt, and the shell of the paddling jacket that would protect me from a soaking with its wrist and neck gaskets.

I launched off the same padding of seaweed I had piled at the high water mark. A swell lifted the bow off the rocks and, as it receded, pulled the stern easily off the tangled heap. Instantly, the wind pushed me out into the chop wrapping around the ends of the island. I paused and looked back at the landing and the standing stone, then turned away and looked to Clare Island.

Once I was out of the wind and wave shadow of Caher, the following seas lifted the stern and tried to twist the boat broadside to the swells. For awhile I fought to keep the bow pointed at the top of Clare Island, the only part I could see above the waves. With every second or third wave, the stern shifted to the right. I would wait for it to pass under me, correct the course, and begin again. It was fatiguing and frustrating, and within a mile I changed tactics. There wasn't any sense in competing with the sea for endurance; if the winds increased, I would need every ounce of strength and a better angle of approach to the island. I let the bow swing out to sea and settled into the smoother flow of paddling in the troughs. Now the sea and winds were coming broadside.

For a mile I paddled ninety degrees from the island, the boat tracking as straight as an arrow in the troughs. I paddled with my face turned to the winds, eyes glued to each approaching wave, guessing at which second it might topple. If I thought it would break at a point where our courses met, I would back off, watch it turn from deep blue to glistening silver, then blinding white as it unloaded the top third of its height. The rumble of broken water would run for ten or fifteen feet, then be absorbed into the next wave. Time and again I watched as waves broke, re-formed, and broke again. The ones that swept under the boat and broke to my right, I didn't worry about. They were noisy and it was tempting to turn and look, but in that instant of distraction, three or four other waves were building and racing toward me.

On a cloudy day, these same conditions would have shaken me; there was too much noise and too many waves to keep track of. Without the sun, the waves would have felt bigger and more hostile, the crossing a desperate struggle both physically and emotionally. Today, it was more of a game, a wild one of guessing when to push and when to back off and let the sea have its way. This was the kind of day I loved. The sea was demanding and required constant attention, but it also fired me with energy.

When I had a better angle for approaching the island, I turned with the wind and felt the first swell lift and begin to surf the boat. A few strokes of the paddle held the boat on the face of the swell and suddenly I was racing with the speed of the seas. Between the large swells were smaller wind waves that the bow sliced through. A wave broke in front and to the right. While it was frozen in those seconds of re-forming, I flew past it and sliced into another smaller wave, throwing spray into the air that washed my face with its coldness. The boat was moving so fast that any forward strokes were useless. I held the blades clear of the water, leaned back, and hoped the bow wouldn't dive into the back of the swell in front of me. A touch of the back of the paddle on either side kept the bow racing straight for the island.

I was miles from land, surfing the waves, and feeling wild and free. Once in a great while, the forces of the sea and the winds combine and flow together in near-perfect unison. This was one of those days and to be part of it was the joy of paddling a tiny boat on the ocean. It was also a time when being alone on all of that vastness was frightening. There was so much speed and power in the waves that I knew if something went wrong, I would be upside down in a second. It was a thin line to dance upon, yet it was so pure in its wildness that I would not have wanted the safety of a windy camp.

It wasn't the adrenaline I was after. It was more a desire to be part of the winds and the sea when they were at their peak. I wanted to know that moment, to feel it through the boat, and hear it in the sound of the winds and the waves. It was a matter of taking a calculated risk in order to be a part of that moment. Whether I was sitting in the cell of a beehive hut and feeling the presence of a monk's spirit, or racing with the power of an ocean swell driving me across five miles of open water, I opened myself to both extremes.

The high I was feeling mirrored the swells driving me toward Clare Island. They had been generated far out at sea and rolled in at different intervals and heights. Between the larger sets I had a chance to rest and breathe easy, glancing over my shoulder and waiting for the next big set. Pivoting halfway around in the seat, I could see them bearing down. They were easy to spot, their faces a darker blue and tossing the smaller wind waves over their crests as they raced forward. As the set approached, I pulled hard on the paddle, let the first wave pass, then sprinted to stay in front of the second. If I caught it right, the wave would pick me up and I would be off and flying again.

In an hour, the distance to Clare had dropped to less than a mile. Ravines, stone walls, and shadowed glens rose from the cliffs whose base was strung with a necklace of glaring white. Closer yet, I could see specks on the island's hillsides, heads lowered and nibbling frantically away as if in a race to graze the entire treeless island. I had timed the crossing well. From the west a band of dark clouds marked a frontal system that promised more rain.

As I followed the curve of the cliffs, the waves gradually lost their power in the lee of the island and the transition from ocean to land slowly began. The square tower of a castle standing solid above a grass-covered point marked the harbor. This was the castle of Grace O'Malley, the pirate and plunderer of the sixteenth century. Granuaile, as she was called, was as feared as any male pirate and demanded payment from all, including the royal vessels of Queen Elizabeth. Legend has it that the queen, who was equally ruthless and murderous, sent for Granuaile and received her at court not as a prisoner but with full honors. A truce was agreed upon whereby the royal Tudor merchants England depended for its wealth would no longer suffer the humiliation and ravages of the Irish pirate. In return, Granuaile's coastal towers stocked with cargoes lightened from the queen's fleet would be hers to keep. Queen and pirate parted as equals. Grace O'Malley retained not only her treasures but also her dominance of the sea and lived on into her seventies. When death finally came in 1603 for the woman who bowed to no man or royalty, she was buried in the twelfth-century abbey on Clare Island. The remains of her castle with its square tower and arrow slits stands guard over the harbor from where her ships sailed.

I paddled beneath the tower set against the last blue of the sky and let the swells carry me toward a sandy beach. Above the beach was a road that connected a handful of white houses on one end, and the ferry-pier and castle on the other. A tractor was parked on the pier beside a stack of lobster pots. Several thick-framed bicycles with wire baskets and rusty rims leaned against a stone wall that crowded the narrow road. The harbor felt friendly, past and present living side by side. It was a good place to sit out the rains that were only moments away.

The waves picked up the light brown of suspended sands and broke with a rumble on the beach. I nosed the bow onto the back of a wave, rode it for a few seconds, then felt the keel bump the sandbottom. Before the next wave could fill the cockpit with a slurry of sand and water, I jumped out, dragged the boat over the soft sand, and set it down beside an overturned rowboat. In those few seconds, I had gone from being a sea creature to an upright land animal. Now part hermit crab and part chameleon, I discarded my fiberglass shell and changed colors as I pulled off the spray deck and sun-faded blue paddle jacket. Moments later, I walked into the pub above the harbor and melted into the crowd of tourists escaping the first drops of rain that splattered the sun-heated road and sent wisps of steam into the air.

I ordered a pot of tea and scones, carried them to a table in the corner, and once again thought how odd the transition felt. A miniature teapot, china plate, and teacup—all so orderly and clean. The clink of spoons stirring tea. Laughter and Dutch accents from a wet foursome sitting on a bench near the window. Was it only yesterday I had crouched on boggy ground beside the pond on Caher? It didn't seem possible for the two worlds to be so different yet so close—a six-mile paddle away.

While the rain came down in sheets and spilled off the slate roof in a steady cascade of mini-waterfalls, I burned my tongue on the hot tea and wrote letters to friends and family. How could I tell them of all I had seen and felt in the last few days? Islands and crossings, encounters with the people past and present, and always one eye on the weather, the other on the sea. The words written on blue aerogram paper that folded with glued edges told so little, yet hinted at so much.

In an hour, the downpour had stopped as suddenly as it had begun. The sun burst through the clouds, poured through the open door with crisp freshness, and the constant flow of water off the eaves slowed to drips that fell in still pools. A few letters written, a bit of food in my stomach, and I was ready to find a camping spot for the night.

I walked into the dazzling sunlight and around to the back side of the pub. It seemed an odd place for a post office, but the fellow behind the bar had pointed over his shoulder with his thumb when I asked about buying some stamps.

In a room barely big enough to fit a desk crowded with papers and stacks of letters bound with rubber bands, the postmistress held her office. She sat with her back to a door that must have led to the pub, and looked out onto the harbor and the mainland four miles away. From her glass-enclosed cubicle, she could see tourists and locals alike queuing up for the ferry. Groceries, mail, livestock, and tourists, they all passed within view of her window on the world. Below the windowsill, the surf broke and melted into the golden sands. I waited outside as a local farmer asked about sending a parcel to some place he wasn't sure had a post office. She assured him that the address on the package was fine; not to worry, it would find its way for certain. There was a familiar ease and trust about their exchange. The farmer with his high rubber boots, pant legs stuffed in the tops, and tattered sweater, left with a wave and a cheery farewell. I took his place at the elbow-high counter, the same height as any mail counter in the world, but with a view that million-dollar-home owners would gladly trade for: a castle, a crescent beach of gold, and the green mainland across dancing blue water.

I asked for a half dozen stamps for the States. After the coins were slid one way and the stamps the other, I asked if she knew of any place to land a small boat on the east side of the island. She hesitated a second, then asked, "What kind of a boat is it?"

I pointed to it resting on the sand below the seawall. Even to my eye that knew the strength of its design and seaworthiness, it looked fragile. She echoed my thoughts. "That's a wee bit of a boat, it is. There's a beach on the far side of the island but I wouldn't be knowin' if the waves are on it the likes of today. There's the old harbor next but it's all stone and no way for ye to land there. It's the beach you'll be wantin' to try."

I thanked her for the stamps and the advice and squeezed past a young couple behind me.

The island ferry silently overtook me as I paddled out of the harbor. Tourists on the upper deck pointed their cameras and waved as the ship ghosted past. The winds that buffeted the paddles and lifted small waves to break on my bow barely breathed on the hundred-foot steel hull. As she crossed the harbor mouth in front of me and turned south, her engines rumbled to life, churning the water into fits of white boils that erupted from her stern. In twenty minutes, maybe a half hour, she would be moored to the pier on the mainland.

I paddled wide of the eastern point of the island where the winds pushed the waves onto the shallows with noisy, continuous breakers. Behind the tip, the waters were calmer, the wind waves were held at bay, with only the swells wrapping around the point to break on the curve of land. The island rose steadily in the soft shadow of grazed pasture. The sun, past its zenith, lit only the tops of the higher hills and cast shadows that reached into steep-sided ravines. I paddled out of the sunlight streaming over the peaks and into the cool dampness of the island's shadow. The only thing that disturbed the peaceful setting was the steady rumble of surf collapsing on cobbles and rock ledge.

Another mile of paddling brought me to a rocky point that lifted and ran like a spine, spilling folds of green to either side and climbing steeply from the sea. Around that point was a rocky stretch and a beach that unfortunately had to be the one the postmistress had told me about. Every few seconds, a line of swell rolled innocently toward the cobbles, until a few feet from the layers of small stones. It suddenly peaked and toppled over itself with a crunching roar. That was one landing I didn't want to tangle with.

Beyond the beach was the harbor, the second possibility. I paddled over and looked at the two arms of rock that reached out from the land and stopped short of closing the circle of stone by the width of two fishing boats. I sat just beyond the entrance and watched the swells reach through the opening and roll high onto a boat ramp of mortar and rock, the only possible landing inside the unused harbor. The swells raced up the ramp at an angle that sent them cascading over the outer edge in a four-foot drop of white water meeting the lift and swirls of the same swell. In an emergency, I might try a landing, but this wasn't an emergency. The safer of the two would be the beach.

I turned the boat slowly around and paddled back for a second look. Dumping surf, a brief lull while the swell pulled back and the rocks drained free, then another thunderous *whumph* that the hills echoed back. I remembered a similar landing, larger waves but on sand. It was a misjudgment of distance and timing that caused the searing pain of a broken rib when the wave tossed me upside down like a piece of driftwood. It had been two years but that second of impact was still fresh in my mind.

I turned away from the beach and looked at the mainland five miles away, an option that I hadn't considered until that moment. I could have returned to the beach at the village, but what would tomorrow's weather bring? The winds could increase or shift to the north and I would be windbound. The afternoon was clear, the winds strong but favorable. Marginal conditions for a solo crossing.

Decisions.

Across the water the mainland was bathed in the afternoon sun. Shadow and light defined valleys and west-facing hills that looked more welcoming than the rhythmic thundering of swell behind me. Beyond the shelter of the island, the seas were lifting as the larger swells straightened from the curve of Clare Island and rolled away in the sunlight. They would be at my back. Five, six miles. It would take an hour, maybe a bit more, depending on how steep they were and what the winds were doing once I got out of the lee of the island. It was a gamble.

Considerations clicked through my mind, familiar ones that had been on every trip I had done. The thoughts weren't linear but more a matter of options weighed against risks. The decisions to push on, retreat, or find an escape route all depended on elements I could not see, the unknown quantity of wind and the blindness of sitting two feet above the waves and trying to guess what the seas three miles out might be like. Somehow, all the options and risks were balanced and the first pull of the paddle started the crossing. I slipped across the line of shadow and sunlight and pointed the bow at a ravine that I thought might be Achill Sound. That shaded ravine and a compass bearing would tell me if I was being set one way or the other with the falling tide.

The first two miles went as I expected, big swells similar to the ones on the Caher crossing with wind-generated waves breaking between and on top of them. I watched the compass, kept the stern perpendicular with the waves, and surfed every swell I could, glad to have the fifty-yard bursts of speed that chewed away at the crossing.

Somewhere in the middle, the waves suddenly felt different. Whether it was the increasing wind or that I was finally out of the protection of Clare Island, I didn't know. Whatever the cause, the six- to eight-footers that had been the norm were now building, steamrolling with a power and speed that kindled a fear in my gut. They were steeper, bigger in volume, and seemed to be growing by the minute. Behind me were walls of water that looked like the side of a mountain bearing down and tossing aside four-foot waves like they were a nuisance. Clare Island was a black silhouette of shadow that disappeared from view as the swells towered over the troughs I sat in. I was certain the tops would crumble and sweep down, burying me like an avalanche. Instead, each time I felt a compressive lifting.

The boat shot upward and forward on the shoulder of the wave, then balanced precariously on the thin crest. One second the weight of my body shoved skyward seemed to force the air from my lungs, and the next instant complete weightlessness as the boat hung in midair before the backward slide into trough. In the belly of the swell, three- and four-footers harassed the boat, seemingly panicked by the larger swells that towered above. I backpaddled, braced, and turned on the top of a small wave, trying to keep the stern into the next swell. Again the massive uplifting, the sudden weight and weightlessness, the winds at the top that tore past my ears and tried to twist the paddles from my fingers. The surreal view of the wave in front racing away and dropping me backwards. Broken water washed over the cockpit and the horizon line changed with each toss of the boat.

There was so much noise: the wind, the breaking waves, and the boat getting slapped sideways as the bow rose out of an unintentional surf and was hit by a broadside wave. There was so much confusion, and yet the boat and my reflexes were working as they should. There was the instinctive reach and pull of the paddles, the midstroke change of thrust from pulling to bracing, and letting the power of a broken wave sweep under the boat. "Break away, my friend, behind, to the side, or in front, but not on me. Spend your energy elsewhere. . . . Yikes, watch that one, it's a roller!" The wave slams me to one side, then lets me go. In my mind I talked to myself, told myself which wave to watch, and to settle down when the coiled fear began to unwind into panic. I listened to my breath, forced it out, slowed it down, and closed the circle around me, mentally pulling in to fifteen yards and locking on to that perimeter defense.

I was amazed at how quickly my body responded to the twisting boat, how my spine pivoted and bent at the waist and somehow kept the boat under me. Visually, there was only chaos, and yet in the water-sky-water turmoil there was a balance and a pattern that my eye and inner ear found and that directed the forward motion of the boat. The miracle was that the boat crawled forward at all. In a world that raced past in blurring sensory overload, the paddle still spun and the hull crept toward the land.

The land: blessed refuge or cursed executioner? It stood firm against the explosive power of waves that climbed high and blackened its face with streams of sea pouring off. Waves filled with power and energy, born a thousand miles out to sea, gathered speed and met the rock with thunderous finality. Vertical walls threw the waves back in sheets of white as defiant as the waves themselves, echoing concussions that measured distance and resonated in my chest. Clouds of mist, ionized vapor that was once ocean swell, hung in midair and gave birth to rainbows.

I aimed for a point at the base of the cliff, the tip of Achillbeg Island, where the tidal flow emptied Achill Sound. Too far to the right and the ebbing tide would stall the boat, freeze it where the waves stood side by side spilling their white tops and not moving more than a few feet over the shifting sands of the bottom. Too close to the cliff base, the world of hidden rocks and boomers that folded with a sickening roar, and the waves would not be the only life broken by the rocks. Between the two forces was a line that neither laid claim to, a channel that felt both the pull of the tide on its edge and the confusion of fragmented swells. It was hallowed ground, a safe refuge that I read partly with my eyes and that of the resistance of the blades pulling the boat toward safety. Progress was measured by watching the cliff face slowly pass to my left.

Minute by minute, the waves receded, took with them the noise of broken water, and I was left with the distant rumble of the sea meeting the cliff behind me. Another quarter mile and I let the boat glide, the paddle resting across the cockpit, my muscles draining from the postadrenaline rush.

I paddled around the last rock that led into the narrows of Achill Sound. The shadow of its bulk absorbed the last whisper of wind and the fading rumble of swell. I slipped into a world that was suddenly tame, quiet in a way that washed through me with assurance. In front of me were cultivated fields gently sloping to the shimmer of sand beaches and the smooth-flowing ribbon of water separating Achill Island from the mainland.

I stayed in the shadow of Achillbeg Island and followed the rocks that gradually gave way to pockets of sand and finally a long, sweeping beach. On the hills above were sheep trails and peeling whitewashed cottages

staring empty and forlorn at the mainland a half mile away. With each
pull of the paddle, the bottom became clearer as it gently sloped up toward
the surface. The last few strokes stirred the sand into swirls. I lay the paddle
alongside the cockpit, holding it against the boat with open palm and bent
elbow, leaned back in a deep stretch and closed my eyes. The gentle lift
and nudge of keel against sand finished the crossing.

Hours later, the sun cast the shadow of the tent off the knoll I was camped
on, and stretched it across sheep track and shorn grass. Below, the boat
was pulled to the edge of the beach where the grazed hill broke off and
the roots of the grass showed through layers of sand and dirt and shell. I
was cleaning up after dinner; rinsing pots, dismantling the stove, and looking forward to sitting and writing. Across a little valley that in ancient
times must have been a marsh or an inlet of the sea that nearly cut the
island in two, I saw a boy walking along the sands. He left the edge of the
beach where the sands were firm and headed toward my camp, leaving a
crooked line of deep tracks.

He waved just beyond calling distance and stepped up on the slope of
the hill. Copper-haired and lanky, he looked to be fifteen, maybe sixteen,
a lad out for a stroll on the land. He disappeared behind a hillock, then
topped the shelf of land below the tent, called out hello, and walked higher
until his head was even with where I sat.

"I saw your tent from our house and was wondering who you were."

He couldn't have been any more up front than that. Whoever this kid
was, I liked him. What struck me was how sure of himself he was. Not in
an aggressive way but certainly not like any adolescent I had known.

He introduced himself as Ruairi (Rory) Bourke and immediately asked
where I had come from and if the boat—"It's called a kayak, isn't it?"—
on the beach was mine. I told him about my trip, where I had started and
where I was heading. I explained that I had to wait for the tide, there was
no way to beat against the strength of the current running between mainland and island, and that it would be noon tomorrow before I would be
away. He knew when high water was and that halfway through the narrows
the tide split, flooding and ebbing from the far end. It was a complication
that I had known of but for a teenager I was surprised he knew the rhythm
of the sea. It was one of many ways of the island Ruairi was to tell me of.

He asked why I was taking this trip. A pointblank question that caught me off guard. There weren't the usual questions about the boat, what the seas were like, or how far I had come that day. He just wanted to know why. I sensed he asked a lot of questions like that. Reaching for answers as any boy will at sixteen, not the hazy esoteric answers of a man almost forty but more direct ones. Answers that he could grapple with, toss around, and either accept or reject. In hindsight, maybe I was doing the same things. I told him I was interested in people, the history of Ireland, and that I had traveled a lot on the sea and loved the birds, the cliffs, and the feeling of wildness on the ocean. It wasn't a complete answer but it came close and I let it go at that. I was twice his age plus a few years, but there was enough boy in me to appreciate his abrupt challenges and questions.

"I can show you the island. There's a ring fort above the cliffs and a holy well." It was more a statement than anything else.

"Okay, let's go." The journal could wait and I was humble enough to know that this lad could probably shed some light on the island. It turned out to be more light than I could have imagined.

As we walked, he told me of the cottages on the hills, one of which his family had fixed up and used as a holiday home. They had been abandoned in the sixties, the same problems of a dwindling population and easier times on the mainland that I had heard before. But this island had a twist of tragedy. Walking past the schoolhouse with its slate roof folded in and grass growing on the chimneytop brought the tragedy out of the past.

It was Christmas Eve, 1965. "The father of eight children—most of the kids in the school—was out on the sea. He fell overboard and drowned. The mother wouldn't stay on the island. She took the children and left. There were only a few families living here and not many children. The government couldn't afford to pay a teacher to live on the island and they shut the school down."

It was the final chapter not only for the school but also for the village. Too many vacant houses already boarded up, then one more tragedy that brought the village to an end. Where the father was going or coming from on that Christmas Eve, Ruairi didn't say; maybe he didn't know. The point of the story was that it was the end of an era.

There was more to see. We left the houses and school behind, their doors nailed shut while the roofs decayed and collapsed.

He told me how in the winter, the gales would blow the seas over the rocks guarding the far end of the lowland. Where we walked would be flooded with seawater. We crossed a bog, Ruairi jumping from clumps of grass and me walking through the brown waters and feeling the land through the stained skin of my feet. We walked not so much across the boggy low valley but along it, first on one side, then the other, depending where the driest footings were. Up on the shoulder of the far hill we followed a sheep trail. Droppings—some fresh, some old—lay scattered amid splayed footprints in the soft mud and trampled grass. They led to a band of thick grass running across the track as true as the trickle of clear water dribbling from a circle of stones dug into and draining off the hillside. This was the holy well.

Balanced on the flat of a stone was a cup. Ruairi leaned over, peered in, and said, "We used to take the money that the women would leave. They'd take some water and leave a few coins."

"What would they do with the water?" I asked.

He shrugged and said, "They thought it could cure sickness. But I don't know what they did with it."

I looked at the little spring, the stones overgrown with grass but still holding a pool of clear water pouring gently off the lip. Fresh water on an island. The basic element of survival woven with the color of superstitions. Who first saw the dampness and dug a shallow pit, watched it fill, and decided it was worthy of more work? No one could assign an age to something so simple, so quiet in its gurgled secrets. I caught up with Ruairi and climbed steadily for another quarter mile until the land abruptly leveled off with the noise of the seas hammering the cliffs below.

In front of us was a sod-covered ring that enclosed much of the level ground atop the cliffs. The wall was four or five feet thick, and so settled into the earth that in places it was barely distinguishable. In other places it was three or four feet high, curving around in a circle that abruptly ended where a portion of the cliff had fallen into the sea. The setting sun picked out the ring in soft shadows and painted the land in rich colors of the Atlantic evening. Within the circle were depressions and mounds whose shadows hinted at other dwellings. The cry of a gull, the return flight of a cormorant winging in from the sea and the boom of swells meeting cliff floated over the ancient site. I stood in the center of the ring and slowly turned, letting the green circle of history soak into my bones.

Through my thoughts I heard a red-haired lad tell me that the shadows of raised earth were an early Iron Age fortification.

Early Iron Age: a thousand years before Christ, pre-Celtic and of a time for which surviving manuscripts tell exaggerated tales of great warriors and impossible feats, stones buried in sod and grass that were ancient at the beginning of the first millennium. Places that were revered because of their mystery. Rock walls and mounds that held the secrets of the past and were the birthplace of Irish folk lore, of heroes, kingdoms and kings. In the light of evening, it was a noble place, sacred in age and powerful in its breadth of enclosure. A place of beginnings and, as Ruairi told me, of endings and sadness.

"The unbaptized Catholic babies were buried here." He said it with little emotion, just a fact of history, another piece of the land and humanity.

The words cut through the ages, tearing through centuries too numerous to count, to a time where religion ripped out the spiritual connection that is as natural as breathing the sea air and replaced it with guilt and fear. As real as my wonder at the earth works was, so too was the bone-sorrow and pity for the mothers and fathers who buried their infants in the pagan ring fort. Not because of the pagan aspect but because of the shame and guilt of the families who were not allowed to bury their unbaptized child in earth that the church had deemed consecrated. What ground could be more consecrated than that which held the spirits of three thousand years of humanity, ground that knew the pain, suffering, and small triumphs of other human beings? If there was any act of holiness in a child being buried on a clifftop amid mounds and rock that were considered unholy, then it was the sacredness of that child being left in the care of a God who could see beyond the limitations of a threatened religion. The unbaptized children would not have had names. Any one of a number of stones that lay in the middle of the ring could have marked the graves of those infants.

We left the circle through the two stones we had entered and continued our walk.

Around every corner was a reminder of how beautiful Ireland is and also how tortured its past has been. Ruairi showed me a stone wall with a break in it and a single heavy slab of rock spanning the opening at waist level. "In the days of the land clearings, this would keep the landlords' cows in but let the tenants' sheep wander out and fall over the cliffs," he explained. The tenants could not afford the taxes of the absentee owners, and this was one of the many cruel ways of ridding the land of the poor. Some of the other ways were not so subtle: the tripod of timbers set up outside the cottage door and a heavy beam swung on a chain to smash it down. The cottages were then burned to the ground. In a land of rain and ocean mist, it took an Irish boy and a long walk on a island of ruins to pull the carpet of green back and reveal both mystery and tragedy.

We eventually walked the perimeter of the entire island. So many piles of stone and crumbled walls settling into the earth. The past and the present, separated by the passing of centuries yet connected by the rocks that refused to go away, refused to be silent. Even as they crumbled and were covered in weeds and green, the stones still told the stories or at least kept them alive for a stranger to hear. All of it was Ireland, a land of stones and history layered one upon the other like the stones of a wall, held together with the mortar of stories.

We ended our walk on the hillside above the family cottage, the valley and beach in shadow and the waters of the sound churning around a buoy in the middle. Flood tide. Ruairi's father greeted us as we came off the hill, and after an introduction, I was invited in for the evening. A fire of drift-wood was set and chairs were pulled close. Geofrey; his wife, Mary; Ruairi; and his sister, Bronwyn, and I sat until almost one in the morning talking and watching the fire. My stories of the sea mixed with Geofrey's life as a vet, and a weekend of solitude that Mary had just finished at a Catholic retreat. There were more stories of the island: how a boatload of children bound for the Scottish potato fields in 1894 had run aground and capsized. All the children drowned. Geofrey told of the conditions in which other migrant children lived, the seasonal shipping of the young to England and Scotland, the poverty they escaped, and the neglect and abuse they labored under. It was child labor at its worst. The stories were told with sorrow and compassion, as if the events had happened just days before.

Long after the family cat had curled into a ball on my lap and fallen asleep, I looked around at the circle of faces staring into the fire, warm, welcoming people who had shared their evening and their stories with me. Late night had turned to early morning and the fire was crackling in a low burn, surrounded by glowing embers. It was time to say good-bye—an awk-ward time when the sharing had to end and we all knew the hours of soft conversation would be like a dream. I had been warmed by their fire, warmed also by their interest in the journey and in who I was as a traveler, as another human being. It was a warmth that I wanted to respond to with a gift of myself, something I could leave them. I wanted them to know how their stories and their kindness fed me with the human contact that I needed to balance out the intensity of the solitude. I had nothing to give but fragments of stories that were not connected by any sense of distance or time, glimpses into my life as a paddler that had held their interest.

As at many other times of parting, I thought of the journal wrapped in its cloudy double plastic protection, the words printed so small, packed into the pages that I was afraid would not hold all the days of the journey. It wasn't the first time that I thought of the journal as a gift. Of taking those cryptic sentences and telling the stories that each one hinted at. Of sharing not only my story but those of the people that I met along the way. I thought how fitting it would be someday to have this family read of the depth of their gift. To read of this visit and understand the importance of it to an ocean traveler.

In the early hours of morning, I said good-bye to the Bourkes beneath a sky that had once again clouded over. The light of the open door spilled into the night, then seemed to draw back into the warmth of the cottage. I knew that feeling of not wanting to cross the threshold of light and darkness, of saying good-bye. I walked back toward the tent, turning several times to look at the yellow glow in their window as I followed the path down to the beach.

I walked past the boat, then up the hill to the tent site. In the pitch black I could see its pyramid shape against the wall of rock that sheltered it from the west winds. Inside, there would be the welcome warmth of the bag, the sleep that I needed. But for just a few more moments I wanted to stand on that shadowed island, become part of the darkness, and recall the day. I wanted to etch it into my mind, savor the images, the feelings in my chest that made it real. Caher, Clare, and Achillbeg: islands stitched together with the pull of the paddle and a tapestry of thousands of years of history. Standing stones, a pirate queen, seas that I danced with, and others that terrified me with their power. A long evening walk, the swirling emotional eddies that pulled me in and let me turn slowly in circles, touching mysteries, feeling fragile beside sod-covered ruins, connecting with the tide of humanity. In the darkness, I was clinging to that day.

I knew that I was just a visitor, that I would leave, and all of the reality of that evening and of those minutes standing in the dark on an Irish island would someday be a memory, a story that I would tell in the hope that friends and family would know the ache in my heart of not wanting the day to end. How would I hold on to that day, keep it from slipping and melting into tomorrow?

And what of the dawn that was only hours away? Of the miles yet to paddle? The seasons moving on, the passage of time? Once again, I felt small, my mind feebly trying to grasp ideas of time and meaning that were beyond me.

In that feeling of smallness, the night with its folds of dark drawn close around me like a blanket, I found comfort. It was a comfort born of the ages I had drifted through, the mystery, the timelessness. I realized it was okay to feel small; and maybe more than just okay. Maybe it was essential to know how fragile the passing of time was and to honor it with awareness and reverence, each moment a gift.

Monks: Yesterday and Today

They never fail who light
their lamp of faith at the unwavering flame.
Burnt for the altar service of the Race
since the beginning.

—Elsa Barkar, *The Frozen Grail*

On the morning of August 12, I woke to silence. No wind popping the tent walls or driving the waves into the steady break of sea against rock. The grass around the tent stood straight up, still as a photograph. It was the oddest feeling of quiet I had experienced. For weeks, the sound of the wind had been a constant part of every waking hour. And in those seconds of half sleep when a shoulder felt the cramped ache of too much time in one position, I also knew that it continued into every night. Now, when I needed the winds to be calm and the seas flat, they suddenly were.

I was camped forty miles north of Achillbeg Island. The previous evening, as so many times before, I had measured the miles of the next day's paddle. With a piece of dried seaweed held at the point on the map where my camp was, I carefully followed the curve of coastline to the next safe landing. At the top of the map was a scale, roughly three inches for twenty miles. I broke the seaweed off where the day's paddle would end and laid it beside the scale. It ran the length of the black line that was broken in five-mile increments. I looked again at the coastline and measured the distance to an inlet that was the only break in the solid wall of north-facing cliff. It was within the first five miles of the day. The winds would decide if I was going to go beyond that break or pull in and wait for better conditions to attempt the fifteen-mile cliff run.

With the previous night's plans tucked away for reference, I was packed and on the water by seven o'clock the next morning. The Broad Haven lighthouse I had camped beside grew smaller with every minute that I pulled away from its automated light. On the foredeck was the map that showed Benwee Head and the coast of County Mayo. In front of me was the real thing: a massive bulk of cliff rising in the light of an overcast morning. Once I was around the headland, the land would fall sharply away to the east, the cliffs leading toward Sligo, then Donegal Bay. In a north or northwest wind this coast would be impassable, the incoming waves rebounding off the cliff and turning the waters into mayhem. Today, by the luck of a calm between weather fronts, there was only the gentle, almost imperceptible rise and fall of a low swell. In the quiet of morning, it was as if the sea was still sleeping, breathing softly, content in its slumber.

I came around Benwee Head with the bow wake carving a perfect "V" through the undisturbed water. As I turned that abrupt corner, the cliffs lined up in a row of peaks that faded into the distance. A half mile offshore stood four major pinnacles, the Stags of Broad Haven. Angular faces: sunlight and shadow split by knife ridges, sheer faces of rock guarding the headland that jutted out of the sea like teeth. Even in the absolute calm of the day, it was an intimidating sight.

For the first hour I was edgy, not wanting to trust the calm and constantly looking over my shoulder to the west for any sign of approaching weather. It would be a deadly place to be caught offguard by the fronts that moved so rapidly here on the west coast. I paddled across the entrance to Portacloy, the rest spot that I had noted the previous night. Again I looked around. There was only the gray of the sky and the occasional brighter spot that hinted of the low clouds breaking up. I gambled and continued past the break in the cliffs. Gradually I relaxed, eased up on the paddling, and sat mesmerized by the cliffs towering over me.

For the next fifteen miles, I drifted and paddled at the base of the walls that soared six hundred feet out of the calm waters. Between sea and clifftop were gannets intent on an east or west flight, and the ever curious fulmars that grew from specks against the heights of gray-black rock. In sweeping approaches, they dropped hundreds of feet and glided gracefully over their reflections until they were a few yards from the bow. A flared wing would carry them ghostlike to one side, then in a slow turn, back again for a second look. Puffins would suddenly surface through the crystal-clear water, look around nervously, and dive again trailing strings of tiny bubbles behind. I paddled within a few feet of the cliffs, leaned back in the cockpit, and stared straight up at the lines of sun and shadow painting the rock in black and white relief. Sea caves echoed gentle rumblings from their darkness, and the precise line of wet rock that marked the rise of the swell dripped with light-tingling harmony.

I paddled away from the walls of rock, headed straight out to sea for a half mile, then turned and paddled parallel with them. In that distance from the cliffs there was no sense of motion, no scale that met my eye with a familiar measurement. The cliffs were still massive, almost bigger because I could see five or six miles in both directions, everything defined by the solid vertical world of rock meeting water. The blades sliced into the motionless sea. Their pull and the surge of the bow wake told my eye I must be moving, but in the flat light and immense scale of silent waters there was little registry of movement; no waves, seaweed, or reflection of sun to mark my progress, only the unbroken line of cliff and the hypnotic smoothness of the water. Any sense of distance paddled was lost until I saw a feather, upturned and downy, floating on its reversed image. I tried to judge the distance, my eyes struggling to find any detail on the film of water it floated on. There was no depth perception, no substance to the water under me, nor to the sky that seemed to be of the same opaque lighting. I felt dizzy; not seasick but unstable. I slapped the back of the paddle on the water and scattered tiny bubbles of trapped air across the surface. The bubbles and the disturbed water textured the surface and suddenly my eye found the balance I was fighting for. I turned the boat again and paddled back to the cliffs.

Hour after hour, I crept along their base and watched their grandeur unfold. Each rock face that I slid past revealed another breathtaking view: more caves, arches, and great slabs of rock that must have fallen in slow motion, separating along a fracture line that left the cliff above with a fresh scar of exposed rock. Hundred-foot sea stacks, daggers of rock surrounded by sea and sky, looked fragile against the backdrop of continuous cliff.

There seemed to be no end to the creative powers of the sea, which had chiseled away, thundered into this impenetrable wall of Ireland, and shaken it until the finest crack trembled open.

After six hours of soaking in the calm and beauty of the cliffs, I finally eased out of the boat on a cobbled beach near Ballycastle. It had been a long day, a day of cliff imagery that filled my mind. As I walked stiffly to the bow and started pulling the boat over a roll of seaweed, a stab of pain shot into my right hip and down the back of my leg. I dropped the bow and slowly straightened up. The pain eased but immediately flared again as soon as I crouched to lift the boat. I walked over the cobbles, trying to flex my back. It was a pain I had felt in the previous week, but never that severe. The six hours of sitting in one position and not having the boat pitching and moving under me must have somehow aggravated the sciatic nerve in my hip.

A year earlier I had been laid up for four weeks with the same pinched sciatic nerve, which made the simplest moves excruciatingly painful. As I set up camp, I remembered how crippling that pain had been, how impossible it was even to walk down a flight of steps. I worried that this injury could be the start of the same inflammation. If it got that bad or anywhere close, how would I continue? Several times that night I woke with a gasp as I rolled over and the pain raced into my hip with red-hot piercing stabs. I lay awake, afraid to move, to aggravate the nerve that had been plucked like the high note of a guitar that had the same lasting pitch reaching into the depth of the muscle. In the dark, I thought about how little control I really had over the outcome of this trip. I had prepared for the hazards of surf and big waves generated by weather and winds. So far, through luck and judgment, I had avoided any major mishap. It would be a cruel irony if it was my hip that brought the trip to a sudden halt. After two and a half months of continuous exposure, what I needed was a break from the demands of the journey. I needed to kick back and forget everything that had to do with surviving on the ocean. It was a life that I loved, but a life that was also wearing me down.

Less than thirty miles up the coast was a monastic community of men and women that I had known for the past ten years. The Spiritual Life Institute was a Carmelite order of Catholic monks. They were a contemplative order with hermitage sites in Nova Scotia; Colorado; and within the past year, in the rural hills near Sligo. I had worked with them on several building projects in Nova Scotia and Colorado, gotten to know them as individuals, and admired their simple way of spiritual living. Months before the trip started, I wrote and told them of my plans. They wrote back with typical enthusiasm, extending a warm welcome and a place to rest if I needed it. Rest was exactly what I needed and I knew their invitation was sincere.

The next day, in near-perfect weather conditions, I crossed Killala Bay and continued due east toward Sligo. The pain in my hip wasn't as severe as the night before, but in the monotony of flat water and low shoreline my mind kept focusing on every little twinge of muscle. Mile after mile, I sat fidgeting and trying to relieve the tightness of muscles stressed with spasms. I tried putting the water bag under my thigh for more support, shifted my feet on the forward bulkhead, and finally found a position where I could paddle for a half hour and not think about the pain.

The coast had changed dramatically from the cliffs of the day before. Now it was one farm after the next, rolling fields dotted with lines of round, honey-colored bales of hay. I spent most of the day a mile or more offshore, watching the fields slowly move past and the plateaulike mountains of Sligo inching closer. I was in my auto-paddle mode, putting the miles behind me and trying not to think of my hip or the boredom of the flat water. I was too far offshore to see the details of the land. I watched the bow wake, the twin lines on either side of the hull reflecting the distorted glare of the sun. As I leaned into each pull of the paddle, the wake would surge gently and shift the warmth of the reflected sun across my face. No wind or waves and no sounds from the land. Just the continuous reach and pull of the paddles and the sound of water falling from the high blade and hitting the foredeck like beats of a drum. The patter of drops from the right blade, the silent pull, and the patter of drops from the left. Hundreds of strokes in an hour, a rhythm that didn't waver. I watched the wake, listened to the drumming, closed my eyes, and felt the pull of the paddle. The routine became rich with simplicity: purity of motion, harmony of paddle stroke and breath.

Five, then ten miles slid by, and still the mountains to the east held their distance. I watched the compass, thought it might be frozen, knew that it wasn't but swung a few degrees off course anyway. The dome of white lines floated slowly in response and I turned back on course. If there had been any seas I would have been paying closer attention to the water, but there wasn't any threat and I was enjoying the freedom of letting my mind wander.

For some reason I happened to look past the bill of my hat pulled low to shade my eyes. It took a few seconds to focus and realize what was cutting through the shimmer of ripple-free water straight in front of me. Behind a slight bulge of reflected sun was a gray-black dorsal fin that split the water as cleanly as a knife. Four or five feet back was another fin, sweeping side to side in a lazy thrust that left a trail of swirls. In those seconds of awakening from our respective stupors, the distance had closed to less than a boat length. As I reached for the camera, the shark must have sensed the presence of the boat and in a thrashing, panicked dive that threw water into air, he was instantly gone. The boil of water quickly smoothed over and the only sign of his passing was the rapid beating of my heart that the explosive power of the shark had startled into action.

For the next few minutes, I kept glancing over my shoulder half expecting to see the dorsal fin following in the boat's wake. The shark was probably hundreds of feet down, much more frightened by the experience than I was. But the sight of those fins slicing though the calm waters left me unnerved.

Toward evening, I landed on a concrete boat ramp behind the protected point of Aughris Head. A thirty-foot wooden fishing boat was winched above the high water mark and held in place by a rusty cable disappearing into a wooden shed. I walked up the steep lane behind the ramp and asked at the first house if I could use their phone. I called my monk friends, told them where I was, and a half hour later they drove up. After a warm welcome of hugs, and assurances that I could stay for as long as I needed, we tied the boat to a trailer behind their car and were off for Holy Hill Hermitage.

We drove up one country lane, down another, then out to a main road where a sign pointed to a turnoff for Skreen. Farmland, the smell of cows, and cars flying past on the wrong side of the road were a blur as I held on to the boat in the back of the trailer and tried to take it all in. One of the monks had offered to ride in the trailer with the boat, but after two weeks without a shower I thought it better if I was the one out in the wind. We turned at the sign for Skreen and a few miles later stopped in front of a massive iron gate set between stone walls. From the car came shouts of competitive joking:

"I'll get it."

"No, I will. You got them the last time."

More laughter, then my friend Kay jumped out and swung the gates open with a creak. The short procession of car, trailer, and cargo continued up a slow, twisting drive and under the first trees I had seen in months. We stopped in front of the old convent, the building they had been given months before and had sweated through restoring. The ivy had been cut back to frame the tall windows, and freshly turned flowerbeds were filled with splashes of color. After weeks of living on the sea and hearing only the call of gulls and the cry of kittiwakes, the songbirds and the smell of land were sudden reminders of life on land.

Kay, Sharon, Eric, and Josephine all piled out of the little car and a plan was formed for the evening. The monks wanted to celebrate my arrival, and I wasn't surprised. There was nothing stiff or pious about them. They were like a family: faithful to their vows of poverty, chastity, and obedience, they also loved a celebration. Sharon had been with the community for almost twenty years and was the senior member. The others were in their thirties or forties and like Sharon had a great energy for life about them. It was decided that we should drive into Sligo for pizza, and later, in place of vespers, we would walk the beach and look at the stars. After a hot shower and a change into the one set of wrinkled street clothes I had, we were off for the big city.

It had been three years since I had seen Eric and Kay in Colorado and longer since I had seen Sharon in Nova Scotia. Josephine had known the community for several years but it was the first time I met her. We devoured three different kinds of pizza and caught each other up with what had been going on in our lives. They told me about other members of the community, what building projects were underway at the three different monasteries, and how their work at the new site in Ireland was progressing. After months of traveling alone, it was exciting to talk about familiar people and places. They missed the other members of their community, the mountains of Colorado, and the deep solitude of their hermitage in the woods of Nova Scotia. Here in Ireland, they weren't getting the help they had hoped for from the local parish. Materials and labor were expensive, and every phase of the building process took weeks longer than anticipated. But none of the delays, the lack of money, or the bitter-cold damp of the previous winter seemed to weaken their resolve to convert the old buildings into a contemplative center of retreat.

One thing that made the evening so enjoyable was the cheerful attentiveness they all expressed. There was no hurry in the conversation; one person spoke at a time and everyone else listened. It was wonderfully relaxing to sit and slowly get caught up.

At one point, Sharon said, "Okay, now we want to hear about your travels."

I sat and looked at them, these four who had dedicated their lives to living as monks in a secular world. Where to begin? My life was so different from theirs. But if anyone could understand the months of moving slowly and deliberately along the coast, being struck silent by the beauty and power of nature, of seeking the solitude of ruins and the mystery of island monasteries, they could.

They listened as I told stories of the people, the seas, and the ruins. They asked questions in sure, soft voices, wanting to know where I camped, how far offshore I paddled, and what I did when the weather was rough. I told them about Skellig Michael, the depth of silence I felt on the remote island, the seabirds that were so much a part of my life, the headlands, and the stillness of spirit I found on the ocean. It all came out in stories that overlapped one another and skipped around the coast with complete freedom. I heard myself talking longer than I had on the entire trip. Once I got going, it was like a dam that had breached, the stories spilling over the lip in a gush of memories and feelings. Halfway through one story, I would think of something I just had to tell them, and would interrupt myself and pick up the first half of the story ten minutes later. As I spoke of the stillness and harmony I had found despite all the struggles of the trip, they listened, and nodded with gentle, understanding smiles. In their peaceful way they let me go on, let the flood of the trip pour out, then recede.

Then they told me about their own travels around Ireland, of the monastic sites they visited, and their feelings of spiritual connection at those ruins. From them I learned about Inishmurray, an island where they had renewed their vows and where Eric had taken his final vows in a seventh-century chapel. They talked of a common spirit amid the stones, a sense of continuing the lives of the monks who had lived there, revering work, leisure, and prayer. When we were finally talked out, we drove to the beach and wandered across the sands of low tide. In the dark, I walked beside the shadows of my friends. One of them would stop and point to a constellation, pick it out of the thousands of stars for the rest of us to see, and name it like a trusted friend. Someone else would point out the Dolphin, the Clown, or the Dog Star, and a dozen other constellations, some I saw for the first time. A shooting star would leave its streak of light for an instant and a chorus of "oohs" and "aahs" would lift into the night. These late night walks beneath the stars were a ritual for them, as were full moon walks or predawn communal prayer. It was all an acknowledgment of God, an earthy mysticism married to the cosmic Christ.

The next morning, I followed their silent robed figures up a narrow set of stairs to the chapel. I was given a seat and book of prayers and shown where the readings would begin. Matins was divided into silent, then communal prayer, the women reading the first half of the incantations and the men responding with the second half. Occasionally, I lost my place and Sharon or Kay would lean over, use the red or yellow ribbon sewn into the binding of the prayer book to turn to another section and point where the next prayer began. Like everything else, it was done with gentleness and caring.

Holy Hill Hermitage would have been the perfect place to rest from the strain of the past two and a half months. My body needed the uninterrupted sleep, the simple, wholesome food, and the quiet of their library where I could sit in a big chair with my feet curled under me and write in my journal. I liked the feeling of the scatter rugs on worn wooden floors, the large, high-ceilinged rooms, and the drapes pulled back to let as much of the summer sun in as possible. There was a bright warmth to the walls decorated with pictures of their other monasteries and the smiling, tanned faces of fellow monks in unplaned wooden picture frames. Dried flower arrangements and the hand-thrown pottery of one of the monks in Colorado gave the kitchen the feeling of a large family home, a place where food preparation depended on a recipe of wooden spoons and whole-grain cheerfulness. In every room there was a feeling of uncluttered peace.

The only problem with my visit was the weather. For the first time in weeks, there wasn't a breath of wind. The tall grasses in the fields around the monastery reminded me how still the sea would be. An occasional breeze would comb through the thick green, turn the light undersides of the grass to the sun, then just as silently leave them as they were. It was as if the wind couldn't be bothered to stir the air on such a fine day.

As much as I wanted to relax, eat well, and sleep without the worry of tides and wind, I knew that the break in the weather was something I couldn't waste. The sea was a difficult taskmaster. Even ten miles inland, far enough away that I couldn't smell the tidal changes or hear the swell against sand or rock, I couldn't deny its pull. That second evening I stood in a field beside a set of old ruins that the monks were slowly rebuilding and watched the setting sun brush the sky with sweeping strokes of pink. The days were getting shorter, the evenings cooler. I was dressed in layers of fleece, my collar soft against the back of my neck to ward off the evening chill. I could stay for a week and rest but what if the fall weather brought more winds and rain? These days of calm winds and sunshine might be the last of the summer.

It was another gamble, whether to sit and rest, or to go with the fine weather and hope the pinched nerve wouldn't get any worse. What made the decision easier was that even after those months of paddling, I still loved being on the ocean. I missed the sound of its movements in the night, of waking for a few moments and listening with a sleepy mind to the rhythm of the waves, checking in with the sea, then drifting back to sleep. As I stood and looked to the northwest, in the direction of the setting sun and the ocean, somewhere beyond the undulating hills of green, I suddenly wanted to know what the sea was doing. I wanted to touch it on this evening of pink light and hear its murmur. The decision to continue wasn't entirely mine. It was in the sky, the still air and the remaining three hundred miles of coastline that were calling me.

If I was going to leave, I needed to get into Sligo and buy food for the next week or ten days of paddling. The next morning, I talked with Sharon and explained the sudden shift in plans. She didn't question me, didn't push for me to stay longer. In her eyes I saw an understanding that was as welcoming as the first embrace on the boat ramp. The day before, we had had a long talk about our shared spirituality. I had told her of my fears, my struggle in balancing my faith with the demands of a troubled world and how it was that I prayed. My life was very different from her monastic life (one that I had considered years earlier), but our souls were on the same journey. It was that soul journey that I think she recognized when I told her I would be leaving early.

It didn't take long to fill the basket with pasta, rice, peanut butter, jam, and brown soda bread. I could feel the sideways glances of people as we made our way down one aisle after the other, Eric in his tan and dark brown monastic clothing and me in wrinkled camp clothes. I wasn't sure if it was our mismatched clothing or our bare feet in sandals that attracted the most stares.

After a few stops for the other errands, Eric said he wanted to show me something. He took a detour from the main road and drove along Ben Bulben, the plateau of green that I had watched from the sea. It rose sharply from the surrounding fields, with treeless slopes that topped out in horizontal bands of eroded rock. Shadows of puffy white clouds drifted over the layers, then floated higher to the crown of green that capped the long finger of mountain. From miles in any direction the mountain was what focused the eye.

We drove onto a road so narrow two cars had to slow to a crawl or pull out on a wide shoulder of weeds to pass. We left the car on the edge of a field and walked through a gate whose wood was softened to a velvety gray by years of weathering. A footpath wound through clumps of thistle and around the odd boulder sitting in the middle of the pasture. Over a slight rise in the field and in full view of the ridge of Ben Bulben stood a circle of stones thirty feet across. In the middle of the circle were three upright stones, capped with a great slab of rock resting at an angle.

I had been following Eric and listening to him tell of the ancient burial sites that dotted the fields around the mountain. As we came over the rise and saw the circle, the gray of the rock contrasted against the green of the field, his voice dropped to almost a whisper. He stopped a few yards from the outer circle and stood silently with me as I looked at the site.

The outer circle was a loose ring of boulders, waist-high and with enough space between each to walk through easily. The spacing seemed almost an invitation to enter. Within, the three upright stones were slightly taller and so closely braced against each other that they formed a darkened chamber beneath the capstone.

Eric stepped closer to the outer circle and rested his hand on one of the rocks. The movement seemed almost involuntary, as if his hand was drawn there by the reverence that so clearly filled him. In his movements and silence I recognized my own feelings. I watched him looking at the stones, then turned and looked at them again. I wanted to ask a question that I had asked myself many times in the past. Eric answered the question before I could put it into words: "These places always feel holy to me."

I looked at him. "You really feel like they're sacred?"

He nodded. "Oh yes, definitely."

He explained how the circle of stones showed the reverence for life that people of four thousand years ago had. The stones would have been dragged many miles over boggy land and carefully arranged, enabling the transition from this life to the next. Where we stood had been—and still was—holy ground. It was in this setting of green, with the dominance of the mountain watching over the circle of stones and inner dolmen, that those people had surrendered their dead to whatever was beyond.

Archaeological evidence suggests that the bodies were cremated and interned with the remains of others beneath the capped chamber. Eric touched those stones with a reverence for that humanity. At that moment of internment they, like we, faced the unknown, the great mystical chasm. They were living, breathing, caring people who felt the pain and anguish of the death of a friend or family member. We are left with the stones of their beliefs, just enough to ponder their existence and maybe probe the same unanswerable depths of our own. Today, we speak of the soul or the spirit of the dead passing from this world to the next. The dolmens that stand like sacred rings on the hills beneath Ben Bulben are clear signs that the tribal people two thousand years before Christ knew of the existence of the soul and of a greater being. It was that connection that made the site a holy place for Eric and validated my own feelings for similar places that I had stood before.

An hour after standing beside the passage tomb, I walked with Eric up the stairs to the hermitage chapel. Father John had returned from giving a retreat and was celebrating mass. Beside my friends cloaked in the tan and brown robes of the Carmelite order, I recited the prayers that I had known since I was seven or eight years old. The greeting, the reverence of the words spoken deliberately and slowly filled the closeness of the chapel and drew us together. I looked at Sharon, and thought of our talk, then to Kay, who had washed my clothes, dried, and folded them; at Josephine, who had cooked a communal dinner for us; at Eric, who had walked with me around the burial ring; and at Father John, who now offered the mass. My mind wandered far from the prayers as I silently thanked each monk for their insight and help.

As Sharon walked forward to read the first lesson, the rest of us took our seats.

She opened a book on the simple podium, studied it for a moment, then folded her hands behind her back and began to read. The lesson was about wisdom, what a treasure it is to value something—to seek with all one's will. The message was familiar, but the words were not. They were stated simply, woven with a clarity and beauty that I had not heard before: words that floated with a poetic ring and settled at the base of a deep breath.

Sharon finished the reading, closed the book, and quietly said, "This ends the first reading from the *The Bhagavad-Gita*, the Hindu holy book."

When I paddled away from the boat ramp, I knew that I was leaving some very special friends. Father John stood at the waterline in a faded T-shirt and jeans. He had given me a ride back to the water and helped carry the loaded boat down the ramp. I turned one last time for a final wave before rounding a point that would take me from his view. My visit had been brief, too short to get the physical rest that I needed, yet I felt refreshed. It was the earthy spiritual life the monks shared with me which had given me that boost. Their groundedness in their faith didn't blind them to the sacredness of other teachings or beliefs. Instead, it freed them to embrace truth where they found it. It was a lesson I could take with me, and become, as Sharon said, "a monk in the marketplace."

I wanted time to ease back into the paddling and reflect on my visit with the monks. The calm waters and the rise of Inishmurray Island on the horizon were a perfect way to renew the paddling. I crossed Sligo Bay to a point of rock that reached out from beneath the fields and ended in fingers draped with the dark green tangle of kelp at low tide. Five miles out into Donegal Bay, the outline of Inishmurray floated in a gray world of sea and sky. I stopped for a stretch and a quick lunch of soda bread on the kelp-covered rocks, then set out for the island.

Halfway across, I could see the walled ruins of the monastery on the highest point of the land and a row of abandoned houses along the shore. Several boats were anchored in the lee of the island, and as I drew closer, I could see people picnicking on the rocks. As I was landing, a couple of men came down and helped carry the boat above the high water mark. They said they had spotted me a mile out and had watched my progress. They had never seen a kayak before and were astonished that I would paddle the five miles from the mainland. They studied the boat, asked the usual questions, then insisted that I join the picnic and tell the others where I had come from.

It was another one of those moments of instant celebrity status when all I really wanted was to explore the island quietly. The trade-off was their wonderfully innocent enthusiasm, the musical lilt of their voices filling the island air, and the baked chicken and potato salad that appeared from a basket packed for the return trip to Donegal. By now I had an abbreviated version of my own trip with which I answered the barrage of questions. I could almost predict word for word the questions that came up. I explained where I had started and filled in the gaps between Dublin and Donegal Bay. As I described the route, I couldn't help but chuckle at their looks of disbelief, and also my own awareness that the west coast portion of the trip was almost over.

As we talked, the last of the chicken disappeared and the kids who had been fishing off the rocks wandered back to the picnic site. The day was drawing to a close, the sky settling in over the island with a closeness that heralded rain. The fishing boat that had brought them out appeared as a white speck on the colorless waters. In a few minutes, the white of the hull could be distinguished from the breaking bow wave and the boat turned in toward the island. Another small group of people followed the shore path down from the island's interior and clambered into a dinghy that had been resting on the rocks.

One other boat was anchored in the natural harbor, its bow line gently holding the boat into the faint breeze that had drifted in with the low sky. Everyone seemed to have one eye on the weather and the other on the mainland, two hours away. The fishing boat idled into one of the clasai', a natural fissure in the sandstone of the island. Even at low water, there was plenty of depth for the boat to pull partway into the ten-foot-wide cleft running fifty or sixty feet through the rock. The fisherman and mate held the boat off the rock walls and everyone jumped aboard. I handed the last of the picnic gear down to outstretched hands, then watched as the fisherman eased the boat into reverse. A swirl of bubbles wrapped around the bow planking as it slowly backed away. The rumble of its engine softened as the captain eased off the throttle. The boat slid backwards through the calm water, then came back to life with a throaty roar as he slipped it into forward and turned the bow toward Donegal. With windbreakers zipped tight and the boat riding a good bit lower in the water, everyone waved. I was left with the island to myself.

Most of Inishmurray was covered in a tangle of bracken, fern, and nettle. It was a half mile wide by a little over a mile long and no more than fifty feet above the sea. I followed the grass track to where it split and turned toward the walls of the monastery. A couple of house ruins along the path stood covered in thickets of bramble that looked intent on pulling the stones from the walls. The path wound through the underbrush, rose out of a slight depression, and suddenly the imposing wall of the enclosure was in front of me. Out of the thicket of briars and ferns it rose like the walls of a fortified city. Eight to ten feet high, perfectly flat on top, and twelve to fifteen feet wide, the walls curved gradually out of sight. Beneath the white-gray sky that mirrored the rock, I walked into the walled monastery.

Within the protection of hundreds of tons of rock were the remains of a chapel, a stone-roofed oratory, a larger church, and a single beehive hut. Mounds of stone covered in grass added to the puzzle of shoulder-high passageways lined in stone. Low ridges of green hinted at what might once have been a wall or inner enclosure. I walked around the first building— the chapel where Eric had taken his final vows—crouched through the doorway, and stood beneath the gable ends reaching into a somber sky. The intricate work of the stonemasons tied one tier of stone to the next and interlocked the corners that held the building square centuries after the last monks had lived on the island.

Across from the chapel was a raised platform filled with rounded beach stones, the "cursing rocks" of Inishmurray. Legend has it that the stones had the power to curse an enemy. By turning one of the stones and invoking its power, bad fortune would befall the accursed.

A narrow walkway bordered on either side by interlocking stone led from the open green of the main courtyard into the labyrinth of passages around the main chapel. It was as if the mounds of grass-covered rock had been pushed back and piled high to protect the sanctity of the church.

Above the shoulder-high passage, I could see the curve of the beehive hut, and around a slight bend, another passageway led to the steps ending at the low doorway. The proximity of the cell to the church made me wonder if this was the sleeping area for the abbot.

I crept through the door of the beehive hut and stood for a moment in near darkness. I couldn't see the stone but could feel its weight in the dome above, its curve wrapping around me. A small opening in the ceiling cast a light that my eyes couldn't gather in. It looked far away, only feet above my head, but filtered by an impossible distance. Gradually my eyes adjusted to the dark. The light from the opening and that of the doorway slowly filled the room, and I could see the roundness of the floor and even the powdery dirt on which I stood. The shadow on my right became a solid bench of stone, its surface nearly flat, with several fitted slabs. A bed of stone? I stood and listened, felt the silence, then returned to the glare of the flat light outside.

I walked around the perimeter of the church to a ramp of stone that led to the top of the wall surrounding the monastery. From that height, I could look down on the interior of the enclosure and see how the pathways laced together the buildings and stonework of the seventh-century monks. Rock walls, gabled peaks, the rectangular shape of the chapels, and the round dome of the beehive hut all lay within the massive ring.

Stone: everywhere I looked, there was the weight and permanence of it. The mounds and depressions softened by the green hinted at more structures beneath the grass.

To one side of the enclosure was a bank of earth and rock, a raised platform alongside the stone-roofed oratory. My eye kept wandering over its shape, seeing something that was there but not understanding it. I climbed down off the wall and retraced my steps through the passage beyond the church and past the beehive hut. I looked at the wall again and knew that it held a secret; it had to be more than just a retaining wall. I walked around it, climbed over it, and had almost given up figuring it out when I stepped on a slab that rocked with a hollow thud.

I lifted the slab, then another beneath it, and peered into a narrow chamber that ran the length of the wall. Long and narrow, it would have been useless for food storage. The only other purpose was as a place of refuge.

I thought of the Viking raids beginning in the last decade of the eighth

century, the plundering of Lindisfarne on Britain's east coast in 793, and
the repeated raids of Iona off the west coast of Scotland in the early ninth-
century. Inishmurray suffered the same pillage, burning, and murder, and
was destroyed in 802. I wondered if the hidden tunnel had been an effort
to survive those raids.

I lowered the slabs back into place and gazed at the walls of the ruins.
A mist had begun to fall. The tops of the stones were darkened, though
the sides were still light gray and dry. I had been far away, deep in the age
of the monks, and hadn't felt the softness of the mist. Now I saw it drifting
in fine shadows between grass and stone. It had moved in from the sea,
wrapped itself around the island, and gently touched the ruins with a fine-
ness that settled tenderly upon stone, lichen, and tips of weighted grass.
The day could have been any day in the ninth-century, the gentleness of
a summer mist healing the terror of a Viking raid that left the island as I
saw it.

I wandered over the rest of the island, looked in through the window
openings of the house ruins, and wondered what it must have been like to
have a seventh-century monastery in one's backyard. The houses stood in
a row facing the sea, as close to the edge of the land as a winter gale would
allow. They crowded the rocks as if the rest of the island was holy. Farther
along, on the eastern tip, was the schoolhouse with its boarded-up windows
and doors. Gulls stood on the shore rocks, their necks pulled in and the
blackness of their eyes staring out toward the mainland, which was hidden
by the weather.

I returned to the boat and pulled the sleeping bag and pad from the
front compartment. The mist was getting heavier and I thought how the
tent would be a sodden mess by morning. Then I thought of the beehive
hut. Why not sleep in it?

I took a few extra clothes for a pillow, the pad and the sleeping bag,
and returned to the ruins. By the time I reached the passageway, droplets
of mist clung to my beard and the wet grass had washed my feet. I bent
low through the thick opening of the cell. In the last of the light, my eyes
adjusted to the interior again, and I made my bed on top of the raised
platform, my feet toward the doorway. As I lay down, I felt uneasy, as
superstitious as any Irishman might who dared to sleep on that bed of stone.
Who or what might appear in the middle of the night standing above me
in the center of the dome? No sooner had I laid down than I began to

think of my tent and a patch of grass above the shoreline. Maybe sleeping in the hut wasn't such a good idea.

I told myself that such thoughts were foolish, pushed them from my mind, and looked at the curve of the ceiling. Each circled tier was shadowed by the one above it, an overhang of two or three inches that gradually drew the circles tighter. A final stone sealed the apex and seemed to hang suspended. The graceful arch floated above me in intricate layers of stone that soothed my superstitions. As the night settled over the island, the details of the ceiling faded and darkness slowly filled the hut. When the last of the light was gone and all that remained was the silence and the imagined touch of mist on blackened stone, I let my eyes close and slept peacefully.

Hours before dawn, I awoke to the same blackness, drifted in and out of sleep, then watched as light slowly reached through the doorway and rekindled the day. I was stiff from not being able to sleep in a curl on my side. I wanted to get up, but lay still and watched the light fill the hut just as the darkness had the night before. Such a simple thing, to lie and watch the light: day becoming night, night becoming day.

When I could see the details of stone, I got up, dressed, and gathered my bed in armfuls of warmth. To the stone and to that which I could not see, I said a prayer of thanks for the night's sleep. I crouched, stepped out into the morning, and walked silently across the ruins and out of the walls that held the history of the island in their embrace.

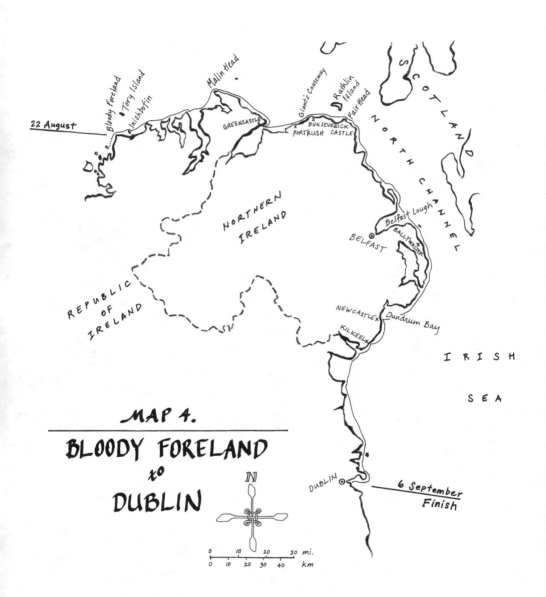

22 August

Bloody Foreland
Tory Island
Inishbofin
Malin Head
GREENCASTLE
Giant's Causeway
Rathlin Island
Fair Head
DUNSEVERICK CASTLE
PORTRUSH

SCOTLAND

NORTH CHANNEL

NORTHERN IRELAND

Belfast Lough
BELFAST
BALLYWALTER

REPUBLIC OF IRELAND

NEWCASTLE
Dundrum Bay
KILKEEL

IRISH SEA

MAP 4.

BLOODY FORELAND
to
DUBLIN

N

DUBLIN

6 September
Finish

0   10   20   30 mi.
0 10 20 30 40 km

Donegal Cliffs and Island Stories

The islander can read an outsider's thoughts
with terse accuracy. You know you have made it
when they invite you into their kitchen.

—Leon Uris, *Ireland: A Terrible Beauty*

Halfway across Donegal Bay I turned to look back at Inishmurray and saw nothing but a bank of fog. In front and to either side of me was the same wet thickness that cut visibility to less than a half mile. The fogbank had been moving in from the northwest, slowly erasing the headland I was paddling toward. Before it faded completely, I had taken a compass bearing and now paddled blind, engulfed in a world of white, watching the dome of the compass holding steady on the bearing but rolling side to side as it countered the action of the waves. A light wind was blowing on my left cheek and raised a small chop, which the bow easily cut through. I stared at the compass, subconsciously monitoring even the slightest shift in the wind and noting the angle of the waves against the boat's course. As long as there wasn't a westerly set to the tide, I would hit land in ten miles.

An hour later, nothing had changed. I didn't know how far land was or if I was still headed for land at all. My face was wet from the fog that occasionally lifted to a mile, then lowered again. Uneasy with the thought of missing the headland, I shifted course a few degrees to the east.

Another half hour, and I was straining to see land where I thought it must surely be. There was nothing but more fog, damp and thick as before.

Somewhere through the fog were the cliffs of Slieve League, eighteen hundred feet of mountain that dropped into the sea. There was a low swell running. I stopped paddling, turned my ear toward land, and listened. No sound of swell breaking on rock. I settled into the paddling again, not alarmed but a little anxious to pick up the first hint of land.

The fog played tricks on my eyes. Depth perception and balance were skewed and time seemed to drag by. The only thing to do was to trust in the bearing, stay focused on the compass or the bow to keep the dizziness away, and keep paddling. There was nothing to look at but the circle of hazy light that I seemed to pull across the bay with me.

In the dampness and glare of white fog, I was all too conscious of my hip. I fidgeted, stretched low over the foredeck, sat up straight, and settled back in the seat again. Nothing seemed to help. My mind was divided between the concerns of the fog and the discomfort. What I needed was a distraction, something to break the monotony. What I almost bumped into was another shark.

I had long since given up hope of seeing the basking sharks that live along the northwest coast of Ireland. Any chop on the water at all would easily hide the telltale sign of their dorsal fin and even in flat water I would have to be almost on top of one to see it. They are twenty-five to thirty feet long, slow-moving, and one of the largest sharks in the world. Unlike the smaller blue shark, which feeds aggressively on other fish, the basking shark is a gentle giant that swims along, filtering the sea for tiny nutrients. The last thing I expected to see coming out of the fog in front of me was the dorsal fin of one of these mammoth plankton feeders.

He didn't seem to be in a hurry, the dorsal fin laying on his side as the shark must have rolled to feed, then coming upright and slowly parting the waves around it. I stopped paddling and watched the shark approach. He cruised through the swell and low chop with the steadiness of great weight, oblivious to the action of the sea. Through the chop, I could see the shadow of his head, three feet wide and spreading wider, back toward the fin.

I had the camera in my hand but was so caught in the awe of watching this giant floating just below the surface that I missed taking the picture. Ten feet in front of the bow, the shark simply sank out of sight. One second the fin and shadow were there, and the next there was only the mixing of a slight boil amid the chop. I looked over my shoulder, hoping to see the fin reappear. There was nothing but the choppy waters fading into the fog.

Three and a half hours after leaving Inishmurray, the north coast of Donegal Bay gradually materialized out of the thinning fog. The filtered sun covered the water in a sheen of oily light and the vague shadow of land became cliff and wave-washed rock. Fog and mist slowly lifted to reveal a rockbound coastline and the broad base of Slieve League shouldering its way into the retreating blanket of clouds. I eased the boat back to the original compass course and headed for a passage between the abrupt end of the mainland and a low, rounded island that lay a mile offshore.

The passage between Rathlin O'Birne Island and the point would bring me around this last exposed headland of the west coast. The swells that I had ignored during the crossing now became more pronounced, steepening and battering the north side of the island in a violent rumble of white. I had left Inishmurray on a falling tide and now the exposed algae-covered rocks on Rathlin O'Birne showed that the tide had run its course. The increasing swell indicated the tide had begun to turn and the seas would steadily build. The only landing in the next fifteen miles was around the point to the north of the island. Glen Bay was a mile beyond that point and a place where I could decide whether to push on or call it a day.

After the monotony of the crossing, it was a welcome change to watch the swells breaking on the rocks around the headland. As the sun burned off the last of the fog, my mind and thoughts cleared as well and I focused again on sea meeting rock. I paddled across Malin Bay, then over to Rossan Point, where collars of white wrapped the base. From the point, I could see across Glen Bay to another point whose base was also awash in breaking swells. I was amazed and a little alarmed at how quickly the seas were building. A swell lifted the stern, pushed it sideways so the boat sat in the trough, then rolled away, blocking the view of the far point. Six-footers were running where there had been two-footers an hour ago. The breeze that had been a gentle caress now rippled the sea with cat's paws and occasionally grabbed at the high blade, then just as quickly let it go: warning of another front moving in. The boat wallowed in the swells, patiently waiting for me to make a decision, seemingly as willing to go on as it was to turn and seek shelter somewhere in the bay that opened into the hills.

I sat with the sea for a few moments, watched the lines of swells wash the cliff base and pockets of steep-cobbled beach with brilliant white, then turned into the bay.

The bay was formed by steep hills rising to the north and south, which dropped sharply and tapered to a beach at the back of the inlet. The west-facing bowl of hills sat drenched in the warmth and light of afternoon and offered a perfect haven from the cliffbound coast. Shaded contours of green dotted with white cottages and flocks of sheep looked out over the tongue of ocean reaching into the land.

As the swells entered the half-mile-wide mouth, they broke over the rocks on both sides in a wild race to the beach. Blackened rocks were left with glistening streams that weakened to a trickle, then were flooded again in a confusion of thundering water. As I paddled further into the bay, the swells grew steeper, and the narrow channel of unbroken water closed in on both sides. Heavy surf pounded the beach and filled the air with mist and a continuous roar. I sat well outside the first line of swell tumbling over itself and studied the surf. Five or six ranks guarded the beach and broke in overlapping lines of deep blue, blinding white, and the dull color of sandy shallows. A half mile of flat beach, then grass-covered dunes stretched out beyond the last waves grinding into the sand. It would be a long carry to high ground once through the gauntlet of surf. If the winds continued to build, the relaunch would be difficult. I backpaddled into the swells that were pushing me closer to the breakers, turned, and headed back toward the mouth of the bay. I remembered seeing a tiny beach between twin towers of black rock, a beach no wider than the length of the boat and one that would be buried by the ground swell thundering into the rocks at high water. If I hurried, I could land before the beach disappeared.

In an hour, I had the boat carefully balanced on a ledge of one of the rocks and my tent pitched fifty feet above on a grassy bench that faced the ocean. The waves that pounded the outer coast and rolled into the bay were thick with the power and volume of a distant storm. They had the clean lines that hundreds of miles of rolling forms: the gathering in of the smaller waves, and the orderly rows of ten-footers that advanced in lines of poetic motion, the stanzas flowing in sets, punctuated by the break-ing of a rogue wave and the crescendo of wave breaking on cliff.

Occasionally, a large wave would stand above the others. From the safety of the cliff I watched as it drew closer, the sun shining on its flanks. It would lift, raising its shoulder above the waves around it, stand proud and magnificent, then suddenly throw itself forward at the last second. The unleashed strength of the wave erupted and shook the air in fury as it folded and tried to pulverize the rocks buried beneath its white foam. Seconds would pass, the groan and rumble of the wave would recede, and the first black ridges of rocks would reappear. Behind it, another wave would begin to climb as the first had, and bury the rocks again in the same thunderous roar. Ten seconds apart, hour after hour, the moon tide and the strength of an unknown storm combined forces to batter the cliffs of Glencolumbkille.

All night long, the assault continued. In the pitch dark I woke many times to the sea and land crashing together and reverberating in my chest. Even with the tide dropping, the seas weren't abating. Was it possible it would ever be calm again? I crept out of the tent and checked the boat. I leaned out over the rocks, shooting a beam of light into the blackness until it pulled from the depths a yellow hull resting silently on its bed of rock. Its graceful lines contrasted with the harshness of the rocks and the tumult that raged all around. Unworried and patient, it sat waiting.

In the morning, I waited for the tide to drop, to pull back and expose that buffer of sand I needed to launch from. The eye-of-the-storm waves had passed. With every hour, the swells would now drop, echoing the rhythm of all things on the ocean, the cycle of flood and ebb.

I sat in the boat and waited for that same rhythm in the swells, spray deck snapped in place, paddle resting across the cockpit, and my knuckles pressed against the packed sand. A five-footer peaked, broke once, reformed, and dumped on the steep beach ten feet in front of me. The last of the wave rushed over the sands and floated the bow. My knuckles ground into the sand, the water rising over my wrists as I lifted with stomach and thighs to free the stern. Ten seconds between waves—ten seconds to make all the right moves or get tossed like a three hundred–pound piece of flotsam. I felt the stern break free, grabbed the paddle, and got three strokes in before the next wave engulfed the front half of the boat, hit my chest with a powerful shove, and filled my eyes and nose with the burn of saltwater. I blew my sinuses clear, shaking my head and blinking my eyes until I could see the next wave. Three more strokes, another drenching, then a near miss as the boat rocketed through the knife edge of a cresting wave that left it hanging in midair. There was a second or two of hopeless flight, then the bone-jarring crash as the boat slammed into the hollow of the next trough. One more wave with the bow climbing high into the air, riding over the softer shoulder, and again falling with a crash into the trough. With each passing wave the crests became rounder and the boat began the slow rise and fall of the deep water swells. The threat of the surf zone fell behind me and the pounding in my chest settled into a quieter beating.

The swells that had hammered the coastline all night brought with them a touch of cool morning air, bright sunshine, and a blustery day that had a feel of autumn to it. I could not have wanted for a finer day to paddle this last stretch of west coast cliff. A six-foot swell was still rolling in from the west. Six feet of height and fifteen feet of width that carried the volume of tons of water meeting sea stacks and rock with sheets of glaring white thrown high into the sunlight. Five hundred–foot limestone cliffs soared into a cloudless sky speckled with the flight of gulls and fulmars. Offshore rocks, towering pinnacles of sunlight and shadow, stood solid while the sea threw rainbows of mist around their bases. In every element—sky, cliff, and heaving blue ocean—there was a purity of energy that soaked into me. The crisp morning air bathed everything in its freshness and flooded my senses with a light so clear and refreshing after the previous day's fog. I breathed it in, felt it wash my face and hands and fill my eyes with its clarity. I sang and laughed, paddled with its coolness on the back of my neck, and dug into the strength of the sea swirling around the blades.

In front and to the left, a wave broke where there had been only deep blue. A rock hidden in the depths must have caught the foot of a larger wave, the rogue one, and blanketed the waters with a blinding rumble of foam, cascading and engulfing everything in its path. It was far enough away that it wasn't a threat. I laughed with it, laughed at the power that could snap my boat in two, re-form, and break it into a dozen smaller pieces. I watched the wave melt back into the innocent roll of the sea, its power hidden until it shook the air with an explosion of white that climbed the cliff face, froze in seconds of brilliance, then fell back. Beneath the smallest sea stack I was nothing but a speck, a dot of yellow lost in the trough one second and high on the shoulder of a roller the next. Around me everything was huge, each wave perfect in form, splendid even in the final moment of destruction.

Again I sang. I had to. I had to lip my voice, mix it with the winds and the seas, and offer it to the wildness and the pageantry that surrounded me. It was either sing or explode like the waves, vaporized by the energy that my body could not contain. Each time a massive roller collided with a reverberating *whumph* against a hidden rock or sea stack, I would sing out, "Yes! More, more. Yes, you are beautiful!" The seas filled me, they rolled through me, and built into breakers of emotion that erupted into shouts of ecstasy. I was caught up in the passion, a wild man singing with heart and voice to the sea and the winds that poured off the clifftops.

The winds fueled the passion. They came in a tumbling mass of cool, heavy air that rolled off the mountains like a river, gathering speed in the ravines and following the contours of the land until it spilled over the edge of the cliff. In a waterfall of wind, they blasted the sea with cat's paws, fanned out a clear warning, and hit with a ferocity that stung my eyes and ripped past my ears in a deafening torrent. They came from behind in gusts that grabbed the paddle blades, yanking them one way, twisting them another, trying desperately to tear them from my grasp. With startling power the winds spirited me across the waves, flattening the paddle jacket against my back and tearing at anything that dared to stand firm against their fury. A minute would pass and suddenly the air was still.

Gentle puffs touched the swell crests, left a fingerprint of contact, as if an apology for their rude behavior, and then vanished. All was instantly quiet; the cat's paws raced away, coloring the seas in front of me with their glitter. The warmth of the sun returned to bathe my face. For three or four minutes, the winds were calm, or at least they stayed high. I watched the fulmars streak across the heights of the cliff, a blur of white that banked and faulted in the sudden collision of updrafts and pillows of air that spilled and rolled off the cliffs as certainly as the waves of the ocean. The fulmar's wings sketched the invisible lines of wind squalls, the gusts throwing them side to side, then suddenly lifting them fifty feet straight up and stalling their flight. For a second, they hung suspended, then turned their bellies toward the cliff and rocketed out to sea, dropping and bringing with them the cat's paws and renewed attack of the winds.

The telltale warning of the cat's paws came straight out from the cliffs, and I struggled to get the bow pointed into the winds before they hit. The winds were so strong they lifted the tops of the waves, flinging them into the air in sheets of pelting droplets that stung my face and hands. The only thing to do was to lie over the front deck, my forehead touching the fiberglass, and the paddle held against the boat with the weight of my body. With each blast I curled my shoulders tighter, pushed harder into the deck, and hoped the wind would blow itself out. The boat skidded backward, over swells and into troughs, and still I lay tucked in my protective curl. If I straightened, the wind would throw me over in the blink of an eye.

Thirty or forty seconds is a long time when you know you're being blown out to sea. What if the earlier gusts were just probes, spin offs from the main body of winds that might now be tearing over my folded form? The wind was blowing over forty knots, stronger than an hour earlier and far beyond anything I could paddle against. I stayed tucked until the blast started to drop. When I thought I could regain some ground, I came par-tially out of my curl, and with the paddles as low as I could hold them without losing purchase on the water, I headed back for the protection of the cliffs. A quarter mile on either side of me, the winds whipped the waters into the same fury that had carried me away from the land. As the seconds slipped by, the winds weakened. It was the lull I had hoped for. I sat upright, reached for as much water as I could with each stroke, and sprinted for the safety of the land a quarter mile away. Another blast caught me halfway, forced me back into a tuck, and I lost most of what I had gained. The thrill of the high winds was long gone. Now all I wanted was the safety of the land.

I headed for the sea stack at one end of a shallow indent filled with soccer ball–sized rocks. Tens of thousands of white and gray rocks, all perfectly rounded, were pushed in parallel shelves that followed the gentle curve of the cliff. Like the levels of a receding lake, the highest line of rocks showed the height of a winter gale, the two lower benches a record of lesser storms. Beneath the layered crescents of mini-boulders, the swells rolled in blue and dumped with a roar that filtered back into the sea. The cove, bracketed by points of cliff that had eroded and left lofty isolated towers capped in green, funneled the swells onto the steep slope of rocks. The only place to land was behind the north sea stack. I watched a swell rake the sides of the stack, noted where it broke over hidden rocks and which shadows it left covered in a smooth mound of blue-green. Two, then three swells rolled in. Each broke with the same fury and the noise that is so unnerving, even when it is expected. With each passing swell I picked out another twenty yards of route that would lead me into the calmer waters behind the stack. I waited for a smaller set to roll in, paddled onto the back of a swell, and rode it through the memorized channel into the shallows.

The winds still rolled off the cliffs, covering the water with a pattern of scales, but under the walls of rock it was dead calm. I found three broken lengths of boards and part of a pallet that I used as a bridge to pull the boat over the ankle-twisting rocks. One boat length at a time, I pushed, pulled, and reset the boards again until it was high above the reach of the swells. It was a lot of work considering there wasn't a square foot of level ground to set up camp. I was stuck. I couldn't risk being out on the water and I didn't trust my luck with setting up camp amid the fragments of fallen rock at the base of the cliff. The only thing to do was wait and maybe the afternoon winds would calm.

I explored the rock-strewn cove bordered on one side by the dumping surf and the other by the sheer cliff and the steep grass ledges that somehow held enough soil for the greenery. Streaks of blackened cliff dripped with the tingle of water seeping from the growth above. In the recesses of shallow caves were tangles of orange and green trawler nets filled with dried weed and knotted around bits of fish crates and pieces of driftwood. A length of hawser, eight inches around and fifty feet long, snaked through the rocks, its braided strands flowing with the smoothness and muscle of coiled scales that disappeared beneath a pile of netting. Tangles of flotsam, rigid with impregnated salt, lay draped over rocks. Beneath the interlocked web of debris, there was only more rock. There were no little crabs that scurried from the sudden sun or even swarms of beach flies. Just the mummified remains of the fishing industry thrown fifty feet above the highest bank of wave-driven rocks.

I found a sheep trail that angled through tufts of grass and switchbacked in dizzying heights above the cove. In places it branched into a half dozen faint paths that probed the base of overhanging ledges. With careful steps and toeholds that left my knees shaking, I inched around the rocks, occasionally loosening a stone which gained speed as it bounced in greater leaps that took it from sight. Out of the rock and shallow soil, stunted clumps of heather grew in dense patches coloring the cliffside and the gray of rock with a delicate fragrance of tiny purple flowers. Their gnarled roots ran like arthritic fingers over the crumbling rock, searching for crevices and clawing into the shallow soil. Close to the top of the cliff, the grasses were bent over the edge in heavy growth. I rested and looked down at the top of the seastack, a lush platform suspended atop the two hundred–foot spire. Fulmars and gulls soared beside its walls and added a dizzying perspective to the heights I had climbed. Further below, the graceful sweep of the cove reached out in a stunning contrast of white rocks embracing an ocean of indigo. All the sounds of the sea were lost. Surf broke silently around the offshore rocks, regrouped in smooth lines, and came ashore in bands of white. Along that curve of rock meeting ocean, I searched for the yellow of my boat and eventually found it: the thinnest sliver of yellow almost indistinguishable from five hundred feet up.

I finished the climb, peeking over the clifftop and gazing in wonder for several minutes at the dozens of valleys, ravines, and hills that rolled away in rugged relief. Instead of the flat blue horizon of sky meeting sea, my eye was treated to distances and elevations that reached back from the cliffs, lifting and rolling with the freedom of untrammeled lands. Backed into a hillside on the edge of that expanse of green were the ruins of a stone building. It sat in a little valley surrounded by hills that climbed to a distant peak. Roofless and blending into the exposed rock of the hills, it looked like a lonely yet beautiful place to live.

I walked the cliff edge, felt the wind streaming through my fingers and whistling in my ears as I threaded my way along a sheep trail atop the precipice, a five hundred–foot drop to one side and the undulating panorama of desolate beauty to the other. The track twisted and climbed over the irregular terrain, leading my eye to the north, where the land slowly dropped back to the sea. I walked to the highest point on the cliff, turned, and looked in each direction. To the east, the winds came over the land with the fragrance of grasses and earth. To the west was the ocean, a deep blue plain spreading to the horizon and meeting the sky in a fine line punctuated with clouds of puffed cotton. To the south, the velvety softness of rolling hills and the perfect forms of green-covered mountains stopped abruptly at the cliff edge. A jagged, torturous line defined the boundary of land meeting ocean. For almost four hundred miles I had followed that line, creeping around headlands battered by the Atlantic, seeking the protection of its coves and islands, and drinking in the nectar of its history.

The five hundred feet of elevation gave me a sense of looking down on the past two months, the memories coming back in waves, one washing into the next, obliterating the image as quickly as another formed. I wanted to cling to separate images but couldn't freeze the flash-memories of fishermen, music, headlands, and ruins. They ran together in a blur of place names, framed in textures of sun warmth, winds, and the gentle touch of mist. The collage of memories tugged at my mind while my heart colored them with emotions of wild joy, freedom, and the floodtide of wonder and awe. In my chest was a tightness that eased slightly with a deep breath but quickly returned as I stood and looked back on the journey.

In another fifty miles, the swells would be at my back, pushing me across the top of Ireland and away from the wilds and the blessings of the west coast. No matter what lay ahead, the unsettling truth was that with each passing swell I would be further from the coast that had so deeply intimidated me and at the same time filled me with its beauty and wild charm. Another breath. Another sigh that the winds carried over the clifftop and out to the sea.

I saw myself as if I were looking down from some great height, a tiny figure standing on the edge of a cliff, surrounded by the dramatic interplay of ocean, land, and sky. There was that familiar feeling of smallness, of humbly standing there, grateful for the privilege of the past two months, and sadly aware that I was saying good-bye. I hadn't climbed the cliff for the purpose of a farewell, but maybe the powerful gusts of wind that had threatened to blow me offshore knew that I needed to begin that process. I still had over two hundred miles to paddle, but I couldn't deny that the trip was drawing to a close.

The west coast, for all practical purposes, was behind me. The massive swells that battered this coast, and the weather patterns that brought rain and winds, and hid the islands in ghostly veils of gray mist, would soon be another memory. It was time to leave this exposed coast and get around the top of Ireland before the fall winds made today's weather look like child's play. I wanted to linger with the memories and etch them into my heart. I wanted to make them as vivid as the winds and the colors of the sea and land that stretched before my eyes.

The ache in my heart was the fear of losing the companionship of the winds and the swells, of losing the soul connection I had experienced on the ocean. I felt as though the ocean knew me better than any human could. I was unashamed to sing in its presence, to cringe in fear at its power, or to stare in utter wonder at its beauty. I had shed tears of humility at the base of towering cliffs, fought with every fiber of muscle and tendon to stay upright in huge seas, and floated naked, my fingers resting on the smooth curve of stones, while a gentle swell bathed me in the chill waters of a sheltered cove. On the sea I was utterly myself. The winds, the seas, and the cliffs that resonated with the booming heartbeat of the ocean demanded that I put all other cares aside and be nothing but a paddler: a child-spirit, present and wide-eyed, willing to be unguarded and open. Maybe what I feared and what caught in my chest was not only the sadness of letting go of the west coast wildness and the exposure of the islands, but the fear of having to be something other than who I was on the ocean. I was afraid of not singing again, not sleeping with the stars and waking with a smile to the call of the gulls or the chirp of a songbird in the grasses. What if I never again felt the power of a wall of green water rising and arching in fluid poetry on its final rush toward the perfection of sea meeting cliff? How could I live without the purity of those rhythms? Who would watch the swells or listen to the silent stones of long-abandoned ruins? Who would acknowledge the lichens or the soft whisper of a wave melting into the trackless sands of a tiny beach beneath walls of cliff? Questions filled my mind, took me away for a few moments, then brought me back to the clifftop. On that twisted sheep track there were no answers to the questions that rose from my heart and were born away on the winds. I turned and slowly retraced my steps.

Two days later, I paddled around a low finger of land that came off the hills and very understatedly marked the turning point for the north coast. I had asked a shopowner how the point had gotten its name, Bloody Fore-land. He said he had heard two stories: One was that there had been a great battle, centuries ago, between two families. The carnage and slaughter were so terrible that the hillside had turned red with blood. The other story was that in the long light of summer evenings, the land took on the color of blood from the setting sun. That evening, I sat off the point and turned the boat to look back at the west coast: the sky was a coil of energy-filled clouds. A shaft of light illuminated part of the meadow on the point, the green radiating a startling, magical light. The remainder of the land and of the hills reaching down to the sea were blackened as if warning of the approaching storm. Clouds moved against one another, mixing into columns of boiling energy that just as quickly parted to let another ray of light touch the sea or land. Again and again, the clouds combined forces, feinted an attack, then backed off as if knowing they could rain down their power at will. It was a sky that promised winds; the rain would come later, maybe the next day, but first there would be this display of gathering energy. After living with the weather for so long, I knew I had an hour, maybe two, before the winds hit. I took one last look at the west coast islands whose outlines faded into the purple-black light, then turned east.

Due north, ten miles offshore, was Tory Island, the faint glint of its lighthouse flashing a white light every thirty seconds. Five miles in front of me was another group of islands, the ones I hoped to find shelter behind. A heavy ground swell was running with the same ominous lighting as the sky and land, huge volumes of silent black water that rolled out of the west, lifted the stern, and passed me at twice my paddling speed. They came and went as if running from something over the horizon, each a reminder that I had better hurry. As I shortened the distance to the islands, the sky closed completely and all depth perception was lost. The islands seemed to float away from me, as if the energy of the approaching storm was pushing them away. A few raindrops hit the broad smoothness of the swells, their splatter a prelude to the gathering storm.

In front of me, the backs of the waves blocked out the islands and all of the coastline beyond. I turned to look back and was shocked at the size of the swells. Black shadows reared out of the dull light, settled into a trough, and rose again much closer, advancing as if they were intent on sweeping over me. I kept paddling, looking over my shoulder as the leading troughs overtook me and the waves towered overhead. The darkness amplified the speed of the waves. They closed the last yards in seconds, lifting the boat high out of the shelter of the trough and leaving me with a view of the surrounding seas that was unsettling. I would rather have stayed in the trough and not seen the oily blackness of rolling seas that reached out for miles in every direction. Those seconds of being raised, like an offering into the sky, broke my concentration, and I knew the bone-deep feeling of exposure, of being the only bright spot on the smoldering sea, an intruder, a yellow target for the waves to find. I stopped looking back, refocused on the closest island, and tried not to think how far from land I was.

The first island I reached was Inishbofin, a mile-long hill, guarded on the west by craggy rocks that the swells thundered into. Around the north tip were more rocks. I paddled wide around them and came into the instant calm behind the island. A broad sweep of beach lay nestled between points of rock to the north and south, a safe refuge from anything but an east wind.

I landed and hastily carried the first load of gear to a flat spot behind the cobbles of the beach. Dozens of holes tunneled into the soft earth and round grainy pellets lay scattered everywhere. The island looked as if it was overrun with rabbits. The tent was up in a matter of minutes and the heaviest stones I could find were piled on the corner stakes. More gear was brought up from the boat: the food bag, water bag, stove, and pots. In the backpack was the camera, journal, and the radio so that I could get the weather forecast. In a half hour I had my camp set up and the stove roaring away beneath a pot of water. The weather report called for northwest winds at Force 6 to 7, swinging to the northeast by tomorrow afternoon, then to the south by evening. A series of low fronts were backed up across the Atlantic and would bring unstable weather for the next few days. I turned the radio off and stuffed it back into the pack. It was the same forecast I had been hearing for most of the summer: shifting winds as fronts moved in, held for twelve hours, then were pushed toward England and Scotland by the next one. I was tired of the constant winds. They had been with me since the very first day of the trip, and the cat-and-mouse game of running from them was wearing me out.

I sat in the tent, holding the warm pot of rice in my hands and mentally clicking off the next thirty miles of paddling. Horn Head was eight miles to the east, then another ten miles to Fanad Head, where I could paddle into Lough Swilly if the winds forced me ashore. From there it was a twelve-mile crossing to Malin Head, the northernmost point of Ireland. On my map, I had drawn spiraling circles and made a note of "large tidal eddies" to the west of Malin Head. This was the area that a lighthouse keeper I met in County Cork had warned me about. I remembered him saying, "If ye hit it at the wrong time, ye might as well get out an' walk, for ye won't be goin' anywhere."

His advice was a simple explanation of the tidal flows around the headland. At the height of either tide, the current rushes around the point in standing waves that no boat challenges. On the other hand, if the tides can be used properly, the passage can be fast and smooth. The tide floods west to east at almost five knots, a terrific assist, until it hits the headland

and sweeps back on itself. The trick would be to approach the headland at the last hour of the flood when the backflow was at its weakest, then sprint the four or five miles to Malin Head and get as close to the rocks as the swells allowed. If the timing was right, the ebbing tide would begin and I would be able to find a countercurrent close to the rocks. Without the wind factor and in the absence of swells on the headland, it was a straightforward piece of timing and fast paddling. With the wind, especially if it was a wind against a tide, the plan would be useless and I would have to come up with another. Because of the strong tides, the only option would be to sit and wait for the winds and tides to flow together.

I finished dinner, then walked down to the beach to wash the pots with a mix of fine sand and seawater. The banks of clouds that had hurried me into the protection of the islands had drawn thick and were now a single, gray blanket that sat heavy on the sea. Smudges of massed clouds slid over one another, partially masking the energy of an hour earlier. Maybe I was wrong about the winds? I returned to the tent, set the stove and cooking gear in one corner, and slipped the headlamp into the pocket of my raincoat. Before darkness closed completely over the island, I wanted to have a look around.

I set off for the southern end, turning around now and again to see the peak of the tent blending into the hillocks of sand and green. A small building of stone—two windows and a doorway that were barely more than a total ruin—was the landmark I would have to find on the way back. I turned and followed an old track that cut across the uneven ground on the low end of the island, then disappeared as it climbed over a ridge toward the crest. The deep ruts lay hidden beneath long grass and occasionally cut into the center where the tractor or cart had lurched out of the mud. As I walked over the crown of a small hill, I felt the first gust of wind coming from the west. It seemed as if it had been waiting for dusk. The higher the track climbed, the stronger the winds became. In the dim light, amid winds that now blew like waves across the grass, I stumbled, gave up on the rutted track, and turned toward the summit.

Along the shadow of land rising into the last light of day was the silhouette of a man leaning into the wind. His pace was unhurried, as if the long summit of the island had been his destination and he had slowed to catch his breath. A border collie appeared on the ridgeline, frolicking and apparently filled with the energy of the evening walk. The sight of this lone figure set against the sky added to the drama of the winds and the sounds of the breaking seas that came with them. The man spotted me as I came out of the shadow of a dip, waved, and waited for me to finish the climb.

When I was almost at the top, the dog bounded off the ridge in a puppylike welcome. He raced toward me, pink tongue hanging out as he circled, then took off in a streak back to the man. It was a good sign: a friendly dog is often a mirror of its owner.

The fellow was indeed friendly. I introduced myself and explained that I had landed on the protected beach, the first safe landing I could find. He told me his name was Patrick Coll. As if to reassure me, he said, "Ah, the beach is fine when the wind is from the west. In an east wind she can be rough but she's fine tonight." Then he asked, "And what kind of a boat are ye in?"

Whether it was the wind or the island dialect, I didn't know, but it was hard to understand Patrick's short sentences. "It's a kayak," I answered, and went on to explain where I had come from that morning and that I was paddling around Ireland, hoping to get back to Dublin before the fall winds set in.

I expected the usual disbelief, the flood of questions, but instead he simply said, " 'Tis a fair bit to go in a canoe." It wasn't a statement of disinterest, but rather a simple fact, as certain as the fact that the beach was a safe landing in a west wind.

A gust tore over the summit and the first drops of rain slapped onto my raincoat. Total darkness had settled over the island and I could no longer see Patrick's face. He said he lived just over the hill, pointing with the glow of his cigarette to the south, and invited me out of the wind for a pot of tea. The shelter of a roof and the chance to find out more about the island sounded like a good way to spend the evening.

We dropped off the exposed ridge, following the dog and another track that I could barely make out by looking slightly to one side. It eventually led us out of the wind to a cottage set back from a grass-covered road. Patrick disappeared into the house and a moment later the glow of a gas lamp flared, then settled into a warm light spilling through the open door-way. When I entered, Patrick was coaxing the first flames beneath a stack of newspapers and peat in the fireplace. The wind funneled down the chimney and sent tendrils of smoke from the crumbled newspaper drifting into the room. He moved the match to another corner of paper, playing it along the edge under the dry black turf. The peat slowly caught, added color and heat to the flames, and established a draft that pulled smoke and rounded tongues of orange and yellow straight upward.

I dropped into the comfort of a worn chair on one side of the hearth while Patrick put the kettle on in the kitchen. I heard water being poured into a metal pot, the heavy *thunk* of the jug being set down, and the *clink* of two spoons dropped into mugs. The raspy whisper of water beginning to heat, and the gentle snap of the fire blended with the sounds of the kitchen. In the warm and snug cottage, the sounds seemed so delicate compared to the pervasive noise of winds and seas that I lived with twenty-four hours a day. I settled into the comfort of the fire as it flickered a reminder of the winds beyond the thick stone walls.

"Doyetakcsugarinyertea?" The words rolled off Patrick's tongue fast and thick as a foreign language.

"I do if you've got it, but black is fine if you don't," I answered.

He brought in steaming mugs of tea, a bowl of sugar, and a fine crystal pitcher of cream. The tea was strong, dark as the night framed in the windows, the cream white and thick as it swirled the blackness into golden brown. He pulled a chair to the far side of the hearth, lit a cigarette before settling, then without coaxing began telling me stories of the island.

"So, yev come to Inishbofin. Oach, there's stories on this island like no other. Yer tent's down by the beach, is it? Well, if ye looked, ye woulda seen a . . . ah, I don't know the English word. Ye see, we speak the Gaelic here. English on the mainland but here it's the Gaelic. A stone house, not a house but it was once."

I was hanging on each word and struggling to tie the sentences together into the story he was telling. "A ruin?"

"Yah, a ruin. No roof but a pile of stone. A man, Porter Kingsley, built it. In the twenties or thirties. His wife and he lived in that hut 'til the day he disappeared. A rich American, he was. Owned an estate east down the coast from here but lived in the stone hut." He drew on his cigarette and took a sip of his tea. "One day his wife came inta the village an' said he was gone. The people searched the cliffs and beach but never found him. A strange story. Some tink there was foul play. Maybe the wife wanted the estate. Who knows."

Another story was about his father and grandfather, who fished the island waters for salmon, "that was before the nylon nets, an' the fish could see the cotton by day. My father and his father would sail at night, in the yawls. Oach, now, they were a fine boat. Graceful, they were. There's one, two left on the mainland, but they're not used. The outboard is better. More money, but in those days they only had sails. Everything cotton, sails and nets. We fished at night. I did as well. Oach, now that's goin' back. More tea?"

"Yes, please."

The tea was poured and the sugar bowl held out in a hand that was lined and cracked at the joints of the fingers. Working hands larger than mine but holding the bowl as gently as a child.

"Me fatha would catch the salmon, and in the winter cod. Mackerel in the summer. More fish than is caught today, fer sure. The fish are gone. Japanese trawlers ripping the bottom up an' takin' our fish back to Japan."

With a cigarette in one hand and the cup of cold tea in the other, he tilted his head, squinted through the smoke, and told one story after the other about the history of the island. In the course of three hours, I listened to this handsome, gray-haired fisherman and pieced together stories that flipped back and forth as if time itself didn't matter as it did in the rest of the world. Fragments of tales. Overlapping time frames, smoke hanging in the air, and the soft burn of the peat. Patrick's dog was stretched out in front of the fire, his black and white coat glistening in the soft light of the gas lamps and the glow of the flames, his legs twitching in dreams.

"Some islanders went to Alaska and the Yukon. Lookin' for the gold. I tink the families live in Seattle now, maybe Montana. Islanders 'ave gone all over the world but I come back every year. Come out in May an' stay till the mackerel and salmon are gone, then back to the mainland.

" 'Ave ye seen McGregor's hut? 'Tis down on the rocks—ye must 'ave seen it. Queerest thing I ever saw. But for a man, Neil McGregor was the smartest. A goldsmith from London, we never knew 'ere he came from or why he came to the island. Didn't ask. The island is that way. Oach, that man could fix anything from a stone wall to a fine watch. Some days I would see 'em on the back o' the island and he'd wave—sometimes he'd walk right past without a word. A queer man, but if there was help needed, he'd be there. I carried him out. Dead, he was. No one had seen 'em an' I went and looked in his shack—ye have to walk to the point an' look at it. Nothin' but a sheep hut, but he lived there closer to the sea than anythin'. On the wall inside are, ah . . . in the Gaelic I can say it but . . . pictures in the stone, chipped, hammered inta the rock."

"Etching? Or carvings?" I tried to find the word he was looking for.

"Yea, carving maybe." Patrick was gazing into the fire with a look of wonder, the stub of his hand-rolled cigarette held loosely between thick fingers and his weight shifted forward and leaning on the arms of the chair. "Ye should have a walk down to his hut before ye leave. 'Tis a lobster, a salmon, and a gull on the stone. I've never seen the likes of them lookin' so real—and in a shack so small you wouldna tink a man could live in it."

"You said you carried him out? What happened to him?"

"He died. He was there on 'is bed. Like he was sleepin'. But dead he was. I carried the body out and a nephew of his showed up to claim him. We rolled a rock agenst the door and 'tis the way it is now."

The stories continued: a meeting on the Aran Islands two years ago, islanders from all over gathering to make their voices heard. They want power and water brought to the islands; they want a share of EU (European Union) money. Ireland is changing and Patrick is worried. He shakes his head and gestures with his hands. The drugs in Dublin, the violent crime of the cities. Again he lifts his hands in the simple expression of a man who doesn't understand the ways of the outside world.

It was late, close to midnight, when I heard footsteps in the outer hall. The dog woke, stood, stretched, and waited for the inner door to open. A tall, trim man, mid-fifties, walked into the living room, looked directly at me, then over to Patrick, and said, "I didn't know there were strangers on the island."

Patrick echoed the man's words, "Oach, ye didn't know there were strangers on the island."

It was an interesting exchange. The visitor then greeted Patrick. "Good evening to ye, Patrick." Patrick returned the greeting, "Good evening to ye, and it's a wind we'll be feelin' tonight and rain before long." After a few rapid sentences in Gaelic and a nod in my direction, Patrick introduced me to his friend. The man wasn't unfriendly but neither was he outgoing: a man comfortable in the presence of other islanders but withdrawn in front of a visitor.

A week later I met a man from Londonderry who had studied the ways of the island people. I told him of my visit with Patrick and the greeting that I had listened to with such interest. He said the islanders were different; they kept to themselves, but if they took you in, you couldn't find finer people. The curious pattern of repeating phrases and parts of a story was a holdover from the days of old, the repetition drawing out the story and making the telling more dramatic and suspenseful. What I had witnessed was the beginning of the story of my visit, a story that would be retold in the village again and again. It was the isolation of the islands that made the telling of stories so important: something to add to the evening hours in front of the fire.

I left Patrick and his neighbor sitting in the warm glow of lamplight and peat, their voices soft and unhurried as I stepped into the chill of the night. Thick, dark clouds raced across a half moon that illuminated the crown of the island. My eyes adjusted to the moonlight and I found the old road leading to the summit, then angling down across the slope of the island in the direction of the beach. My feet raked the sodden grasses and the wind found its way through the flaps and pockets of my raincoat. A light flickered on the northern horizon, then swept across the darkened sea in a solid beam. It swung in a smooth arc, the pinpoint spreading out as it probed the blackness, sweeping the sea and reflecting off the clouds. The beam blinded me for a second, then raced away and sent its message of light into the Atlantic. Every thirty seconds the light returned, flared across Inishbofin, touched the mainland two miles behind me, then faded again as it reached into the black horizon. The light was from Tory Island, built high on the cliffs so that it could be seen thirty miles out, its four-second beacon guiding fishing boats and shipping into the restricted waters between Ireland and Scotland. In a howling gale or star-filled summer night, the light kept a vigil over the waters. I thought of Neil McGregor and the nights he must have shared with the silent and lonely repetition of the beam.

I let the slope of the island pull me down to the beach and to the ruins that stood against the skyline. The toppled pile of stones near the campsite now had a story that accompanied me on my walk. A few hours earlier the island had been a place of refuge, a rockbound shelter that blocked the onslaught of westerly swells. An Irishman, a peat fire, and a sleeping dog had brought the place to life. Now the night was filled with tales of island hermits, canvas sails, cotton nets, and the voice of a Gaelic storyteller. I zipped the tent shut and settled in for the night as the light on Tory Island filled the space with a soft glow.

By morning, the winds had dropped to barely a whisper. The forecast was for a northeasterly, Force 5 to 7 by midday. If the report was right, I wouldn't be going anywhere beyond the protection of the cluster of three islands. I had breakfast, then walked over the ridge and down to the row of houses crowded around the village pier. Lobster pots, fish crates, and netting with small oblong floats rested against and on top of the stone wall that ran in front of the whitewashed houses. Three men stood at the top of a concrete boat ramp, leaning against a rusty winch and looking out across the narrows to the mainland. They wore dark trousers and worn black jackets over white shirts. Crumpled caps, each worn differently—one pushed high on the back of the head, another down low to shade the eyes.

At first I thought they were waiting for someone to cross from the mainland, but after a half hour of standing and chatting with them I realized that they probably did this every morning. We talked about the weather, how fickle the winds were, shifting and covering the sea in whitecaps. I asked about the winters, what the seas were like and if they fished at all once the weather turned.

The fellow who did most of the talking cocked his head to one side and simply said, "Ah, the winter seas er rough, and there's no fish to be had."

The other two men echoed his reply. "Oh aye, rough, very rough. No fish a'tall."

Without looking at the other two, the first fellow said, "We'll go to the mainland in September, won't we?"

The reply was a curious partial echo, expressed on a sigh as if it were inevitable. "Oh aye, in September, in September."

The echo seemed to be a way of reassuring each other, of making a statement and trusting that your neighbor or fishing partner was there to back you up.

A couple of men who looked as if they must be in their eighties shuffled down the pier and climbed into one of the small open boats. Their clothes were the same as the younger fishermen I stood next to—the same, but more worn and hanging loose without the bulk of muscle to fill them. There wasn't a word said between them as one went forward, the other aft. Gnarled fingers cast off the lines with a splash and the man in the back pulled twice at the outboard before it sputtered to life. They sat on the wood seats, a last-minute shift in weight to trim the boat, each with one hand on the gunwale and their caps pulled low over their eyes. They disappeared around the end of the pier, in the direction of the mainland.

The sheltered harbor was the center of island life. Doorways faced the pier, a dozen houses, some boarded up as if a reminder, like the old fishermen, of days gone by. Oars, nets, and open doorways looked out on the harbor. A couple of men were chatting on the far end of the row of houses, enjoying the morning sun, talking to each other but looking in my direction. A beautiful young woman with ringlets of flaming red hair came out of one of the houses with a wooden tray of salted fish. A child of four or five ran to catch up with her as she carried the tray to the stone wall bathed in sunlight and began spreading the fish out on the stones. Out in the middle of the harbor were five or six miniature wooden fishing boats, each brightly painted, the hulls black below the waterlines, blue or green above, and the pilothouse another color. The boats were two or three feet long and perfectly built so they rode over the tiny waves without taking on water. One fisherman told me when a child wanted his or her boat, one of the adults would row out and get it.

I wandered out to the end of the pier, aware that I was being watched. Massive rings, rusted smooth, were pinned into the concrete and held the lines of fishing boats. More lobster traps and coils of tangled lines lay heaped to one side of the pier. Smells of fish and drying seaweed hung in the air. They were the smells of a working pier that spoke of early morning departures when the winds were calm and the open boats could work the seas.

By the time I walked back to the boat ramp, the fishermen were gone. Most of the men were out fishing and the only signs of life were two aproned women standing in a doorway above the harbor. A peaceful silence floated over the village and along the grass road, bordered on both sides by high stone walls. I walked up the road—more of a path because there wasn't a single car on the island—to Patrick's house, the last one before the track faded into the meadows of the island. I turned in the general direction Patrick had pointed when he told me about Neil McGregor, and started across the island.

A stiff wind flattened the grasses and snatched at the bill of my hat. The waters around the island were black, menacing and flecked with the roll of whitecaps. The winds were coming in early. From a knoll overlooking the northeast point of the island, I could see the hut that had been the island hermit's home. As I drew closer, I was struck by its size. It looked like the shelters I had seen on Blasket Island that had been built for the sheep. Nothing more than a five-foot by eight-foot stone shed with a flat, tarred canvas roof. The stones were carefully laid so that no mortar had been used, the roof no higher than my chest. Rather than being built in the shelter of a draw or snugged against the slope of the hill, it sat forelorn but solidly, a few yards above a finger of rock that reached into the sea. In a northeasterly blow it would have been drenched by spray.

I rolled the rock away from the door and was surprised at how smoothly the hinges swung open. I squeezed through the child-sized doorway, sat on my heels, and looked at the home of Neil McGregor. A small window of glass held in place by tiny stones and bits of rolled cloth offered what little light was needed to fill the claustrophobic space. Below the window, on the ledges of several stones, were the melted remains of thick candles, the dripping wax hanging in suspended droplets as if the flames had just been blown out. Bits of newspaper had been jammed into spaces where drafts must have whistled. The hut was tidy, the dirt floor packed solid and swept free of any loose stones. On the wall beside the door were the etchings Patrick had told me about. When I saw them, I understood the look of wonder that had come over his face.

The etchings were the patient works of an artist. A salmon leaped from the surface of one stone, its back arched, its tail rippling the water in concentric circles. Fins, an eye, and the curve of mouth and gills gave the fish life. It hurled itself out of the coarse grain of the stone and floated into the shadowed light of the hut. I forgot it was still part of the stone and half expected it to have the feel of fine wet scales beneath my fingertips.

On another rock was a gull standing as only a live gull would, almost arrogant in its posture of supremacy. The curve of stone held the gull's shoulder in perfect proportion, its back feathers tapering and layered into a resting stance.

The third image was that of a lobster: each leg, antenna, and the segmented tail was painstakingly cut into the stone. One claw was bigger than the other, the larger one used for crushing and the smaller for feeding and tearing.

The stone art and the manner in which the hut was built spoke more of Neil McGregor than the stories I had been told. I could almost hear the tapping of hammer and chisel emanating from the squat hut on a windy winter's night, see the soft yellow light of a flickering candle casting shadows on the stone as he added detail and life to his work. One man alone on the edge of an island, tapping out an image while the waves broke over the point and the Tory Island light swept the skies with its watchful beam. His world would have been rich with the life of the ocean and the winds that either scattered the clouds or bound them together in quilted gray layers. Whatever secrets he lived and died with on that remote finger of land, I wanted to believe he had found peace.

A gust of wind rushed over the hut, swung the door on its hinges, and mixed with the noise of the waves. Once again it was the stones, those that had felt the cut of the chisel and held the winds at bay, that knew the stories and lessons of the past. The hut that had sheltered the life of Neil McGregor now held his thoughts and soul within its walls. Most of his story would never be known except by the winds, the gulls, and the seas that washed the rocks in front of his hut. I closed the door, gently placed the rock against its base, and left the hut as I found it.

By the time I reached the tent, the winds were piling small breakers on the beach. The tent was straining at its tether of rock-buried pegs, the rip-stop nylon stretched taut and billowing in with each fresh gust. The waters on either side of Inishdooey Island, a half mile away, were covered in breaking rollers.

My visit to Inishbofin had been intense. Suddenly I wanted some distance from it. I wanted to see it as I saw Inishdooey, far enough away that I could look at it as a whole rather than a compilation of stories. The trip had been filled with these moments of intensity that needed distance for perspective. The day was windy, maybe too windy to be out on the water, but now that I knew the stories of the island and had met its people, I wanted to see it again as an island: a green hump of hillock and ravine, rising out of the sea and having a life and spirit shaped by the winds and waves that wrapped around it. The winds were too strong to venture far, but a camp on Inishdooey would give me the perspective I wanted.

Before leaving Inishbofin, I needed water, and walked back over the island to fill my water bag. The village spring was along the track near

Patrick's house. As I approached, an older lady was coming up the track with a bucket in each hand. She wore two sweaters over a printed dress that ended midcalf above a pair of boots. She was thickset, her sleeves pulled halfway to her elbows, and wisps of wavy gray hair catching in the stiff winds. We met near the spring, a circle of stones almost hidden in the grasses spilling over its rim. She was breathing hard from the walk up the hill and set the buckets down beside the spring.

"Good morning," I said.

"Good mornin' to ye and 'tis a fine day. You'd be the man camped on the strand that Patrick was tellin' about."

I liked the woman's direct manner. Who I was was neither a question nor a statement that needed acknowledgment. It was simply a fact of the island. Talk of my visit must have spread house to house as quickly as the wind carried the smoke of the peat fires.

"I am. I wanted to get some water, say good-bye to Patrick, and head out before the winds pick up too much."

"Ah well, ye won't be finding Patrick on the island. This mornin' I saw him off to the mainland with the other men. He won't be gone long but for sure he isn't home. An' where is it yer' off to today?"

"Patrick told me there's an old chapel on Inishdooey and some cottage ruins that I think I'll have a look at. I want to get over before the seas get too choppy."

The woman's jaw dropped and her composure suddenly changed as if a cloud chilled a memory. Her eyes grew wide with fright and her response surprised me. "Oh sweet mother of Jesus, don't be tellin' me you'll be goin' to Inishdooey on a day the likes of this. For if ye do, I won't be sleepin' tonight." She was looking at me as if I were a son setting out to fish during a hurricane. "Ye can't be goin' out there with this wind. 'Tisn't a place to land with the seas and wind as they are."

I didn't know what memories haunted her, but I had heard enough tales of drownings in my trip along the coast to know that I had inadvertently touched a tender spot in her heart. Fishermen, and the woman who wait for them, know the tragedy of boats gone missing, and on an island as small as Inishbofin, with the men fishing the rough waters, I was sure there were stories of men lost at sea. I wanted to take back my words and leave the woman with only the cares of drawing her water. But I couldn't retract them, or hide my intentions. The only thing I could do was try to reassure her, point out the direction of the winds and how I planned to get onto Inishdooey.

"Patrick said there's a cobble beach on the near end of the island. I'll be in the lee and it's only a half mile. If the winds stay east or northeast I'll be over there in a half hour. I'll be fine. I don't want you to be worrying about me," I explained.

The woman looked a little relieved when she heard I had talked it over with Patrick. "Ah, but the winds. I wish ye hadn't a told me ye were goin' to Inishdooey. But if yer to go, then ye best be quick. 'Tis true there's the cobbles, but the wind is still strong. Oh mother of God, ye best be careful. I'll be sayin' a prayer for ye."

I thanked her for her concern and dipped the buckets in the well for her. We said good-bye, then walked down opposite sides of the hill, she to return to the village and me to the strand and the sea.

I paddled across to Inishdooey, landed in the shelter of its lee, and found a ravine, barely out of the wind, to set up camp. I had made a half mile of progress into the remaining two hundred fifty to Dublin. On days like this, when the clouds dragged their darkened tails across the wavetops, the distance to Dublin seemed long.

Inishbofin sat framed in the opening of the tent, an island filled with stories and cloaked in drifting mists. When a squall rolled past and the island cleared for a moment, I could see a low, dark square above the point where the waves washed white. It was Neil McGregor's hut. From a distance the hermit's home looked terribly lonely and exposed.

The first rain hit the tent with the flat beats of a drum. I was writing in the journal about my visit to Inishbofin. I would look up in thought and watch a bead of water run down the outside of the tent. It would start slowly, then gather speed as it collided and absorbed the weight of other drops. At the bottom of the floorless tent the droplet hit the sewn seam and hung for an instant before another followed the ease of its wetted path. The drop swelled until a gust of wind shook the tent and sent it, and a half dozen others, into the woven mat of fine grass and tiny rosettes of green leaves. I let my thoughts grow with the same weight, gathering, collecting memories of conversation and textures of Inishbofin that I penned along the lines. When I had tired of writing, I gently bent the edge of the journal with the flat of my thumb and watched the pages of black writing flip past. Page after page of cryptic lettering floated from one cover to the next, ending with a dozen blank pages that would soon hold the remaining days of the trip. In my hand, I held a thousand miles of paddling memories. The past three months had been intense, perhaps more so than I realized. I looked across at Inishbofin, saw the island set against the sea and the mainland through a transparent veil of rain, and knew that I would need the same distance from the trip to fully appreciate all that I had experienced.

I closed the journal, noting the dings and soft depressions in the leather cover and admiring the worn look of it. All the gear had that same patina of heavy use, the scratches in the brilliant gel-coat finish of the boat, the slight play in the shaft of the paddle where the two pieces had originally joined tightly, and the blackened outside of the pot where the stove had heated many meals. My tent leaked more than it did at the beginning of the trip, and the bottom of my left sandal was split from miles of walking and climbing. They were all simple things, little scars that I noted and was secretly proud of. They spoke to me of shared travels. Back home, I would not think twice about the sole of my sandal. When it eventually split in half, I would more than likely go out and buy a new pair. But in a place where the track of a raindrop was watched with quiet attention, there was time to be aware of the little things that held my simple life together.

I brushed a droplet of water from the closed journal and looked up at the seam of the tent straining against the winds. The prayer pennant with my friends' names and mildew-spotted outline of the Olympic Mountains hung damp in the peak. A gust of wind buffeted the tent and the pennant swayed gently. My clothing, the sleeping bag, and the pages of the journal and letters that I had written were damp. I thought of sunny days when I had spread the colors of my gear across the loft of wind-blown grasses. The gentle warmth of dry days would certainly return—days when the gear would be dried again and the seas would roll easily and allow me to continue.

I pulled on my raincoat, zipped into the chill of the hood, and stepped out into the mist drifting like fog over the island. A flock of sheep lifted their heads in a wave of panic as I walked over a rise in the land. The ones closest to me turned and bolted, panicking the others in a stampede that flowed like water over the contours. Blasts of wind pushed me off the top of the hill and into what little protection there was in the ravines. The island was shrouded and cut off from the mainland by clouds of fine moisture, not rain but wind-driven vapor that condensed on everything it touched. It was like a fine veil of shimmering cloth blown on the winds, drifting until the lower reaches caught on the top of the island, then set-tling over rock and grass with the same moist breath. Looking back, I could see my path cutting through the soft glimmer of weighted grasses, my feet having disturbed the delicate silver.

This island was the last one I would visit on my journey. I wanted to remember the feeling of this walk: the winds, the cool wash of mist, and the purity of island isolation. I crested a gentle rise running the length of the island and looked toward Horn Head, straight into the winds that came tearing out of the east. There was nothing to see but the lines of black waves covered in breaking white crests. They advanced out of shadows, one minute a quarter mile out, and the next barely beyond the reach of the last rocks. I wanted the mist and fog to lift for just a few minutes, long enough for me to get a glimpse at what lay beyond the gray blindness. I was wet and chilled but still I watched the sea. Somewhere through that drifting veil was a route that would lead me over the top of Ireland.

Northern Ireland—Tidal Terrors

The sea has never been friendly to man.
At most it has been the
accomplice of human restlessness.

—Joseph Conrad

The day I rounded Malin Head, the sea was suspiciously calm. I had awakened early, timed the tides, and sprinted to within two miles of the headland before backing off to a pace that eased the burn of shoulder muscles. I didn't trust the calm, or the puffs of east wind that floated over the bow and caressed my face. The day before had also been wind-free and sunny, contrary to the weather reports that had called for Force 5–7 winds out of the northwest. Throughout the summer, the reports had been unerringly accurate—often foul, but accurate. Now, on a day that was sunny and warm, the morning forecast haunted me with every puff of wind that rippled the faces of the swells.

In front of me, the cliff broke off in dazzling sunlight, its face painted with the sharpness of rock and brilliant green ledges. It was a picture out of one of those expensive coffee table books: stark light and shadow lifting the rock from the sea and thrusting it into a cloudless sky. I imagined the text beside the glossy photo: Malin Head, the northernmost point of mainland Ireland. What the picture wouldn't show, of course, were the swirls that were beginning to form at the base of the cliff; the first hint of the turning tide. The reality of the tide interrupted my daydreaming. It was still two miles to the village of Malin, where I knew there was a sheltered harbor. The puffs of wind were now a gentle breeze. Was it pure coincidence, or were the winds and the tides connected like two finely balanced gears that had slowly begun to turn? There was no time to bask in the moment of accomplishment, of reaching this northern headland I had heard tales of for the last two months. The wind was against the tide and already a few whitecaps were forming a mile offshore. I needed to get clear of the headland before the predicted winds developed.

The weight of the boat resisted the first paddle strokes, then slowly gave in to its own momentum. The compass swung to the southeast and all the stories and worries of the headland fell behind me. I was "over the top" and on my way to what I thought would be an easy wind-down paddle to Dublin.

The day after I came around Malin Head, the winds and rain returned. The low-pressure system that had been forecast a day earlier arrived in the predawn hours with fierce winds that hammered the tent. By dawn, the sea was churning with black rollers and streaked with the familiar trails of broken white waves.

Out of the past week, there had been two days of calm winds. The air temperature had dropped considerably, and I was in a race with the approaching fall weather. I waited all morning, hoping that the forecast was right: diminishing winds by midday, picking up again by late afternoon. By one o'clock the conditions were marginal, five- to six-footers that raced out of the northwest with occasional breakers. I loaded the boat and launched through a narrow slot in the reef I had camped above.

Two months of paddling on the west coast had sharpened my skills and accustomed me to paddling in rough conditions. After a half hour of getting bounced and twisted by the following seas, I settled into a rhythm. It was a slow paddle, with every fourth or fifth stroke a low brace, as waves broke over the stern and threw the boat on its edge. I would lean on the paddle, let the wave pass, sometimes washing over the cockpit, then calmly bring the boat back on course. I was matching the rhythm of the sea, not trying to overpower it, but letting it push me steadily along the base of the cliff.

From a height of three or four hundred feet, my situation would have looked perilous, the boat occasionally getting buried and skidded sideways by breaking waves. A strange yellow boat crawling ever so slowly amid coal black waves. While I paddled cautiously but comfortably through the seas, someone spotted me from the clifftop, and thinking I must be in trouble, reported my position to the local sea and cliff rescue unit.

Two hours later, I rounded Inishowen Head and paddled into the protected waters of Lough Foyle. I landed below a grassy park in the village of Greencastle. The rain had stopped and the clouds were beginning to thin. There was no one in sight as I climbed from the boat, then pulled it above the high water mark on the ramp. The day's paddle was behind me, and I was already thinking of what food I needed to buy for the next few days. I tucked the paddle and life jacket into the cockpit, shouldered my pack, and walked to the local shop.

With a pack full of bread, rice, and pasta, I returned to the boat and was carefully fitting it all into the rear compartment when a dark blue Land-Rover, with RESCUE printed in orange on the side panel, tore into the parking lot above the ramp. Gravel shot out from the tires as it came to an abrupt stop. A bearded fellow jumped out and hurried down to where I stood, straddling my boat, wide-eyed and wondering what all the commotion was about.

The first words he fired in my direction confused me even more: "Were ye out around Kinnagoe Bay two hours ago?"

Kinnagoe Bay? I had never heard of it, but maybe it was one of the small bays that I had cut across between the headlands of the cliff. "Well, I've just come from Culdaff. It's a bit more than two hours since I left there, but I don't know where Kinnagoe Bay is. How come? What's going on?"

"We had a call of a canoeist in trouble, an' before we launch, we're trying to get some more details."

There was some confusion as to exactly when and where the boat was spotted and even what color it had been. Whoever had called in had either not given the crucial information or it had been lost in the phone calls and radio transmissions that had sent volunteers out to the clifftops. As the fellow grilled me with questions of times and distances that I didn't normally think about, I was certain it was me that everyone was searching for. I knew how rough the outside waters were and I doubted that anyone else would have been paddling in those conditions. I never thought to ask him how he found me on the boat ramp below the level of the street.

Maybe I had made some forgotten comment about paddling on the sea to the grocer when he cheerfully asked if I was enjoying my holiday.

The fellow asked me to accompany him to the rescue center. As we sped along the village streets, I thought about the phone call I had made two days earlier to the Malin Head Marine Emergency Service. I had called them for the sole purpose of preventing this very thing I was now entangled in. For the last thousand miles I had kept the various rescue centers informed of my route and plans. They had always been cooperative and enthusiastic about the trip. Now I felt guilty for causing all this confusion.

The rescue center was on the second floor of an old military building on the edge of town. We climbed a set of dimly lit steps that opened to a small room looking out over Lough Foyle. Above a desk with several radios and a phone was a map of the surrounding area. Yellow and red pushpins dotted the coastline. Three other rescue volunteers were waiting, all fellows about my age. Introductions were made, but I was too confused to remember names. The time of my arrival in town and the details of my boat were written down while one of them tried to get in touch with the caller who had originally contacted the unit. They were trying to put the pieces of the puzzle together and determine if there could be more than one kayaker/canoeist.

More calls were made and gradually the tension began to subside. Someone at another location had talked with the original caller and determined that it was indeed a yellow canoe that had been spotted. Another call was made: the search was being called off, the rescue boat wouldn't be launched. The phones stopped ringing and everyone, including myself, sank a little deeper into the worn chairs at the rescue center.

Now that the emergency was over, everyone wanted to know more about my trip. When did I start? Where did I camp and what was the west coast like? Mugs of tea were filled, and cream and sugar passed around. Suddenly the distinction between rescuers and rescuee had melted with the last garbled radio message. Now we traded stories of the sea. I told them of places in their own country they hadn't seen, and they told me of the local waters, which they knew intimately. They knew nothing of kayaks, and I knew little of their job of pulling people from the cliffs and waters around the region. What we all shared, though, was the sea, that common denominator which had brought us together in a cramped room looking out over the lough.

We parted company at the village pier, all of them standing on the boat ramp and patiently watching as I slid into the cockpit, fastened the spray deck, and slowly backed the boat away. I took a group photo, called out a last farewell and thanks, then paddled back toward open water.

The day after the confusion of the search, I crossed the mouth of Lough Foyle and entered Northern Ireland. Throughout most of the summer, I had been listening to reports of the violence and tension that were smoldering in the mixed Catholic and Protestant neighborhoods. During the two-hour crossing, I watched the low shoreline gradually draw closer and wondered what lay waiting for me. My mind was half on the Troubles, the riots and bombings, and half on the increasingly powerful tides for which the waters up ahead were notorious. Ten miles ahead was the Giant's Causeway, a three hundred-foot cliff of hexagonal basalt columns where the tides swirled in massive overfalls and standing waves. Beyond that was Rathlin Island, then the coast of Scotland, which funneled all the power of the Atlantic tides into a fifteen-mile channel. By chance, I was arriving just as the moon was at its fullest: spring tides, the most powerful of the month. I couldn't remember who had first warned me about the area, but I had heard it from more than one person, a warning of extreme caution.

A westerly swell was gradually developing, three- to four-footers that I ignored but would later remember. My mind was on other things, the searing pain in my hip that was part of every day, and the unknown politics I was paddling toward. My concerns were focused on finishing the crossing and getting some local knowledge before the tides carried me below the cliffs and into Rathlin Sound. I turned the bow toward the seawall at Portrush. Suddenly any bias that I had toward the Troubles was forgotten. What I needed was information. I didn't care if it was Catholic, Protestant, Irish, or English.

I paddled into the flat waters of the Portrush marina and tied up in front of a yacht moored to the visitor's float. It looked like a working boat, the sails furled but not tightly stowed on the boom, the hull and chrome stanchions covered in powdery streaks of salt. I met Roy, the owner of the boat, and Jim, his companion, who had joined him for portions of his sail around Ireland. They had left Dublin five weeks earlier and had just pulled into Portrush for customs. Like me, they were homeward-bound, on the last leg of the journey back to Dublin. Jim was catching a train that afternoon, and Roy was waiting for a favorable tide to cross Rathlin Sound and find shelter in one of the island's harbors. He said they were off Malin Head in the roughest seas of the entire circumnavigation when they heard the radio transmissions about a lost canoeist. We compared notes on the weather and seas, and where we had both been. It was ironic that we were just a few miles apart, different boats and journeys, but all of us dealing with the same seas that had eventually pushed us over the top of Ireland. There was a sense of shared camaraderie; again, it was the sea that was the common denominator.

Roy brought out his charts. We sat in the cockpit of his boat, enjoying the sun and figuring out the best time for both of us to get through the sound. The overfalls—places where the bottom conditions threw the tidal currents into standing waves—were clearly marked below the Giant's Causeway, Benbane Head, and further down the coast at Fair Head and Torr Head. The key was to reach these headlands at the right time. Too early and the tide would be against us; too late and the overfalls would have already developed and could be a problem. We figured the distance to the first headland, the Causeway, how long it would take both of us to reach the cliffs, and what time the current would turn. The time of the tide change was different from that of the current and everything was figured from tables based on high water in Dublin. After double-checking the calculations we figured I had three hours before I had to leave. Roy would leave an hour later, and probably cross the sound as I came around Benbane Head.

Roy needed time to prepare his boat for the crossing, and I wanted to get another opinion on the currents in the sound. As I walked up the gangway that tied the float to the city pier, a group of people gathered to look down on the two boats. I turned and looked too. I had pulled my boat up on the float, and it sat like a nursing pup beside the bulk of the bigger sailboat. Both boats had a weathered look to them, a shared journey of a thousand miles, five weeks for one, three months for the other. I smiled and headed for the harbormaster's office, which straddled the seawall and looked out over both the sea and the harbor.

After confirming the current times with the harbormaster, I walked around town and treated myself to a couple of pastries at a bakery. Portrush was the biggest town I had been in since Galway. I sat at a table outside

and watched the bustle. The sidewalks were full of shoppers, mothers pushing prams through the crowds, and lines of three or four people patiently
waiting to enter small shops. It was a busy place, but no less friendly than
any other town of its size that I had visited.

I checked my watch, then walked around the block and down a side
street to stretch my legs. As I turned the corner, I stopped and stared at a
building fenced off with fifteen-foot-high wire. Coils of more wire with
glistening blades set in the rings ran on top of the fencing. Strands of
barbed wire held the coils in place and stretched tightly between concrete
pillars supporting a locked steel gate. A sign identified the building as the
headquarters of some organization of Orange Men. I didn't fully understand
what the Orange Men stood for, but I knew they represented the Troubles—the Protestant side. The sight of the razor coils was a harsh reminder
of the news that preceded each evening's weather report. I suddenly felt
vulnerable, and wanted to put distance between me and the tension that
ran like an electrical charge through all that fencing.

I hurried back to the boat, relieved to deal with the threat of the sea
rather than the ugliness of politics and religion.

When I got back, a newspaper reporter and a photographer were waiting.
The harbormaster, or maybe the customs official, must have called them.
With a ringed notepad, the reporter scribbled down my responses to his
questions while the photographer moved around us, the click of his shutter
interrupted by the soft whir of the motor-drive. A dozen or more people
crowded around and listened as I explained once more where I had come
from and some of the highlights of the trip. I struggled to find words to
describe the richness of the journey, all the emotional and spiritual connections that were woven within the challenges and beauty. I was embarrassed by the attention, wanting to be cordial and hospitable but at the
same time wishing we could have found a quiet corner to talk.

After the interview, the crowd stayed and watched while I prepared to
leave. As I checked the hatches and spare paddles, remounted the compass,
and tethered the camera again, I caught fragments of conversation drifting
down from the pier.

"He's come up the west coast."

"Right round Ireland."

"Is he goin' through the sound?"

I finished my pre-paddle check, slid the boat into the water, and carefully climbed in. I snapped the belt around my waist, looked up at the crowd, and saw an old man standing quietly to one side. He was tall and square-shouldered, a big man even in his late years. Our eyes met and for a few seconds we just looked at each other. He nodded and called out in a strong, gravelly voice, "God bless ye, lad."

There was such depth and sincerity in his voice. It burrowed through the layers of tides, times, current speeds, and warnings that had preoccupied me. Above the heads of those who sat on the edge of the pier and watched, he had unashamedly called out his blessing. It reached inside me and found a place that needed that reassurance. Something within let go and tears blurred his silhouette. I lifted the paddle in a salute and heard my voice crack with emotion as I called out, "Thank you." There was nothing more to say. I backed the boat out of the shadow of the pier and into the warmth of the sun.

As I approached the opening in the seawall, the bow rose and fell with a warning of what lay beyond. I waved to a fisherman standing on the end of the seawall and turned the boat toward open water. The swells had built during the three hours I had been in town and now rebounded off the outside of the seawall in five- and six-foot peaks. I swung wide of the breaking waves and let the flooding tide carry me behind the protection of the Skerries, a chain of small, low islands that ran parallel to the shore-line.

It was five-thirty in the evening, the air crisp and the water sparkling under a blue sky. I held the paddle clear of the water and twisted left, then right, the blades slicing the air as I loosened up my shoulders and lower back. I was nervous, my stomach jittery. Too quickly the tide pulled me from behind the Skerries back into the swells. Portballintrae lay curled around a small cove a half mile to my right, the swells breaking white on the rocks around the village. If the Giant's Causeway was too rough, maybe I could turn around and get into the protection of the cove. Maybe.

Through the passage of time and the stories that the Irish are famous for, the Giant's Causeway has been linked to one of Ireland's greatest Celtic heroes, Finn McCoul. In Irish mythology few champions are credited with as many feats of strength or victories in battle as McCoul. In Celtic times it was not only strength that the warrior boasted, but also intelligence and cunning. It was this trickery, and the magic Finn McCoul possessed, which saved the lands of Eire from the wrath of a Scottish giant.

The Causeway legend tells of Bennendonnor, an evil giant from the western isles of Scotland who built a great land bridge between Scotland and the northern cliffs of Ulster. Upon seeing Bennendonnor coming across from the distant islands, Finn McCoul became frightened by the terrible size of the giant. He quickly changed into the form of a enormous baby, huge even in the larger-than-life world of the Celtic storytellers. As Bennendonnor strode across the basalt bridge, he saw this infant and re-alized this land of green hills and oak forests must be inhabited by people even larger and more powerful than himself. In his fright he turned and escaped back to Scotland, destroying the Causeway as he fled.

Today, the only remains of the Causeway are the columns of six-sided basalt that emerge from the sea like steps and climb to form the face of the cliffs looking out toward Scotland. On the Scottish side there is an island called Staffa whose base is composed of the same columnar basalt. On one side of the island is Fingal's Cave, a sixty-foot high, two hundred foot-deep cavern through which the sea surges. The columns rise like great pipes of a massive organ and were the inspiration for Mendelssohn's *Hebrides Overture*. During my circumnavigation of Britain, I paddled into the echoing cathedral of the cave and understood Mendelssohn's awe. The power of myth and music are our human response to the overwhelming beauty of nature.

As I crossed the shallow bay off Portballintrae, the land reached further into the sea. The softness of grass-covered hills gave way to ledges of red and gray that climbed steadily to the sea cliffs of which the Irish myth was born. The closer I got to the cliffs, the faster the current flowed. I was two hundred yards offshore, watching the brilliant colors of the rock slide past, and with each passing minute becoming more alarmed by the increasing speed of the tide. The energy of tides and cliff was building as the current pulled me faster and closer to the rocks. I paddled another hundred yards offshore, the tide racing me toward the banded cliffs that towered overhead and plunged into the sea.

I sprinted another fifty yards out. It didn't seem to make any difference. I was still losing the buffer that I wanted as the swells kept exploding beneath the cliffs. Any thought of turning back was useless. I was caught in the power of the tidal stream and being swept toward a line of white water a few hundred yards in front of me. I was committed.

The first rebounding waves broke the rhythmic rise and fall of the swells, slapping the side of the boat and sending a cold splash of water into my eyes. I grabbed the camera and got two pictures of the cliff. In the view-finder, it looked so innocent, the rich cream, tan, and rust strata glowing in the evening light.

I snapped the bungee cord over the edge of the camera and grabbed the paddle just as the tide swept the boat into the chaotic heaving and twisting of the standing waves. An incoming swell and a rebounding wave collided a few feet in front of me. The boat powered over the shoulder of the waves, was jerked skyward, then suddenly was airborne as the waves split and left a hollow where they had slammed through each other. The bow fell five feet and met the next violent upsurge of peaked wave, crashing through it and struggling to rise as the sea poured over the front half of the boat. As the kayak started to recover, a rebounding wave from behind lifted the stern and drove the bow deeper into the wave. The boat stalled, sluggish from the weight it was trying to shed. Another wave from the left arched overhead. I snapped the paddle into a low brace, tucked into the wave, and felt its cold weight collapse on my back. Seawater flooded my eyes and filled my sinuses. I straightened, spitting and blowing. The rear wave and the sideward slam of the second one had twisted the boat seaward. I was being pushed sideways into the waves, which were getting bigger and steeper the closer I got to the headland. I backpaddled on the right. Another wave tossed the boat high, almost out of the water. When it slammed into the waves again, I was suddenly back on course.

Amid the pummeling and deafening roar of the breaking waves, I could hear a deeper rumble of the swells hitting the cliffs. The swells. Damn it! They had been there since the crossing of Lough Foyle that morning. I hadn't paid any attention to them. They lifted and rolled under the ranks of standing waves, confusing them, tossing them aside, then rebounding and turning the sea into a riotous panic. There was nothing to do but hang on and try to ride it out.

My breathing was shallow and rapid, my heart pounding wildly. I had to calm down or panic would take over. I took a couple of deep breaths, concentrating on my breathing and letting my shoulders drop. Some of the tension let up and my chest muscles relaxed. I reached for a wave with the left paddle and changed to a low brace as the boat was thrown over from a wave on the right. Another breath. A smooth exhalation, then out of the low brace and reaching forward for the next stroke. I focused on a ten-yard circle around the boat, watching individual waves, trying to guess how they would hit, and backpaddling or sprinting, depending on when I thought they would break. I timed some perfectly, flying over the transparent crests, two-thirds of the boat out of the water, rocketing into the sky at a thirty-degree angle. A split second later, the bow was buried in the following trough, and I could hear the roar of the wave breaking behind me. Other waves I mistimed completely, crashing into a trough and looking up just in time to tuck and take the wave over my head.

For the first fifteen minutes I worked the boat through the seas, judging distances, changing course, aware of how far the next band of standing waves was and how best to approach it. I moved further out into the tidal stream to miss a series of breakers, then angled back in toward the cliff.

Somewhere between the Causeway and Benbane Head, I spotted the red pilothouse of a fishing boat rolling wildly in the sea ahead. We were on opposite courses, a hundred yards apart and closing rapidly. The sound of his engine was muffled when he was half hidden in the troughs, then suddenly louder and straining as the boat lurched into full view. Between crest and trough I caught a glimpse of the fisherman, hands firmly on the boat's wheel, leaning sharply into each violent roll. As we passed, I saw him lean over the wheel and stare in disbelief. The wipers repeatedly cleared the window of spray and framed the look of shock on his face. He stepped to the side window, leaning through the lowered top half. My boat climbed sharply, then slammed down. I let go of the paddle and waved with one hand, desperately wanting to grab the shaft again but holding my hand high, hopefully sending a message that I was okay. The antenna on the pilothouse slashed the air as the boat rolled from side to side. The last thing I wanted to see was him reaching for the radio. He returned my wave with a shake of his head that I had seen dozens of times. With hand still high, I whispered a plea, "Please don't call." In seconds, our sterns crossed. A half minute later, I chanced a look over my shoulder. He was nowhere in sight.

The closer I was swept to the headland, the steeper the seas became and any pattern to the breakers was lost. Time and distance began to blur with each new drenching and the sensory overload of breakers hissing, rumbling, and slapping into each other. Gradually the thought process that is linked to vision, the ability to see what is ahead and come up with a plan, was eroded. I tried to hold on to the mental picture of the waters but lost that as well. I was still warm, reasonably dry, and strong. I just couldn't see or think fast enough to counter the waves slamming in and driving the boat in three different directions: up, sideways, and surging forward.

I closed my defensive circle around the boat to the length of a paddle, exhaled with each wave breaking over me, and mentally pulled in tighter. This was the roughest water I had ever been in, a new physical limit whose boundaries I didn't know. I slipped into survival mode, turned my mind inward to ward off the panic that was just below the surface, and let my reflexes take care of staying upright. "Stay calm. Breathe deep." Another sickening launch into the sky was followed by a drop that I was braced for.

The image of a child's wooden toy broke through my concentration. It was the small figure of a clown with a round weighted bottom. No matter how hard it is knocked over, the little figure rights itself: the red nose and smile rocking back and forth, always coming upright. "Weebles wobble but they don't fall down." The commercial jingle played over and over in my head. It was absurd to be thinking of a wobbling clown when around me the seas were stirred as if by the giants of old: how dare a craft as fragile as mine mock the legends and try to slip past the Giant's Causeway? Humor didn't belong in the near panic of the moment, but there it was—a clown and a new mantra that I couldn't get out of my head.

I don't know how long the seas threw me side to side, burying the boat, then tossing it in the air at will. Judging from the map and the speed of the tide, the passage beneath the Giant's Causeway and around Benbane Head could not have lasted more than forty minutes. It felt ten times that. When the tide finally pulled me from the last of the standing waves, my legs and arms were quivering. I was weak, nauseated. I headed toward a finger of rock that broke the rush of the swells and formed a tiny harbor below a white cottage. A narrow road ended at the boat ramp where several boats were pulled high above the surge. I wanted to get to a phone and call the Marine Emergency Service. I was worried the fisherman had reported me.

I landed under the curious gaze of two men in a mud-spattered Land-Rover. A third fellow leaned against the cab. Their conversation stopped as I hurried toward them, dripping wet and trembling from the adrenaline letdown.

"Is there a phone close by?" The rudeness in my voice surprised me. I was still in survival mode, seeing things black and white. The adrenaline had left my body but my mind was still firing with electrical snappings. All I could think of was the search efforts of two days earlier.

The man behind the wheel was middle-aged, huge farmer's hands resting easy on the wheel, while his arm lay on the window opening. His coarse-woven blue sweater had a hole at the elbow and was pulled halfway up his thick forearm. He heard the rudeness and answered my question with another, "Where is it you've come from?"

His bluntness mirrored my abrupt greeting and broke through my thoughts. I was embarrassed. With less haste I explained, "I've just come from Portrush, around the Causeway. It's the wildest water I've ever seen."

He glanced at my boat drawn up beside the small, open fishing boats. "Ye came around Benbane Head in that?"

I nodded. He shook his head, turned to the fellow beside him, and said something I couldn't hear. He looked back at me and said, "Yer a hard man to come around the headland on a day the likes of this."

I was losing patience. I didn't care what he or anyone else thought of my boat or me. I just wanted to find a phone.

"How far out were ye?"

I thought it was an odd question. "I was close, maybe two hundred yards out," I said.

His reply left me stunned, "Ah, it's a good thing ye weren't further out or ye woulda' been in the Ripples."

The Ripples? How could anything be bigger than what I had just come through? And what if I had gone further offshore to escape the rebounding waves? I didn't want to think about it.

I asked again about a phone, this time explaining that I had passed a fishing boat and was worried that he might have reported me to the Marine Emergency Service. The fellow asked what color the boat was. I told him. He knew the fisherman and didn't think that he would have called, but told me there was a phone a quarter mile up the road.

I found the phone booth beneath an oak tree at the junction where the single-track road met the main road. It looked out of place, the kind of red Victorian phone box you would expect to see in London. Its heavy steel frame was painted bright red, the deep chips revealing layers of paint.

The operator connected me to the rescue center. They didn't know anything about me, which was a relief. I explained what I was doing and that the Marine Emergency Service in the South had me on file as the American Canoeist. They found the computer entry and logged me in. I was now officially on their records.

I camped that night behind a stone wall near the cottage, the winds reaching over the wall and slamming into the tent. I lay awake listening to the hypnotic roll of surf against rock, the tearing of gale-force winds, and the splatter of rain on taut nylon. Rathlin Sound still lay in front of me, then Fair Head and Torr Head. What would they be like? As bad as Benbane Head? I rolled over, trying to block out the noise of the wind and the memory of the standing waves. It didn't work. The terror of the waves beneath Benbane Head haunted me. I tried lying on my other side, then on my back. I was exhausted, needed to sleep but couldn't. The winds. Always the winds. Even at night.

With the noise of the winds, and the waves breaking on the shore a hundred yards from the tent, I dozed fitfully. The night and my troubled dreams were filled with the disquiet of the sea. Through the fog of exhaustion and confused sleep I felt the ground roll beneath me, then change to water and breaking seas, seas that towered overhead, black and horrifying. The boat was getting buried by tons of water and I couldn't get the paddle into position. Something was holding my arms. I strained, thrashed against whatever was holding the paddle, and felt my body soaked in sweat. The boat was going over! I panicked.

I jerked upright out of the nightmare, my heart pounding wildly, my arms straining against the zippered bag. In the blackness a gust of wind slammed into the tent, drowning out for a moment the sounds of the sea that even in sleep I could not escape.

The panic of the dream subsided and I lay back down, trying to calm my heart with deep breaths. I pulled my fleece jacket tightly over my ears to muffle the noise of the winds and tried to sleep. Near dawn, after hours of listening in the dark, my eyes finally closed and I slipped into a distorted dream of wind and waves.

Farewells and Transitions

Farewell! A word that must, and hath been—
A sound which makes us linger;—yet—
farewell.

—Bryon, *Childe Harold*

Long after the sun had risen and warmed the sides of the tent, I stirred from sleep. The unending night of winds and dreams faded as I unzipped the tent and looked out on a sea reflecting the deep blue of a clear sky. The previous night's winds had calmed, but the sea still ran white and broken, the memory of the winds written on the face of the steep waves.

By midmorning there wasn't a hint of a breeze yet still the seas rolled in, breaking with flying spray on the rocks near the boat landing. In the still air were sounds of songbirds, while overhead gulls stretched their wings in effortless flight, finding lift on the last breath of the storm's passing. Whisps of steam rose straight up from the walls of stone beside the tent, whisps that carried away the night's dreams and the memories of the previous day's paddle.

Despite the calm winds the seas were far from settled and after the fright of the previous day a walk was far more inviting than the waves crashing against the rocks of the harbor. I met the owner of the cottage at the head of the boat ramp, John Johnston, who told me about a castle that overlooked the Giant's Causeway. He gave me directions to the ruins, and with pack and camera I set off along the coast road to Dunseverick Castle.

From the edge of the road I looked across a steep ravine and up to a mesalike pinnacle of rock surrounded on three sides by the sea. John had given me a pamphlet that told the history of the ruins: the site was believed to have been one of the first three fortifications in Ireland, and later, the seat of the kingdom of Dalriada, which had included the western islands of Scotland. I remembered wading across a bog in Scotland, during my circumnavigation of Britain. In the middle of that bog was a towering mountain of rock swept by drifting clouds of mist. It was Dunadd, the coronation place for the kings of Dalriada.

Now, I stood gazing at the ruins of another stronghold of that kingdom—ruins that looked out on the same sea I had paddled ten years earlier. Dunadd; Dunseverick: the prefix "Dun" the ancient word for fort. Threads of my own history reached across the sea and tied both forts together, then wove deeper into the fabric of place and clan. Dunseverick had been the thirteenth-century stronghold of the O'Cahans, the O'Kane tribe, my mother's maiden name.

I followed a path leading down the ravine then crossed the land bridge, the only way to approach the fort, and felt the exposure, the eyes and strung bows of history carefully watching as I climbed the narrow rocky entrance. No wonder it wasn't until A.D. 924, almost two thousand years after it had been built, that Dunseverick had fallen for the first time.

I walked over the ridges of grass-covered sunken walls, stepped over ramparts, and silently visited my blood history of six hundred years. My uncle had told me that the O'Kanes had been storytellers, poets, and musicians. Now I knew they were also warriors. This fortification had been theirs, seized brutally from others, then eventually taken again as the clan weakened. No words came to mind as I walked the green platform above the seas then stopped and let the cloak of the past wrap itself around my shoulders. Words, thoughts were not part of the moment.

Part of me was beneath the organic layers of grass, dirt, and toppled stones. My own genetic makeup, blue eyes, and fair skin were rooted in the soil, washed with the mist and sea air. I was a traveler connecting the ages, weaving them like the Celtic patterns of interlocking circles. The ages were connected by legends, myths, genes, and this traveler. All were one, separated by the transparency of time.

How could I leave a place of such bone-soul connection? Was it purely chance that I had found refuge from the seas a mile from that place of my ancestors? And what of the powerful feelings I had had at Dunadd, the sixth-century Pictish fort I had visited ten years earlier? I knew nothing of either fort until by chance I had come upon them. Was it purely chance?

Beneath the layers of my own experiences lies the ancient past, which I cannot ignore. It is a nebulous world of connections and intuitions that I am certain of, yet cannot defend with any realism, any logical societal yardstick. But within that mysterious world lies the ultimate reality: the truth, the passing of eons that hold all human questions and struggles of existence like beads of dew on a spider's web. Identity. Roots. I had a hunger for something more certain than the transparent world of today. I wanted to travel deeper, to origins that approach the great unknown of beginnings, then follow time back to the present, the me, and into a future where I leave something of who I am.

I hadn't thought of defining my journey with any purpose other than to live on the sea and paddle slowly around a country that intrigued me. It was odd how the journey had evolved: the calm waters of the east and south coasts where the sun shone and the days were gentle; the west coast, which had been so threatening, yet yielding in its gifts of ruins and wave-battered cliffs; and now the north coast where I found my emotions running as powerfully as the tides that swept the journey toward its finish less than two hundred miles away. It was appropriate that the moon should be full, the tides, both emotional and of the sea, running at their greatest.

I could not sort the mystery of my connections to the past, nor could I define or defend them. I could only breath them, feel them, know that they were real. And maybe in those moments when the past is part of the present, when the crumbled walls of a fort stand high again above a wind-blown sea, when storytellers are welcomed from distant lands for the gift of their tales, and the rhythm of monks living in beehive huts on isolated islands comes alive: maybe it was at those times that my soul absorbed something which my mind could never understand.

Perhaps this journey was not what it appeared. It wasn't an expedition but an introspection, a bridge between the ages, connected by the silence of a heart and quieted with the rhythmic pull of a paddle. The three months of the journey had been a gift, a precious gift of time. As I walked atop that pinnacle of fortified ruins, I knew that I wanted to share that gift, to try to pass on the stories and the whispered magic of this land wrapped in the mists and thunder of the Atlantic.

I walked around the uneven ground of the fort once more, and gazed out to the headland where the standing waves were white against the blue of the rollers. I wanted one last look and feel for what my ancestors had gazed on, an image that I could take with me as I turned and followed the path past the vine-covered tower, then down and across the land bridge connecting the fort to the mainland.

As the tides slackened, then slowly began to turn in my favor, I repacked the boat for the final push through Rathlin Sound. While my thoughts were on the waters ahead, I tried to stay focused on the moment, attentive to each piece of gear that had its assigned place within the hatches. The gear stowed in the hatches may have seemed chaotic but there was an order that I understood, an order that I would feel in the way the boat sat on the water.

John helped carry the boat down the ramp in front of his cottage and watched as I buttoned everything up. Before closing the front hatch, I reached for the journal and walked back up the ramp. While the tide rose beneath the stern, lifting and gently setting it back down with each breath of the sea, we traded addresses. The back pages of my journal were filled with the names of all the people who had helped me along the way.

John held the bow as I balanced on the rear deck, then quickly slid into the cockpit and snapped the spray deck in place. A few more words were exchanged, luck was offered as a blessing, and I was off again.

As I paddled away from Dunseverick, I looked out toward Rathlin Island and didn't see a single whitecap. The evening was still. If the calm held, I could be through Rathlin Sound and around Fair Head before the tide would again turn. Maybe the winds would be kind and allow me to slip into the Irish Sea without a repeat of what had happened at Benbane.

I paddled with the tide through the narrows behind Sheep Head Island, then on to Carrickarade Island, where a rope bridge swayed under the weight of tourists silhouetted against the sky. We waved. Cameras were pointed in both directions, and the tide hastened me past.

Three miles offshore, Rathlin Island was aglow in the rich evening light, its pastures and rockbound shoreline bathed in brilliance. In front of me, Fair Head reached out into the tidal stream toward the tip of the island, crowding the tides that poured through the constriction. Beyond Fair Head, softened by fifteen miles of distance, were the rounded contours of another landmass. It filled the space between mainland and island, distant but rising into full view as the tide pulled me closer to Fair Head. When I realized what I was looking at, I could not take my eyes off it. It had been ten years since I had visited that land, thirteen since living there. It was Scotland's Mull of Kintyre.

I was shocked at how close it appeared. The map clearly showed the distance and it should have been no surprise to suddenly see this bulk resting solidly on the near horizon. This place where Ireland and Scotland cautiously reached into the Atlantic had become a focal point. I had calculated tidal flows and distances from here to Dublin for the past week. Yet with my concerns on standing waves and wind directions, I hadn't thought of the impact of this first view. Now, in the absence of threatening winds and with the current pulling me through tidal swirls and boils, I realized that Scotland's presence meant the last of the open ocean. This wild ribbon of water was pulling me out of the Atlantic and into the relative confines of the Irish Sea.

Maybe on a stormy day I would have welcomed the shelter of turning this point. But in the softness of the evening, I felt an emptiness seeping into me. I wanted to hold everything around me: the tide, the warmth of the sun on my back, and the three landmasses that crouched like lions over the convergence of waters. I wanted more time. Time to take stock, to feel the moment that was slipping past like sand through a clenched fist. I couldn't stop the tide; couldn't slow the boat speeding toward the headland that would take the last view of the north from me. And yet I needed to follow the tides. Wasn't that what I had waited for? A calm passage through hazardous waters? I was swept with the conflict of wanting to finish the trip but also to hold on to the passion of the open ocean.

Fair Head loomed massive beside the swift waters, basalt cliffs standing black and vertical against an evening sky. Beneath it, almost at the water's edge, lay house-sized chunks of hexagonal towers that had slipped from the cliff face, falling and crushing into fragments other columns that lay shattered into perfect six-sided blocks. I tried to imagine the earth trembling as each behemoth thundered into its place of rest.

Twenty feet out from the cliff, I shot through the inner tidal rip—a noisy, violent chop of three- to five-footers. It was less than two hundred yards long, a boisterous child compared to Benbane. It lifted the boat, tossing it playfully, then chasing me into a shore eddy on a surfing wave.

The tide carried me past Fair Head, then faded as the cliff pulled back, melting into a steep hillside of meadow bordered by thickets of trees. The last rays of sun illuminated the varying shades of green and created a lush oasis beside the churning waters. It was a perfect place to spend my last night on the edge of the Atlantic.

I sat in the tent doorway after a hot meal of rice and tomatoes. The sky was swept with the soft pastels of evening; deep blue overhead, fading to lighter blue, washed-out yellow, peach, and pale orange. Beneath the clear sky I was cold even in my fleece clothing. Summer was drawing to a close.

Across the Irish Sea a light flickered on the Mull of Kintyre. There was no sound but the soft reach of the sea over kelp-covered rocks. My movements were gentle and meditative as I dismantled the stove and slid it into its bag, then rinsed the pot and spoon and placed the cooking gear near the front of the tent. Such a simple ritual. I let the sleeping bag fall from my shoulders, stepped out of that warmth, and walked up a track toward the headland. Beside the sea, and over a hill covered in low trees, I walked and listened to the evening—no destination or thoughts, just a peaceful emptiness that welcomed the end of day. Out of the shadows of trees and into the light of the moon: I turned and faced it as it rose above the outline of a coastal hill. Full and brilliant, it crept higher until its cratered roundness was complete as it cast its silver light upon the water. Sacred and celestial, it hung suspended, silently pulling tides and emotions, filling shorelines with the sea and my spirit with awe.

In the moonlight I heard the sounds of the tide, a rushing murmur close to shore and the thin rasp of breaking waves further out in the darkness. Tomorrow, that same flooding tide would carry me south into the Irish Sea. Six, maybe seven more days and the circle would be completed. After three months of paddling, it was hard to imagine that the end of the trip was so near. Scotland's shadow to the east and the quieted seas reminded me of the planning stages a half year earlier; how I had known this last leg would be a time of recollection, of transition. Soon I would have to give up the freedom of the tides and the paddle, and find my place in the world that I had slipped away from. It would be another transition, a new challenge. What would I take with me when the trip was over? Would the memory of this night and so many other moments of the journey stay with me to remind me of the rhythms and peace I had found in the last months? It wasn't the first time I had asked those questions, but now with the trip drawing to a close, I was haunted by their depth.

For the second time since leaving Dublin, the compass swung to a south-easterly heading as I rounded Torr Head. The tide surged over an orange buoy, four or five knots of current washing over it with the power of a whitewater river. The buoy disappeared, then popped to the surface and was jerked under again as I flew around the point.

Twenty minutes later I was off Runabay Head, three miles down the coast, and plowing into a countercurrent that the minor headland had turned against me. Confused by the land that reached into the powerful tidal stream, the tide was split into four or five parallel currents that ran opposite each other. After years of running rivers and paddling on tidal waters, I could read the subtle differences in the texture, color, and ripples that marked the lines of current. By cutting across eddy lines, anticipating the sudden grab of an opposing current and pushing hard against it, I could cross from one to the other and find the south-running streams. The morning's paddle was a waltz with the currents leading me southward.

As the miles slid by, I settled into the rhythm of this new coast. It felt gentler than the north, tame compared to the west coast. The land rolled off the hillsides and met the shoreline not in cascading cliffs but in a mix of tilled meadows and dark forests that flowed over the contours and softened the harshness of ravines. It was the trees that I found so striking. For weeks on end I had seen only the stark beauty of grasses and flowers clinging to the wind-shorn land. Cliff, worn fields of thin soil, and ledges of white-gray rock had been my land references for a thousand miles. Here the trees were like billowing curtains, swaying, and whispering a message that the winds carried in waves of turned leaves.

The sea was also different. It had the strength of the tides, but it didn't roll with the same energy of the ocean or break on the shore with a familiar rumble. Except for the tides, it felt lethargic, as if it had given up competing against the restrictions of land.

The most significant change on the east coast, however, was the amount of shipping and land traffic. High-speed ferries crossed from Scotland and back again three or four times in the course of my day. Freighters and tankers made their way to and from Belfast, still a day's paddle for me, but only hours for them. They were five or ten miles offshore, but their presence hinted at what I would find further south. A half mile to my right, cars sped along the coastal highway at the base of the hills. They zipped into view, disappeared for a few seconds behind rock barriers, then tore around the next bend and in a flash were gone, replaced by another and another in what looked like a race. Of course, it wasn't a race. It was the motorized world that I had forgotten about. Heading toward Belfast was like slowly coming out of a dream—one that I wanted to fall back into. But I knew that I had to awaken and face reality.

Late in the day on August 30, I paddled into the mouth of Belfast Lough. If I had another couple hours of energy I would have made the six-mile crossing and found a place less urbanized on the south side of the lough. A headwind had taken the last of my patience and strength, and I didn't want to cross the busy shipping lanes leading into Belfast. I landed at the Whitehead Sailing Club and as soon as dusk settled in, I rolled the sleeping bag out on a cement walkway beside some overturned dinghies. As I slid into the bag, I thought of the contrast between this camp and others that I had made on the beaches and remote islands of the west coast. I soon became exhausted and sleep washed over my thoughts.

Two or three hours later, I woke to a terrifying rumble that shook the concrete under me and filled the night with the screeching of metal on metal. In a scream of panic I bolted upright in the bag, my heart pounding in my chest and sweat covering my body. A train slowed to a crawl fifty feet above me, its engine laboring with the brakes to bring it to a stop. Five minutes later, the roar of its diesel kicked in again and the train pulled away.

Concrete streetlights that stole the magic of the stars and the sounds of a city kept me awake most of the night. I woke stiff and dry-eyed long before dawn, waited for first light, then paddled out toward the shipping lanes. The tide was slack, a good factor for the crossing, but even if it had been running I would have left Whitehead anyway. I suddenly wanted to finish the trip. Trains, cars, and concrete that came down to the sea were not the memories I wanted of Ireland.

A mile into the crossing I saw a dot on the eastern horizon that grew by the minute. To the west a freighter was outbound from Belfast two miles up the lough, while another was turning and entering the lough from the south. Both were slow, moving predictably in their courses. It was the high-speed ferry on the horizon that I worried about. By the time I passed the channel marker, it had closed within five or six miles and looked like something out of *Star Wars* racing across the flat water. Its wedge-shaped catamaran hull split the sea and the morning calm like a demon possessed. I stopped paddling, astounded by the speed and the noise of what was bearing down on me but confident that I was out of its way. Forty knots of glistening white steel tore past with the roar of a jet, sending a five-foot breaker rolling to either side. By the time the wake washed under me, it had mellowed into a smooth roller. One threat was gone and two remained. I turned up the lough and angled in behind the first freighter, sprinting toward its stern as it passed, and pivoting around to look for any more ferries. The second freighter was two miles away. A thin line of smoke hanging above the stern marked its progress. I would pass easily behind it.

During the hour-and-a-half crossing, the tide had turned, giving me a two-knot assist by the time I reached the south shore. The sun had burned off the last of the morning haze, reflecting off the pondlike water and making it feel hotter than it really was. Despite having had little sleep I felt good, and pushed hard all morning, enjoying the silence of no wind and watching the low shoreline slide past with the hours. By noon, I was twenty miles down the coast and listening to the last quart of water sloshing in the water bag beneath my thighs. I was a mile offshore and just starting to turn toward the town of Ballywalter when the sound of drums floated across the still air.

I had heard about the Orange Men parading through Catholic neighborhoods. The evening news was filled with reports of the violence revolving around the parades, but this was the first time I had heard the repetitive slamming of the drums. I could feel the intimidation, the hatred behind the paraders as the drums echoed across the water. I didn't understand the politics, but it was hard not to have sympathy for the people whose lives the drummers marched through. I turned away from Ballywalter, the sound of the drums following me as I headed south. I didn't need water badly enough to paddle into possible trouble.

Another ten miles down the coast I landed on a gravel beach and walked up to a cottage that sat picturesque above the water. A woman answered the door and looked at me with distrust while I explained where I had come from, and asked if I could fill my water bag. In her eyes I saw a mix of fear and suspicion. It was clear I was an unknown, a threat. She said she would have to get her husband and half closed the door as she turned away.

I listened to tense, muffled words, then approaching footsteps. The door was briskly opened. A man in his fifties, gray hair and thin-faced, stood with clenched fists on his hips: "What is it you want?"

I explained again that I was traveling by canoe and that I was out of water and only wanted to refill the bag, which I held out. His wife came up behind him and while he watched me, she took the bag and retreated into the house again. I apologized for intruding, made a comment about the beautiful day and got little response. He asked what kind of a boat I was in. I explained, hoping that it would lead to more conversation, but it didn't. I felt pity for the man. Through the mask of tension I was certain there was a spark of curiosity toward me. I imagined what he must have seen in the twenty years of war in Northern Ireland; sandbagged checkpoints, helmeted British soldiers, and angry mobs throwing curses, stones, and firebombs. It would not have mattered what side a person was on. Maybe I would be equally suspicious of a stranger at my back door asking for water.

His wife handed the full bag past her husband, then stepped back again. I wanted to give them something in return, a kind word or an insight into who I was—something that would melt the distance between us and maybe heal a little of the distrust they had for me. The seconds passed slowly. There was nothing I could do but bow slightly and thank them. The door clicked shut as I turned and stepped away from the house.

The next day, I paddled across Dundrum Bay and into Newcastle, my last mail stop on the journey. During the crossing I had seen a military patrol boat sitting offshore and had heard automatic gunfire from a wooded valley deep in the bay. I landed at Newcastle with trepidation. I was only twenty miles from the southern border and was looking forward to getting away from the tensions.

As I pulled the boat from the water, an older man in a fisherman's sweater walked over and asked me where I had come from. I pointed to St. John's Point, eight miles across the gray chop, and told him I had started in Ardglass that morning.

"Ardglass? You've come a fair way already; and in this wind?" It was half question and half statement.

"Yeah, and it's the wind that's the problem. It's supposed to kick up this afternoon so I'll have to find a place to sit it out."

"Where is it yer goin'?" The man's tone was very different from the fellow at the cottage and I started to relax.

I told him about the trip and had barely finished when he offered the use of the old lifeboat house for a place to stay for the night. He introduced himself as Hugh Paul, the harbormaster and a member of the Royal National Lifeboat Institute for fifty years. Anything I wanted, including a shower at the new lifeboat house, I was welcome to. His generosity erased the fears I had of being in a northern town.

After a hot shower, I walked into the center of town and found the post office. Five letters were waiting for me. I slid the letters into the pack and found a café beside the busy coastal road. For an hour I sat and slowly read, then reread the letters, sipping tea and thinking that soon I would see my friends and family again.

Two camouflaged trucks interrupted my thoughts. They rolled by a few yards away, the benches in the back filled with helmeted soldiers dressed in the same patterned colors as their trucks. Heavy-treaded tires, whip antennas, and rifle barrels caught my eye. I remembered walking past the police station surrounded by concertina wire and surveillance cameras, and the rip of automatic gunfire out on the bay. Hugh had told me the gunfire was from a training center for the Ulster Constabulary Force. Two more truck loads of young British soldiers sped by.

The sidewalks were thick with people enjoying the sun. There were young couples with children and dripping ice cream cones. Two elderly woman, arms linked, one of them holding the leash of a tiny dog in a red body harness walked by. I looked at the people around me. No one even glanced at the trucks that moved in line with the other traffic.

I walked back to the boat, sorting out the news from America and the images of a holiday coastal town in a country that was unofficially at war.

The Newcastle Sailing Club was hosting its last race of the year and the harbor was crowded with people, sailing dinghies, and empty boat trailers. A woman my age was looking over my boat as I walked up. She asked if the decal on the bow really meant that I was paddling around Ireland. I said yes, then answered her questions about the trip. We introduced ourselves and she told me she had grown up in Newcastle but now lived near Belfast. She had come down to visit her father, a retired doctor, and one of the original members of the sailing club. Aurila wanted me to meet her father. She invited me to dinner. On the way back to the house we walked though the old Ansley Estate, which had been given to the city as a beautiful wooded park. We walked along shaded paths beneath beech trees, flowering rhododendrons, and massive cedars. Being in the forest and listening to a noisy bubbling stream reminded me of places back home. It was hard to imagine that less than thirty miles away there were riots and armored troop carriers patrolling divided neighborhoods.

My evening with Aurila and Dr. Gibson reminded me just how austere my paddling life was. While Aurila made dinner, Dr. Gibson invited me into his sitting room and we talked about the sea. It was a strange feeling to sit there and hear stories of sailing in Scottish and English waters, and down to the Azores and back, while my senses soaked in all the textures and smells of a real home.

The chair felt so comforting, deep but firm, and holding my tired muscles as I sank into its comfort. Around the room were pictures of sailboats and framed art that reflected the contents of the room. There were ceiling-high windows with curtains gracefully drawn back. My mind suddenly had a thirst for the finery. Shapes, colors, and the mitered joinery of the furniture held my eye. It was all so innocent and marvelous, those little things that I had become sensitized to.

Dinner was another plethora of textures and tastes; rolled cloth napkins, placemats, and chairs pulled around a large dining table that had a feeling of many family gatherings. Wine, hot bread and melted butter, steaming vegetables, potatoes, and meat. It had been months since I had sat down to a full-course meal. There was plenty of food and easy conversation that made me feel like a member of the family. We talked about our different lives, of sailboats, thoroughbred horses, and travels by kayak. It was an evening of equal sharing, of three people sitting in Northern Ireland not caring about religious or political differences, but rather enjoying and learning from each of our stories. The evening passed too quickly. A spare room was offered but I declined as graciously as I could. I wanted to be up early to catch the tide and it would be easier if I slept in the lifeboat house. Dr. Gibson drove me through the empty streets of Newcastle. We parted with a warm handshake at the harbor, my feelings for Northern Ireland tempered by the kindness of strangers who had invited me into their home.

The next day another northerner touched me in an equally trusting and reassuring way. I had paddled into Kilkeel, a fishing harbor packed with trawlers three deep to the pier, and the strong odor of fish crates and nets. I needed to buy film and asked a man sitting on the stone wall above the harbor if there was a shop close by. He was probably in his late fifties, though he looked much older. He was thin, unshaven, and gray-looking. His arms were crossed within the folds of a worn black jacket, white shirt opened at the collar, and legs stretched out and relaxed as if this was his routine on a sunny day. He told me the village of Kilkeel was actually two miles inland, then nodded toward a bicycle leaning against the wall and said, "Ye can take the bike and I'll watch yer boat while yer away."

His sudden offer caught me offguard, and it was a few seconds before I got past my feelings of surprise to thank him. The bike was a fifteen speed, stuck in one gear. He warned me the left brake didn't work. The right one wasn't much better, but there was air in the tires and it sure beat walking two miles.

The dilapidated bike was a gift that spoke of the frail man's rich spirit. I pedaled away from the pier with the fenders rattling at every pothole and my heart refreshed by the kindness of a stranger.

The ride into the village was symbolic of entering the motorized world I had watched from the sea. Even in a small village there was merging traffic, a stop light that I almost missed because of the brakes, and a new sensory overload of taillights in front, the sounds of engines and tires coming up from behind, and the smell of exhaust. It wasn't only the brakes I didn't trust but also my rusty reactions to a life that had a different pace from that of paddling. There was too much noise and movement, not of waves, but of cars and trucks that seemed to move very fast. I found the chemist, the drugstore, where I bought film, and returned to the pier happy to have survived my excursion. The man was sitting where I left him, talking with two fishermen off a boat that had tied up since I was gone. I thanked him for his kindness and we had a laugh about the almost nonexistent brakes. "Aye, she needs new brakes, she does, but I only come from down the street aways."

It was clear the brakes probably would never get fixed. The sunshine and the activity of the harbor, the boats unloading fish and taking on crushed ice, were more important. It was the Irish way of letting things be. The bike might fall apart on one of his rides to the pier, but someone would pick him up and he would take his place on the stone wall where everyone knew him.

I left the men talking about fishing as I pushed the boat into knee-deep water and carefully climbed in. I was glad that my last visit in Northern Ireland was so memorable. The gentleman's kindness, and his old bike were better images than that of drums and truckloads of armed soldiers.

I pushed the button on the edge of my watch. A pale green light showed it was almost nine o'clock in the evening. I released the button and darkness replaced the technology of black digits on ghostly green. I lived by two clocks, that of the plastic band on my wrist, and nature's clock of six-hour tides and the seasonal length of days. A month earlier, it would have been almost eleven o'clock before it got this dark. My eyes hurt from trying to see the lines in the journal. I could have used the headlamp but its harsh light would have pierced more than the approaching darkness. I gave up on the writing and tucked the journal away.

I could not remember an evening so still. Not a breath of wind to move the fabric of the tent, nor that of the sea a few yards away, which had risen with the flooding tide as gently as the whispered secret of a child. I had sat on my heels earlier and watched the tide creep slowly toward the polished curves of a fist-sized rock. Without the disturbance of breeze or ripple, it had seemed to struggle over tiny pebbles blocking its passage toward the stone. Ever so slowly it rose higher, fingers probing over pebbles, watering their hidden colors of subtle greens, pinks, and onyx black. Minutes later, the waters pulled by the moon crept around the sides of the bigger stone, wetting its smooth curves but not reaching behind it. The tide seemed to wait for some silent signal, holding out for an eternity as I watched, then suddenly releasing the tension of hesitancy, and in a heartbeat surging around the stone.

Now in the encroachment of darkness I felt the night tide surround my tent. It had crept in with the same patience of the sea, stealthily claiming everything as its own. I was camped on the south side of Carlingford Lough, back in the Republic of Ireland. Fifty miles to the south was Dublin, and if I could stand two hundred feet above sea level, I would see the glow of the city warming the night skies. I thought of the glass-smooth sea creeping over pebbles and stones, and the thunder of thick ocean swells crashing against cliff faces. All of the images in my mind seemed related: Dublin, the beginning and the end of the trip. The sea, silent or thundering, but feeling the pull of the same moon. Day and night tied together by the tides that I pulled the boat through. It was all coming to completion, the circle closing as certainly as the rising tide and the fullness of night.

The next morning I woke at 4:00 A.M. I had left the tent flap open and could see the sky full of twinkling stars. I was instantly awake and decided to break camp and paddle by their light, and that of a half moon shimmering on the flat sea.

Paddling with the night was like being with a friend who I knew had a gift for me: the promise of light, of dawn hidden in the folds and coolness of her sky. The paddles stirred the clear depths into swirls and pinpricks of light that reversed heaven and sea. I held the end of one blade, reached deep beneath the waters with the other, and swept the paddle forward and back, playing in the darkness. A child, watching the curtains of phosphorescence spinning, then fading into the black of night and sea. I stirred the depths again and the lights reappeared, dozens of spinning swirls lighting the edge of my paddle blade, teasing my eyes with the clarity and brilliance of their light show. I thought of the great basking sharks of the west coast, the gentle behemoths whose life depended on these tiny lights of phytoplankton for food.

One by one the stars faded and the sky to the east changed from black to gray, then purple, and the first hint of pale blue washed in yellow and orange. The night gracefully surrendered the heavens to the new day and to the sun that edged over the horizon in a burning rim of orange.

Two days later on September 6, I paddled against an ebbing tide into the mouth of the Liffey River. A ferry, brilliant white with a green shamrock on the stack, was slowly moving away from the loading dock, turning into the river from where it would begin its passage to Wales. Seven stories up, passengers waved and pointed their cameras in my direction. The throb of the ship's engines resonated through the hull of my boat while the paddles slid silently into the murky waters that I had left on June 1. We crossed paths less than a hundred yards apart—one journey drawing to a close while another was beginning.

Further upriver a welder hung suspended over the side of a ship, the sparks arcing over his helmet and sizzling into the wake of a passing tug-boat. Praying mantislike cranes waited at empty docksides for the next ship to be unloaded. The air was filled with the sounds of trucks, jets overhead, and the acrid smells of creosote pilings and diesel exhaust.

I waited for a coastal freighter to overtake me, then crossed the river to a floating dock in front of the Stella Mari Sailing Club. The end of the trip was fifty yards away. I took a few more strokes, wanting to feel the last pull of the paddle, then rested it across the cockpit and watched the distance drift to a close. The boat stopped a few yards from the gray-weathered wood of the dock. I looked at the grain and splits in the dry wood, then over to the ferry dock, and downstream to where the river turned and blocked the view of the sea.

I was stalling. I didn't want to take those last few strokes. The trip was moments away from ending and I wanted to remember each second and freeze it in my mind. My heart didn't want to reach for that dock and end the journey, but when the tide began to pull me back downriver I knew I could wait no longer. I paddled to within an arm's length of the dock, reached out, and touched the wood with my fingers. With that touch the circle was completed, fused like a giant ring encompassing all of Ireland as well as my heart.

I climbed from the cockpit for the last time and stood on the dock holding the boat by the safety belt I had worn for the last twelve hundred miles. The falling tide and the weight of the boat tugged gently at the webbing as if anxious to be off again. However, I was content, satisfied to end the journey where it had begun. I didn't have any great sense of elation or celebration that the trip was completed. Instead, there was a feeling of simple satisfaction, of having lived the journey well, giving myself com-pletely to it and returning to this place of beginnings filled with the treas-ures of its gifts. It wasn't the completion of the journey that I had set out to accomplish but rather to learn as much as I could about this island country, to visit it with a still heart and to meet the sea on its own terms. I had done all of that and in the process I had unraveled a twelve hundred–mile tapestry that now lay warmly wrapped around my heart as a reminder of the journey. Within the textures and colors of that tapestry were stone ruins, sea cliffs, the smiling faces of fishermen, and the fibers of my ancestral roots woven through centuries of stone and lichen.

It would be months before I understood the depth and significance of my trip. I was still six thousand miles from home and there were many things left to do before I could rest. I still had to get the boat on the ferry back to Wales, and deal with the logistics of getting it and myself back to the States. I pulled the stern out of the water and levered the boat onto the dock. Two older men scrubbing the underside of a sailboat on the club's boat ramp looked over at me, their long-handled brushes frozen in dripping silence as they stared. The look on their faces spoke clearly of what they thought. "Now where do you suppose he's come from?"

I took the two-piece paddle apart, tucked it into the cockpit, and walked over to say hello.